The Sweet Life

The Sweet Life

Marcea Newman's Natural-Food Dessert Cookbook

WITH LINE DRAWINGS BY LINDA STINE

Houghton Mifflin Company Boston

1974

A PORTION OF THIS BOOK HAS APPEARED IN *Prevention* MAGAZINE.

FIRST PRINTING   H

Library of Congress Cataloging in Publication Data
Newman, Marcea.
    The sweet life.
    1. Desserts. 2. Cake. 3. Cookies. I. Title.
TX773.N47   641.8′6   73–22254
ISBN 0–395–18484–3
ISBN 0–395–18627–7 (pbk.)

PRINTED IN THE UNITED STATES OF AMERICA

*In memory of Rose
my mother, teacher, friend*

From Pure Joy springs
all creation; by Joy
it is sustained, toward
Joy it proceeds and to
Joy it returns.

— Tantra Asana

Acknowledgments

I wish to thank the following people whose dedication and sincere friendship made this book possible: Sara Sterman, who with utmost devotion gave her time, patience, knowledge and love; Russell Amanzade, who gave his typing skill, patience and time; Brendon Bass, who donated his knowledge of the English language, patience, time and taste buds; and friends who guided me through the lightest and darkest moments. My sincere gratitude to all those who tested, tasted, criticized and helped me to understand.

Contents

Foreword

During the past five years, I have been living and studying a way of life based on "natural" laws. Living according to these laws simply means being in harmony with nature, being conscious of the changes that occur daily and flowing with them. This awareness has given me a new perspective about myself in relation to the universe and the natural laws which govern all things, visible, invisible, large or small.

Health and happiness are inseparable; where one exists, so does the other. Aware of this fact, I began to change my diet simply to fit into the natural cycle in which I wanted to live. As I became more sensitive to the variations in season, foods grown at different times of the year, climate and my own condition, I began to select my foods intuitively, according to these changes. Altering my diet seemed strange and almost impossible at first, but after a short time I realized that I was not only changing my eating habits, but my way of eating was changing me.

My understanding grew, making it easier for me to adapt to any situation, anytime and anyplace. I began to understand why sickness arises, and view it not as something bad, but as a kind of signal that nature uses to try to make people see that they are breaking her laws. If one eats in an orderly fashion, in season, according to the weather and one's condition, then sickness can be greatly reduced.

This book is the result of a strong desire to share these experiences, and the enlightenment received through them, with you.

MARCEA NEWMAN

The Sweet Life

I. Natural Necessities

Equipment, Techniques and Ingredients

From Grandma's apple pie to chocolate hot-fudge sundaes, desserts are an integral part of the American diet. However, what was once an occasional treat has now become a national pastime.

In 1850, families consumed two pounds of sugar a week. In 1900, most American families consumed five pounds of sugar from Sunday to Sunday. This did not include the sugar in fruits or other natural sources such as vegetables or grains, but only commercially "refined" sugar. Today the average American family consumes more than four hundred pounds of sugar yearly, a very far cry from dear old Grandma.

I remember my mother, who was European and definitely a woman of the old school, filling the air with the aroma of her homemade breads, cakes, pastries, cookies and pies. She would usually bake on Fridays, baking enough bread for the coming week, and an extra cake or pie or two as a special treat for us or the neighbors.

Using her own basic recipe and then elaborating on it, she would create pineapple-cherry upside-down cakes, honey-walnut cakes, fruit cakes, marble cakes, apple pies—there was no end to her ingenuity. In addition, she would always make something from dough that she could shape with her hands — turnovers, babkas, strudels, cookies, never measuring by the cup, but instead using her intuition and her eyes.

I never realized how much influence baking with my mother had on me until I began to bake by myself. I remember watching, fascinated, as her hands kneaded and shaped the dough for strudels and turnovers, filling them with poppyseeds, prune butter, or apples, raisins and nuts. Sometimes I helped, cleaning mixing bowls and spoons by licking them, cutting out cookies with an old glass or just playing with the dough.

Today in my kitchen I have returned to using the natural ingredients that my mother used when she first started making desserts as a young girl in Europe. She once told me the story of how she rarely had to go to the store in town to buy ingredients for baking. My father, her boyfriend at the time, grew wheat and millet on his farm a few houses away. So she would get the grain from him and then bring it to her father, who would grind it into flour in his mill. Eggs she obtained from her chickens, milk from the family cow or goat, water from the well, and butter was freshly churned by her mother. Even sea salt was always in abundant supply because her cousin who lived near the ocean dried and sold it for a living. She never used refined sugar in her baking or dessert making, but relied instead on honey or fresh fruits for sweetness and taste. When fruit was in season she would pick and use it; when it wasn't in season it wasn't used.

When she came to America, everything changed. There were no flour mills close by where she could get freshly ground flour, no trees or vines to pick fresh fruit from, and she couldn't keep chickens, goats and cows in an apartment. No longer surrounded by foods in their natural state, she began to adapt to her new way of life, still trying to choose the best-quality products at the local stores. She had to choose from more refined packaged foods and settle for whatever fresh foods could be obtained.

When I began to bake, it was even more difficult to find ingredients that were not only "natural" but wholesome as well. Every item that I bought for baking and dessert making, I discovered, had something added as well as something taken away.

Strange as it may seem I never questioned "refined" foods until, after I became ill, a doctor recommended that I change my diet to regain my health. He strongly suggested that I substitute "natural" foods for refined foods and completely eliminate sugar from my diet, except the sugar from natural sources such as fruits, grains and vegetables.

This suggestion led me to a natural-food store, where I began to read more labels. All was supposedly "natural" and, in most cases, "organic." There was no evidence of bleached or bromated flour. The oils were "crude" and "unrefined," looking clearer and smelling like what they were extracted from — the germ of corn, sesame seed, safflower, sunflower, soybean or olive. Salt with its natural minerals was not refined with additives to make it "whiter" and "free-flowing." Spices were not adulterated with artificial coloring or preservatives and were grown "organically" if possible.

Sugar was nowhere to be found, because sugar as we know it today is not in its natural state, but is highly refined. Even the so-called "natural" or "raw" sugar has been refined and then changed back to brown, its original color, to make it look "natural." The only sweeteners sold in the store were natural sugars such as maple syrup, fruit concentrates, honey, apple butter, apple juice or cider, glucose syrup and sorghum molasses.

Many of these products were labeled "natural," "unrefined" and perhaps "organic." Confused by these terms, I asked what they meant and whether they had any real significance. The owner explained to me that "organic" implies that the foods were grown without chemical fertilizers, synthetics, herbicides, fungicides, pesticides or any chemical at all. The farmer depends on the health and vitality of the plant to resist disease and he uses natural fertilizers and cultivation methods to control the weeds. He further stated that these products were kept under natural conditions without the use of pesticides while they were being shipped to the store.

The word "natural," he explained, has an entirely different meaning. It means that no additives or preservatives of any kind have been added to the food *after* it is grown. He further went on to say that many people today use chemical preservatives or additives unknowingly or even knowingly, without considering the effect these may have on their bodies. Many people have been convinced that additives will impart a better taste, color, texture and even aroma to foods. Often additives are used as a selling device to make foods more appealing to the senses, to enrich foods because the refining processes have stripped them of their natural vitamins and minerals, or to prolong shelf life. He warned me that chemical additives may injure the body when ingested daily.

Preservatives and additives, which are found in most refined products today, were not used years ago because food was preserved by natural methods such as canning, pickling or drying, or by using salt, a natural preservative. A small sign hanging on the wall in the store made it all clear: ADDITIVES AND PRESERVATIVES SHOULD BE HARMLESS TO MAN OR THEY DEFEAT THEIR PURPOSE.

Necessary Equipment

Just as good natural foods make more nutritious desserts, proper kitchen tools are necessary for the preparation of good-quality culinary delights. By using the cooking and baking utensils suggested, you will find that your desserts are not only more delectable, but truly wholesome as well.

J. P. Beach, editor of *You and Your Health*, has pointed out that aluminum "exerts an irritating action on the mucosa of the entire gastrointestinal tract before absorption, and, as aluminum salts, on the tissues and organs of the body after absorption. Thus, it is a common cause of constipation, colitis, and ulcers . . ."

Aluminum and the aluminum compounds formed in cooking, he says, combine with alkaline saliva and the alkaline juices of the duodenum to create gas (similarly, many commercial bakers use aluminum to blow up products and make them light). This gas-making process is continued throughout the digestive system, irritating and damaging the tissue. "These poisons," Beach says, "back up into the liver and kidneys and produce the symptoms of metallic poisoning."

Aluminum and its compounds, Beach goes on, also destroy vitamins in the food (testified by Docket No. 540, Federal Trade Commission, Washington, D.C.).

If you boil ordinary drinking water in an aluminum dish or pan for half an hour, and immediately pour it into a clear glass container, you can see the aluminum compounds, mostly aluminum hydroxide. In cooking, more or these particles are released from the aluminum, enter into the food and are absorbed by the body as well.

I recommend that you choose baking and cooking utensils made of earthenware, stoneware, porcelain, cast iron, enamel or glass, and avoid aluminum and all synthetically coated equipment. For the same reason avoid wrapping food in aluminum foil for baking, cooking and storing.

Mixing

Glass or porcelain mixing bowls
Wooden spoons
Measuring cups, stainless steel or tin for dry ingredients, and glass for liquids
Measuring spoons
Flour sifter or strainer
Wire whisk
Rotary hand beater or electric mixer
Rubber spatula
Suribachi (see p. 54) or mortar, and pestle

Baking and Cooling

Jelly roll pan, 11 x 16-inch
Pastry brushes (to oil pans and brush top of pastries)
Baking sheets, 2 inches smaller than the size of your oven
Loaf pans, 6 x 3 x 3-inch
Tube pan, 6-inch or 8-inch
Square pan, 6 x 8-inch

Layer cake pans, round, 7- and 8-inch; depth, 1 and
   2 inches
Springform pans, round, 6-, 7- and 8-inch*
Tart tins
Cupcake tins
Assorted tins and molds
Wax paper (also for rolling out dough)
Cake racks
Bottle (for cooling tube pan)
Oven thermometer

Cooking

Double boiler
Saucepans
Candy thermometer

* Springform pans are best, because it is easy to remove the
cake from them without disturbing the shape.

Asbestos pad
Wok or cast-iron pot (for deep-frying)
Oil skimmer

Decorating

See p. 41

Shaping

Flute-edge pastry wheel
Cookie cutters
Rolling pin
Pestle (to roll out soft doughs)
Pastry cloth
Knife
Baker's scraper (to clean pastry cloth, and cut
   sections of dough)

Basic Techniques

Everyone has his or her own way of explaining
how to beat, sift, fold, mix, and when to boil, steam,
bake or fry. Directions will always vary regard-
ing baking terms and techniques used, as well as
ingredients called for. Following are some basic
tips that I hope you will find helpful.

   Along with these techniques, there is one ingredient that I feel is most essential — good intuition. For me, baking is an art that I have translated
into measurements and step-by-step instructions. I
feel that one should come to it with the same en-
thusiasm and creative spirit one would bring to any
art form, like painting or writing or making music.
Truly, what could be more artistic and creative
than the preparation of food that is both attractive
in its dress and delicious in its substance?

   So please, experiment with these recipes, suggestions and methods, find your own way and ulti-
mately bake according to your own good judg-
ment and intuition.

Beating

   There are two ways to beat depending upon
what you want to accomplish.
   The first way is to fill the eggs with air. For this
method, use a rotary hand beater, wire whisk or
electric mixer. This method is used mainly in cake
batters.
   The second type of beating is for mixes that are
fairly stiff and are already combined. This is best
done with a wooden spoon, rotary hand beater or
electric mixer. This method is used in éclairs and
yeasted batters.

Folding

   Folding is perhaps the most important technique
for working with batters that use only eggs as a
leavening agent. It is the gentlest way of combining two or more ingredients to retain the air that
you have beaten into them. It should be done with

your hand, preferably, or, if you wish, a rubber spatula, to avoid beating. If you are folding in dry ingredients, sift them, and then sprinkle them on top of the mixture. If the ingredients are liquid, pour them on slowly, gradually folding them in.

Folding with your hand allows you to feel how light and delicate the mixture really is.

To fold by hand:

Spread your fingers open and cut through the mixture to the bottom of the mixing bowl.

Move your hand across the bottom of the bowl and up the side.

Bring hand up, holding some of the batter. Rotate hand so that you drop the mixture.

Repeat whole procedure until all the ingredients are combined, but feel delicate and light.

Mixing

Use a wooden spoon to mix, moving batter in a clockwise or counterclockwise motion without changing direction. If you overmix you can spoil the texture of delicate pastries. Usually one mixes only to combine the ingredients well and evenly. Overworking an unyeasted mixture can lead to a tough batter that is not easy to work with. When a "pancakelike batter" is called for in a recipe, the batter should have the consistency of thick pancake batter; it will drop with difficulty from a wooden spoon. Adjust liquid content accordingly.

Sifting

Sifting dry ingredients removes any lumps that might have formed and gives the dry ingredients more air so that you will have less difficulty in combining them. (Sift before measuring — 1 cup of unsifted flour measures more than 1 cup after sifting.)

When you are sifting chestnut flour, there are many lumps that will not pass through the holes of the sifter or strainer without your assistance. Push the flour against the holes of the sifter so that lumps break down and pass through more easily.

Remember, the only purpose for sifting or straining flour, salt and spice is to make them easier to fold into a batter. The part that remains in the sifter is the most nutritious part of the flour, containing vitamins and minerals, and should not be discarded. It can be used in puddings, breads, etc.

To sift:

Place measuring cup on piece of paper. Sift flour into cup through strainer or sifter. Do not bang cup down. When filled, level off top.

Cooking Methods

Boiling

Boiling in a saucepan over a flame is a good method for heating up liquids that do not contain any flour.

A double boiler is needed to cook custards, creames* (see p. 55) or any delicate flour-liquid

combination. These may overcook or scorch if left directly on a flame. It is not necessary to stir as often when cooking in a double boiler, but the cooking time must be increased.

Steaming

This is a very old, but popular method of preparing puddings, pastries, candies or even cakes, allowing the flavors to permeate more evenly

---

* "Creame" is spelled in this way to indicate that it does not contain any dairy products.

through the dessert. When women devoted more time to cooking and baking, they wouldn't think twice about steaming something for 2 or 3 hours.

Oil a coffee can, cake pan or mold. Fill two-thirds full with batter and cover tightly. Place on a rack in a large, heavy pot filled with enough boiling water to come one half to three quarters of the way up the side of the mold.

Cover the pot and steam on a medium-low flame 2 to 3 hours or longer, keeping the water constantly boiling. If the cake is too moist on top after steaming, preheat the oven to 350° and bake uncovered 10 to 15 minutes to remove excess moisture.

Deep-Frying

(For unrefined oil, see "Preparation of Oil" in opposite column.)

Heat oil on a high flame. To test readiness, drop a few grains of salt into oil. If salt rises to top immediately, oil is ready. Reduce flame and begin to fry. Do not put more than 3 or 4 small pieces of dough into the oil at once. Overloading lowers the temperature and tends to make the oil bubble, preventing dough from cooking properly. Remove and drain on brown paper bags, egg cartons or white paper towels for maximum amount of absorption.

Remove excess particles from the oil with an oil skimmer each time before reusing. To reuse oil from fish-frying, cut up a potato and fry it in the oil before deep-frying the pastry.

Preparation of Oil

(This step is necessary only for *unrefined* oil.) Place 1 quart oil (equal parts sesame and safflower, or all safflower) in a heavy skillet or wok. Cook over medium flame until oil begins to move. (If oil is overheated, it will smoke and will be unfit for use in cooking.) Turn flame off immediately. Cool.

Baking

Preheat oven to suggested temperature 15 minutes before baking (use an oven thermometer to assure correct temperature).

If the oven is too warm, leave the oven door open for a few minutes to lower the temperature.

Never overload an oven — when both racks are filled with pans, the heat cannot circulate evenly around the pans.

The top rack of an oven is used only for last-minute browning. Placing baked goods on the top rack will often result in a browned top and a bottom only half baked.

Basic Ingredients

Agar Agar

See Kanten

Almond Milk

See Sweet Almond Milk

Amasake

This can be used as a sweetener, wine or leaven-

ing agent, depending upon how long you let the mixture ferment. It is a delicious substitute for liquor in fruit cakes (before blending), or can be boiled and blended with lemon juice and vanilla as a creame-puff or éclair filling (see Creame Puffs, p. 82).

Apple Butter

Made from fresh apples which have been cooked down to a soft, butterlike consistency, apple butter can be used as a sweetener or filling.

Apple Cider (see also Hard Cider)

Cider is the fermented or partially fermented juice of apples. Organic apple cider has no preservatives, so it must be refrigerated at all times to retard natural fermentation.

Apple Cider Jelly

Apple cider jelly is a concentrated form of apple cider, produced by boiling down the cider like maple sap, until it jells.

Apple Concentrate

Apple concentrate is made from apples that have been washed and pressed into juice. The juice of the whole apple is cooked over a long period of time. It is so concentrated that ¼ cup of concentrate will make two glasses of apple juice. Although it is known to be a natural sweetener, it is difficult to ensure that the apples it was made from were organically grown.

Apple Juice

Apples are crushed to a pulp, and then pressed to obtain juice. The juice is pasteurized to keep it from fermenting and turning into cider. It may be used in place of any other liquid in any recipe to enhance the flavor.

Apricot Purée

See p. 66

Arrowroot (see also Kuzu)

Arrowroot was named by the South American Indians, who used its fresh roots to heal wounds made by poisonous arrows. Arrowroot is used as a thickening agent in place of flour in many instances, because it does not lose its thickening power when combined with very acid fruits. If overcooked, it has a tendency to lose this good quality.

This thickening agent has properties very similar to those of cornstarch, but is of better quality. It is a light starch used in glazes, cake batters, doughs, puddings, pie fillings and other dessert mixes. It is very helpful in holding dough together while rolling it out; just sprinkle some on the cloth before you begin to roll. Arrowroot can also be used in food for sick people and children, because it is easily digested.

Barley Malt Syrup

This syrup or extract is naturally processed by sprouting barley in water. When the sprouts are ready, heat is applied to stop the sprouting and dry out the malt. Use it as a concentrated sweetener in or on any dessert.

Beet Juice

Boil beets in salted water until soft. Strain off liquid and use for tinting icings, crusts or cookies.

Bulghur

To make bulghur, whole wheat is roasted, cracked, parboiled and dried. Bulghur can be used to give a fluffy, light texture to cakes. It is available in natural and Middle Eastern food stores, and can be used in place of couscous.

Corn Sugar

See Sorghum Molasses

Couscous

This is made from the middle of hard semolina wheat which has been precooked before being dried to make it easier to prepare and to give it a lighter, fluffier texture. It is similar to bulghur and is a staple food in the Middle East, served steamed with various other foods and condiments in Tunisia, Morocco and Algeria.

Couscous is available at natural and Middle Eastern food stores and may be used flavored, as a separate dessert, or combined with flour and other ingredients to add lightness to cakes.

Dried Fruit

Sun-drying is the only natural way to dehydrate food. This drying process evaporates the water from the fruit, so that there is not enough moisture to support bacteria.

The fruits are first picked, washed and peeled, then blanched with steam and spread out on a large tray to dry in the sun. The contact with the air tends to darken the pulp. If the dried fruit you purchase is not darker than fresh fruit of the same kind, it usually shows that sulfur dioxide was used to preserve the color.

If a recipe calls for dried fruit, soak the fruit in liquid to cover until soft.

Tropical fruits, fresh or dried, that are available in the United States are fumigated, and therefore not suitable for natural-food cooking.

Eggs

See Egg Story, p. 18

Flour (see also Flour Story, pp. 13-14)

There are many different types of flour available in natural-food stores. It is important to know how they differ from each other, so that you will be able to work successfully with each one of them.

Brown Rice Flour

This is the most suitable flour to use to achieve a crunchier, sweeter taste and texture.

Chestnut Flour

Ground from dried chestnuts, this flour is sweet enough to be used without any additional sweetener, especially if cooked for a long time as a creame (see p. 55), or for toppings and fillings (see pp. 50–54). Chestnut flour can also be used in combination with whole-wheat pastry flour in pastry, to add crunchiness to pie crusts and cookies and to lend a distinctive flavor. It is obtainable at natural-food and Italian-food stores.

Corn Flour

Made from corn, this flour has a sweet flavor and a delicate quality. It is more finely ground than cornmeal, and is used mainly in fillings.

Corn flour should be used as fresh as possible, because it can develop a bitter taste if kept too long.

Sweet Brown Rice Flour

This flour contains more gluten than brown rice flour, and is best used to make candies, steamed desserts or crunchy cookies. (The Chinese use sweet white rice flour for most of their desserts, which are usually steamed.)

Whole-wheat Flour

Whole-wheat flour is mainly used in breads, although a small amount can be used along with whole-wheat pastry flour in yeasted pastries. Because it absorbs more liquid and contains more gluten than whole-wheat pastry flour, it can make doughs tough if overworked, but it can also provide a greater rise for certain yeasted products.

Whole-wheat Pastry Flour

Some of the best, lightest and most delicious cakes are made from whole-wheat pastry flour. Because it contains the bran from the outside of the wheat kernel, it is slightly brown and a great deal more nutritious than white pastry flour.

Roasting Flour, Rolled Oats and Seeds

Roasting flour, oats and seeds improves the flavor of desserts and toppings in which they are used. Prepare as follows.

Cover the bottom of a dry or oiled heavy skillet or frying pan with the rolled oats, flour or seeds, and heat over a low flame.

Move the ingredients from side to side, in a clockwise or counterclockwise motion, until they are lightly browned and begin to have a strong sweet aroma (when roasting chestnut flour, roast until the flour is a medium shade of brown).

Remove from the pan, and place on a plate to cool before using (never add warm flour to cold liquid, as it will get lumpy).

Roasting flour adds more flavor, but overroasting can produce a bitter taste.

Grain Coffee (coffee substitute)

Because of the harmful effects that caffeine may have on our systems,* more and more people are discovering "grain coffee." This tastes very much like coffee but contains cereal, fruit and roots. It is available in both instant and regular form. The instant is most convenient in dessert making. All

---

* Dr. Irwin Rose wrote in *Science Digest* that caffeine, found in all coffee, has the ability to make your heart beat 15 percent faster, make your lungs work 13 times harder and make your stomach secrete up to 400 percent more hydrochloric acid. Coffee has been linked to ulcers as well as heart disease. Caffeine naturally occurs in coffee beans, cocoa beans, tea leaves and cola nuts.

recipes when listing grain coffee refer to the instant kind.

When a recipe calls for at least ½ cup of liquid, regular grain coffee may be substituted for the instant.

To prepare: Bring liquid to a boil, add grain coffee and perk or simmer 10 minutes. Strain. Substitute for the liquid called for in the recipe.

Grain Syrup

Grain syrup is a natural sweetener that can be made at home by anyone. It can be used as a topping for a cake, or in the same way as maple syrup or honey. Make a large quantity so that you can try it in various ways to see which suits you best.

To prepare, see p. 52.

Hard Cider (see also Apple Cider)

Hard cider may be made by leaving cider at room temperature for two to three days in a loosely closed container, until the top of the cider is foamy and it has a sharp, fermented taste.

Kanten (Agar Agar)

Kanten (usually sold under the name Agar Agar) is a vegetable gelatin made from seaweed, and a rich source of essential minerals. It is used mainly as a thickener, adhesive or emulsifying agent. Having the consistency of gelatin, it will set in a warm or cool spot in approximately a half hour.

Kuzu (see also Arrowroot)

Kuzu is the powdered root of the wild arrowroot, gathered in the high mountains of the Far East. Used medicinally for many years in the Orient, kuzu is traditionally taken as a thick beverage to soothe and strengthen the intestines and all internal organs. It is available at most natural-food stores.

Kuzu is also used as a thickening agent in place

of arrowroot. Use a few tablespoons more liquid when substituting kuzu for arrowroot.

Maple Syrup

Maple trees are native to the northeastern part of the United States, where the Indians used the sweet sap of the tree for making sugar and syrup. The sap of the maple begins to flow usually at the end of February or the beginning of March, and continues for 3 to 4 weeks.

The Indians tapped the tree by cutting through the bark, and guiding the sap into containers, using curved pieces of bark. The sap was concentrated by dropping hot stones into it, thereby boiling the liquid. Freezing this and removing the ice that formed on top produced sugar.

Today, maple syrup is extracted by drilling holes or tapping by hand into the side of a tree and inserting wooden taps to let the sap flow out into the buckets. The sudden change in temperature from a warm day to a freezing night stops the sap from flowing, and the warmth starts it again in the morning.

After the buckets have been filled, the sap is taken to a "sugar house," poured into large containers and cooked over fires, which boil the sap down and concentrate it. It takes forty gallons of sap (the sap of about nine maple trees), to make one gallon of syrup.

Unfortunately, today many trees are being injected with formaldehyde so that the sap will not coagulate, plug up the hole and stop running. Formaldehyde not only feeds into the syrup that is sold, but is harmful to the tree, shortening its life by many years.

Syrups are graded A, B and C, depending on the boiling temperature and how long the syrup has been boiled. Grade A Extra Fancy is made from the sweetest sap, and has been boiled the longest amount of time. The lighter the color, the higher the quality.

Rich in minerals, maple syrup is one of the few naturally occurring sweeteners found today. Because it is so concentrated, it goes a long way. So remember, use maple syrup sparingly.

Miso

Miso, a paste made of fermented soybeans, salt and water, is used in place of salt, but mainly as a protein supplement in dressings, sauces, breads and soups. Miso should never be boiled, since boiling destroys the vital enzymes.

Molasses

See Sorghum Molasses

Mu Tea

Mu tea is a 16-herb mixture, popular for its unusual taste. It may be served either hot or cold, plain or mixed with apple juice. Because of its delicate flavor, it can be used as a liquid in various desserts, in place of or in addition to other spices. It adds zest to pie crusts, pastries, cookies and even cakes. Try substituting it for all or part of the liquid suggested. To prepare, boil 1 bag of mu tea in 4 to 5 cups of water for 20 minutes. Let simmer for 10 to 15 minutes. You may reuse the bag to make a weaker tea.

Nuts (see also Seed and Nut Butters)

Various kinds of nuts can be used creatively to enhance texture as well as flavor in dessert making.

Shells of walnuts and almonds are bleached, and shelled nuts are bathed in chemicals to help dissolve the outer shells and skins. But it *is* possible to find nuts that are organically grown and not adulterated with chemical preservatives in natural-food stores.

Roasting imparts a richer taste to any dessert using nuts. Purchase nuts without any additives (salt, oil or chemical dyes), and prepare as follows:

Place the nuts on a baking sheet, giving them plenty of room. Preheat oven for 10 minutes at 325°. Bake nuts, stirring once or twice, until lightly toasted. Overroasting will make them bitter. Store in an airtight glass jar if not to be used immediately.

Do not roast nuts too far in advance, because they tend to get soggy and stale. Nuts that are to be crushed, chopped or ground should be roasted immediately before using. Crushing nuts releases their oils, enhancing the flavor.

Oats

Rolled oats are not just a popular breakfast cereal. They are used in many cakes, cookies, fillings and toppings, and in pie crusts as well.

Buy only "rolled oats," or "old-fashioned oats" at the market or natural-food store. "Instant Oats" or "Quick Cooking" oats have been heavily processed.

Whole oats or steel-cut oats have not been subjected to the heat and pressure of rolling, and are a nutritious substitute for rolled oats in many creames and fillings.

See directions for roasting oats (p. 9).

Oil (see also Oil Story, pp. 16-17)

The best oils to use for most baking and dessert making are unrefined corn-germ oil or unrefined corn oil. They are nutritionally rich and unprocessed, giving a delicate, almost butterlike effect in cakes, and making the flakiest pastry dough imaginable. If these oils are unavailable, the next best oil for desserts is unrefined sesame oil. Because these oils are unrefined, they should be kept refrigerated after opening.

Raisin Juice

Blend together 1 cup soaked raisins plus soaking liquid, ¼ teaspoon salt and 1 cup more liquid. If desired, you may add 1 teaspoon vanilla or orange rind. Use in place of apple juice or cider.

Raisin Purée

See p. 66

Rind

Fresh rind is the freshly grated skin of an orange, tangerine or lemon.

I searched many natural-food stores for organic flavorings in the form of dried orange, tangerine or lemon rind when I began to bake commercially. The only rind available was colored, sugared and chemically treated, so I had to make my own. Here is a quick and easy method for making your own rind. Made this way, rind can be stored indefinitely, so make extra.

Slice an organic fruit into quarters.

Peel off the skin and discard the white pulp beneath the skin (this white is very bitter, and should not be used).

Dry the skin, preferably outside in the sun, until it becomes hard and dry.

Blend skin in a blender 3 to 5 minutes until it turns into a fine powder.

Store in a tightly sealed container in a cool place.

If you do not have a blender, grate the outer rind on the smallest side of a grater, use immediately, or dry as above.

Rolled Oats

See Oats

Salt

See Salt Story, p. 17

Seed and Nut Butters (see also Tahini)

Seed and nut butters are made by grinding roasted or unroasted seeds or nuts to a creamy texture. The most commonly used are peanut butter, almond butter and sesame butter.

Unlike tahini, which is made from hulled sesame seeds, sesame butter is made from whole, roasted sesame seeds. Substituting one seed or nut butter for another, or for tahini, can enhance flavor and add variety in texture to your desserts.

Seeds

Sesame seeds not only provide us with sesame oil, sesame butter and tahini, but lend a decorative effect to glazes and any pastries, as well as a crunchy texture to cookies. They are a rich source of calcium and protein. Sesame seeds should be lightly roasted before using.

Sunflower and poppy seeds are also rich in oil and delicious in cookies, cakes, breads, candies and pastries. They make a fine snack that is rich in vitamin E, and give an attractive appearance as well. Sunflower and poppy seeds too should be lightly roasted before using.

Sorghum Molasses

There are about four kinds of molasses sold to-day. "Unsulfured" molasses is said to be made from the juice of the sun-ripened cane. "Sulfured" molasses, believed to be a by-product of refined sugar, picks up sulfur from the fumes used in the process of converting sugar cane into sugar. "Black-strap" molasses, another by-product of the sugar industry, results from boiling down the sugar several times during the refining process. It is the discarded residue of the cane syrup, after the sugar crystals have been extracted.

Sorghum molasses, produced mainly in the United States, is the most pure and least processed of all. It is the concentrated juice of sorghum, a relative of the millet family, a cereal grain related to corn. The sorghum stems are crushed in a similar way to sugar cane, and boiled to obtain sorghum molasses, a syrup used in cooking.

(Corn syrup or corn sugar, such as "yellow D" corn sugar, is a product of cornstarch produced by treating corn with sulfuric or hydrochloric acid, then neutralizing and bleaching it with other chemicals. Because it costs less to produce than cane or beet sugar, it is used in tremendous quantities in canned fruits, juices, pastries and other processed foods.)

Sweet Almond Milk

There are many recipes in other cookbooks that call for the use of milk. Here is a suggested substitution for cow's milk that sweetens as well as gives the dessert the added body it needs. (Use also as a cool drink in the summertime, adding any flavoring desired.)
1. Blanch ¼ cup almonds (p. 46) or any nut.
2. Place almonds in a blender with 1 cup of liquid (apple juice or cider gives it a pleasant taste).
3. Blend 3 to 5 minutes or until nuts are completely dissolved in the liquid.

Use in place of juice or cider in most recipes. (It is best not to substitute almond milk for juice or cider in the recipes for glaze, because the nut milk can detract from the clear, shiny effect of the glaze.)

Tahini

Tahini is made from hulled sesame seeds which have been lightly toasted to preserve their inherent nutritional value. Tahini that appears loose and liquidy may have been adulterated with poor-quality oil and chemicals.

Tahini contains lecithin, phosphorus, calcium, iron and vitamins B and E, and is abundantly supplied with protein.

Tahini can be used to make a delicious malted, blended with oat meal, vanilla and raisins, as a milk substitute, or spread on bread or crackers. It is used in baking as a flavoring, filling, icing or sauce.

Fresh tahini has a creamy consistency, and if tightly covered and stored in a cool place, it should keep for many months.

Tamari

Tamari is a naturally fermented soy sauce, made from wheat, soybeans, water and salt, which has been aged in wood for at least two years. It provides vegetable protein, natural sugars, oils, vitamins and minerals. Tamari is useful as a seasoning for vegetables, soups, grains, casseroles, sauces and salads, and can be substituted for salt.

Tofu (Soybean Cheese)

Tofu (pronounced "dofu" in Chinese) can be purchased at most natural- or oriental-food stores. It is made from soybeans by soaking, grinding and boiling, thus separating the outside of the bean from the liquid. To this liquid (soy milk) lemon juice, vinegar or any strong acid is added, until the mixture starts to curdle. The liquid is strained through cheesecloth and discarded; and the solid tofu remains.

High in protein, tofu is used almost daily in the Orient. Its light, delicate texture embellishes any dessert, in creames or fillings, or as a basic ingredient in a cake frosting or custard. It has the ability to adapt to a creamy consistency and can jell into any shape or form without a binding agent.

Remember to keep it covered with water and refrigerated until used.

Vanilla

Vanilla is a natural flavor found in the form of a bean or liquid. Sometimes vanillin, an artificial flavor, is added to liquid vanilla. It is best to avoid this kind. If pure vanilla extract is unavailable, substitute the bean for the liquid, preparing as follows:

Soak bean until soft in the liquid which you are to use in a dessert. Slit the bean vertically and scrape out the inside. Soak both bean shell and inside in the liquid for several hours. Or cover and simmer at least 30 minutes. (The longer the soaking or simmering, the more flavor will be added to the liquid. If you do not have time for the long soaking or simmering, you may omit this step, as cooking will also help to bring out the vanilla flavor.)

Remove bean and use liquid. Or, if the mixture is to be blended and bean is soft enough, cut it into small pieces and blend it with the other ingredients.

If neither bean nor pure extract is available, substitute grated tangerine, orange or lemon rind in proportions of 1 teaspoon rind to 1 teaspoon vanilla.

Yeast

See Chapter 5, "Higher and Higher"

About Natural Ingredients

The natural sweetness and fragrance of freshly pressed, organic apple cider, the strong rich taste and texture of whole grains ground into flour, the clear golden color and distinct aroma of unrefined oil, and the natural color and flavor of the sea's greatest gift to man, salt — these are the basic tools of my art, fine dessert making.

I would like to share with you what I learned about the different qualities of basic ingredients such as flour, sugar, oil, salt, eggs and milk, and why I chose certain natural, organic ingredients over refined ones.

Flour Story

In prehistoric times, flour was milled by the pounding of grains between two stones. In time, the lower stone became hollowed out and the upper one rounded, making the mortar and pestle or saddlestone. About 300 B.C. the rotary mill (so called) quern was developed. This mill enabled the grain to be poured down through a hole in the upper stone, slowly feeding down to a lower stone and a stick. This stick, serving as a lever, turned the upper stone against the lower. Slaves or large strong animals turned the larger millstones to grind the grain into fresh flour or meal.

A hundred years ago our grandparents and great-grandparents made their own breads, cakes, cookies, pastries, pies and puddings using freshly ground whole-wheat or other whole-grain flours. The bread we eat today is no longer the "staff of life" which nourished and sustained our grandparents, for it is largely made from "refined" white flour, either bleached or bromated or both.

In the past century, commercial flour has been stripped more and more of natural vitamins and minerals. To begin with, most wheat today is grown with chemical fertilizers, pesticides or herbicides which lower the protein content. Then, in the refining process the outer coating, or bran, of the wheat, is removed and the flour is usually bleached by chlorine gas to make it "white." The outer bran is the part of the grain which contains most of the proteins, minerals and vitamins, and is one of the richest sources of vitamins B and E. This coating, which also provides roughage or lubrication for the intestinal tract, is broken up in the milling of whole-wheat flour so that the digestion of foods made with this flour is actually more difficult than that of unmilled whole grains.

Third, the grinding itself exposes the grain to oxidation which quickly destroys a great deal of nutritional value. Fourth, commercial processes to make the flour store longer (have a longer shelf life) destroy almost all of the wheat, or add chemicals which are easily absorbed by the starches inside the kernel. In this way flour can be stored for years at any temperature and shipped to all parts of the world, with never a rancid taste to spoil it. Synthetic vitamins and minerals are added not to "enrich" but actually to "restore" some of the nutrients that would ordinarily be present in the whole grain. No wonder bread and other flour products sold today all have the word "enriched" on the label, for almost all the valuable natural nutrients have been removed.

During the First World War, a doctor by the name of Sir William Wilcox discovered that an epidemic of beriberi (an extreme deficiency of vitamin B) in India, which had been destroying the British troops, did not affect the Indians. Once Sir William investigated the matter, he found that the Indian troops had been fed their native flour — stone-ground whole-wheat — while the British troops had been treated a little better and were fed white flour instead.

Flour is available in many different qualities, each one used for a specific purpose. I suggest that you buy whole grains if possible, and that you grind your own in a grain mill (obtainable in a natural-food store), to secure the least amount of nutritional loss. If you cannot grind your own grain, the next best thing to do is to buy your flour no more than a day before baking from a reputable natural-food store that receives fresh shipments once or twice a week. If flour is allowed to sit on the shelf after milling for more than ten days, it may lose almost all nutrients. Since it is usually necessary to keep flour at least several days after it has been milled, be sure that the store, as well as you, keeps it refrigerated and away from light. A cold temperature does not eliminate nutritional loss completely, but does slow it down considerably.

Sugar Story

The true meaning of the phrase "white sugar" came to me one day when a friend served me honey for my tea instead of sugar. She explained that she had stopped using sugar when she found out that all commercially packaged sugar was without nutritional value and even harmful to the body. Giving me some literature to read on the subject, she emphasized that sugar, "white" or "natural raw," was grown and processed in the same way. Synthetic fertilizers and weed sprays were applied to the growing plants, and when harvested they were put through cleaning, decolorizing, purifying, sterilizing, crystallizing and drying processes. Reading and listening to her, I began to see that by the time it reaches us, sugar has been stripped of all its natural vitamins and minerals and become truly valueless as a food.

Our grandparents were led to believe that "raw"

sugar was inferior to the refined, white product because it was dark and full of impurities. Actually the reverse was true: the dark vibrant color was proof of the presence of natural minerals. But in 1898 certain sugar refiners procured a chemist who was willing to say that upon examination "raw" sugar was found to contain "disease-producing insects." It was then proposed that only "refined" sugar be sold because "those terrible creatures do not occur in refined sugar of any quality," and so a law prohibiting the sale of unrefined sugar in this country was passed. Today, "raw" and even "brown" sugar is made by processing white sugar one step further — putting molasses back into it for color and flavor. Sugar is heated in the presence of lime which eliminates the calcium salts and destroys almost all of the vitamins. Then it is put into contact with lime, carbonate of soda, carbonic acid and sulfurous anhydride and cooked several times, cooled, crystallized and put into a centrifuge. The remaining molasses is then treated with strontium hydroxide in order to extract the remaining sugar. Then the sugar is purified with carbonic calcium acid, bleached, filtered through charred animal bones and dyed with a coloring derived from tar.

Refined sugar of whatever color is highly touted as an energy food, but this is another misconception. According to Dr. McCracken of the University of California, pure or almost pure sugar (sucrose) such as refined sugar is the worst of all foods. It is absorbed so rapidly into the body through the bloodstream that it may trigger an over-production of insulin; this reduces the blood sugar to harmfully low levels, a condition known as hypoglycemia. However, sugar obtained from natural foods, such as grains and vegetables, is absorbed into the bloodstream gradually, does not upset the delicate balance of high and low blood sugar levels, and gives the body more energy to work with.

The amount of sugar primitive man could eat was limited by the amount of food from natural sources his stomach and intestines could hold. When he ate sugar he was also eating protein, vitamins, minerals and other valuable food elements along with it. Because his sugar supply came mainly from natural fruits and from vegetables as plant starch, his body was able to break down the sugar into glucose gradually, thus not straining the body.

But modern man eats pound after pound of refined sugar without being restrained by any natural fiber. Not getting any nutrients with it, especially those which are necessary to help metabolize the sugar, he strains his pancreas and other internal organs by eating sugar in the form of sucrose. *The stress of bypassing the natural digestive process of breaking sugar down into glucose causes undue strain on the body and can lead eventually to severe illness.*

A number of other ill effects can be produced in the body by sugar. Dr. Dennis P. Burkitt of the Medical Research Council of London has stated that refined sugar alters the bacteria in the lining of the intestines. Such altered bacteria are capable of breaking down bile salts to form cancer-producing material. Dr. Burkitt said, "You can put the whole thing down to food — especially white flour and sugar."

There is also ample evidence to prove that refined sugar encourages bacteria that eat up B vitamins and kills certain bacteria that help produce vitamins and enzymes in the body. In order to digest sugar (which has lost its own vitamins during the refining process), the body must take vitamin B and minerals such as calcium from the heart, liver, kidneys and nervous system, resulting in other deficiencies as well. The instant energy or "sugar rush" occurring immediately upon sugar entering the system, paralyzes the stomach until acids are mobilized to neutralize it. This over-production of acids is counteracted by an emergency mobilization of stored minerals. Calcium is the first mineral to be used and is therefore the most easily depleted mineral in the body.

Furthermore, when we have an excess of sugar in our bodies, the liver stores it, and when the liver is overloaded it returns the excess sugar to the blood in the form of fatty acids. These get circulated throughout the body, are stored as accumulated solid fat in the thighs, buttocks and other less active areas and can cause the heart to become sluggish and perhaps even to stop. Thus even though sugar is not fat it can *change* into fats when taken excessively.

Other symptoms have been related to the over-consumption of sugar. These include loss of appetite, fatigue, tooth decay, depression, difficulty in thinking, rheumatism due to a calcium-phosphorus imbalance and even mental illness. Refined sugar irritates the mucous membranes, tissues, blood vessels, glands and digestive organs because it is unnaturally concentrated.

To me, it is senseless to try to use "better" sugar, when in effect it is all the same. I strongly recommend that "refined" sugar be eliminated entirely from the diet. Choose instead a natural sweetener such as maple syrup, sorghum molasses, apple concentrate, honey, barley malt syrup, apple juice, cider, apple butter or apple cider jelly. (Of course too much of anything, including unrefined, natural sugars may also be harmful to the body.) Carrots, beets, parsnips and other vegetables and fruits contain many valuable nutrients as well as natural sugars. None of us needs refined sugars because our bodies convert more than half of our food into blood sugar that will satisfy our sugar requirement. So bake with natural ingredients that will make your desserts taste better and your family and friends feel better.

Oil Story

Oils are usually obtained from seeds, flowers, beans and the kernels of native and tropical fruits and grain. Seeds constitute one of the most important sources of man's food supply, because within their structures are the elements and properties essential to the beginning and reproduction of life. Most of the oils we use are pressed from oil-bearing seeds such as safflower, sesame, sunflower, soybean and the germ of the whole corn kernel.

It seems that one of the chief aims of the food processing industry is to make food look "pure." Food processors remove valuable nutrients which give natural color, odor and flavor in an effort to make foods look whiter, brighter, lighter and clearer. Oil is no exception.

Most of the cooking oils commonly sold today are refined so much that they are usually flat-tasting, odorless and dull-looking, but according to the manufacturer they are "pure." The refining process subjects oils to heating, the addition of acids, bleaching and the alternation of extreme hot and cold temperatures. These treatments are not without their ill effect:

Dr. Roger Williams has recently published a book, called *Nutrition Against Disease*, in which he outlines the dangers of refined oils. In tests which compared refined oils in relation to unrefined oils, it was shown that refined oils actually increased the cholesterol level of the blood and increased the danger of heart disease. Refined oils are sold under nationally known brands labeled as cold-pressed. These can be easily distinguished by their light color and lack of odor and taste. In his book, Dr. Williams suggested that all consumers take the extra time and trouble to seek out unrefined and pressed oils and that the threat to health posed by these refined oils was too great to be overlooked.
– Paul Hawken, President, Erewhon Trading Company, Inc., Boston

Unrefined oils, on the other hand, still contain original substances which give natural flavor, odor and color not usually present in a refined oil. As a consumer, you can tell whether an oil is truly unrefined and pure by using your senses. An oil that has not been chemically refined will be darker, thicker, and have an odor and flavor similar to the source from which it was pressed.

It was a pleasant surprise to discover oils that were not bland, tasteless or odorless, and that could be used for cooking as well as baking. Nutritious and flavorful, these unrefined oils provide vitamins A, E and K along with lecithin, which helps to break down cholesterol deposits in the tissues of the body.

Saturated fats are mainly responsible for cholesterol deposits that form in the tissues, clogging the arteries and veins. One way to distinguish between unsaturated and saturated fats is by observing them at room temperature: the saturated fats are solid, but the harmless unsaturated fats are liquids otherwise known as oils.

I recommend that you use good-quality, unrefined oils, such as corn, corn-germ, safflower, sesame, soybean or olive when cooking and baking instead of refined oils or butter or shortening. You will be amazed at the difference in taste, texture and aroma of your products, and at the same time the improved health of the persons who enjoy them.

Store your oils in a cool place to assure their freshness.

Salt Story

Salt has always been one of the most common and important ingredients of life. Thousands of years ago it was the only preservative used by man. At one time it had religious significance, for it was the symbol of purity among the ancient Hebrews, who rubbed newborn babies with it to ensure their good health. The Old Testament tells the story of Elisha throwing salt into a spring to purify its waters (2 Kings, 2:19–22). In the Near East, salt used at meals is a sign of friendship and hospitality. The Arabs say, "There is salt between us," meaning we have eaten together and are friends. Salt was once so precious that Caesar's soldiers received part of their pay for the purpose of buying common salt; it was known as their *salarium*, which is where our word *salary* comes from. From ancient times through the Renaissance, some of Europe's important highways were salt-trade routes; even before the Romans, the Celts would carry salt from western Austria to the Baltic Sea where they would exchange it for amber.

All salt was at one time essentially sea salt. Today, there are three main kinds of salt on the market: unrefined, sun-dried sea salt, iodized salt and refined table salt. Salt found inland, in rock deposits or in springs that flow through them, can be traced back to the ocean that covered the earth millions of years ago. Earth movements isolated parts of this ancient sea, which evaporated, uncovering these beds of rock.

Unrefined, sun-dried, white sea salt contains many minerals that are not found in refined table salt: gold, iron, copper, calcium and magnesium are present in small quantities, and these are important to our digestive processes.

In ancient times people kept crude, gray sea salt in a jar for at least one year. During that time, the magnesium absorbed water from the air and went to the bottom of the jar. The top salt became less salty and purer and was used in cooking and baking. Usually this salt was roasted to make it drier and ground into a finer powder before it was used.

Most salt found in the stores today has had the trace minerals removed, supposedly to make it taste "saltier" and look purer. The refining process subjects salt to great pressure and steam heat, causing it to crystallize instantly. Although this method saves money, the crystal produced is not only devoid of its trace minerals but also slow to dissolve and difficult to digest.

Try this experiment to see if your salt has been "refined." Place a teaspoon of salt in a glass of water and stir it once. Look at it a little while later to see if there is any sediment. Natural, unrefined sea salt has a tendency to disappear in the water within a few minutes leaving the liquid clear (a residue or cloudiness in the water may indicate the presence of impurities). But the refined table salt will require longer to dissolve.

Commercial table salt sold in the stores may also contain additives. Calcium bicarbonate is added to keep it dry and pourable, and iodine, which is commonly used to prevent goiter,* may also be added. Dextrose, a simple sugar, is added to stabilize the iodine, because it is very volatile and oxidizes in direct sunlight. Then other additives are used to keep the salt looking white.

It is important that we use salt that is as pure and unrefined as nature intended it, salt that has not been treated with chemical additives but extracted from the sea and allowed to dry naturally in the sun. Therefore, when you buy salt remember that, while it may be the smallest ingredient you use in quantity, it is just as or even more important than the other ingredients in your cooking and baking. It can bring out the delicate flavors of other ingredients, sometimes actually making them sweeter.

* Iodine is naturally supplied by the following, in order of highest iodine content: kelp, Agar-Agar, Swiss chard, turnip greens, summer squash, mustard greens, watermelon, cucumber, spinach.

Egg Story

Eggs are prepared by nature to serve as food for the growing, unborn bird; they contain all the minerals and vitamins essential to support life. Thus they can be good food for humans too, if not taken to excess. But the quality of the eggs we use depends upon the food we feed the hen and the environment in which she lives.

Commercial chickens are usually raised to yield the greatest amount of eggs or meat, disregarding the natural environment and diet of the birds. Stimulants are used to increase the productivity of the chickens. Amphetamines and arsenic are sometimes put into their feed to increase their appetite so that they will weigh more and draw a better price at the marketplace. These additives result in large chemical deposits in the commercial eggs and chicken meat. Furthermore the meat- and fishmeal fed to these chickens are of the lowest pos-

sible quality, and full of preservatives, hormones and weight-gaining stimulants as well. Other unnatural ingredients in commercial eggs include antibiotics, phosphates and meat steroids.

The best eggs to buy are those marked "organic and fertile." This indicates to you that the birds that laid the eggs have been fed high-quality food without additives or preservatives and that the eggs are complete and whole. These eggs have many natural growth-promoting hormones which can be lacking in sterile, nonorganic eggs, as well as having natural lecithin.

Hens produce richer, more nutritious eggs if they are allowed to run freely on the ground in uncluttered pens and to mate freely. Healthier and happier chickens, and eggs with more vitality can produce healthier and happier people.

Milk Story

About 80 billion pounds of milk or milk products are consumed by Americans each year.* In order to fill the demands of such a huge consumption, cows are unnaturally confined, given antibiotics and hormones and forced to produce excessive amounts of milk. This is not only unnatural, but unhealthy as well.

Milk is a secondary food when one considers that vegetables are the first products of nature. It is necessary for infants to consume mother's milk, because they cannot digest primary food, nor can they assimilate vegetables and cereals. After the teeth grow in and the digestive system matures, it is no longer necessary to drink it.

Frequent consumption of milk reduces the digestive power of the mouth, stomach and intestines and can also decrease the transmutation ability which can lead to allergies. Cow's milk and milk products are saturated fats, known to be a source of danger in relation to the cholesterol build-up, causing high blood pressure, heart failure and hardening of the arteries.**

Dr. H. M. Sinclair, member of The Royal College of Physicians, teacher of human nutrition at Oxford, noted a lack of unsaturated essential fatty acids in cow's milk. According to *Consumer Bulletin*, March 1960, "Dr. Sinclair has been cautiously against the overfeeding of children, particularly with cow's milk and butter."

Otto Carque, in *Vital Facts About Foods*, says, "Milk and milk products are far from being absolute necessities for the maintenance of the health and vigor of the race. The milking of animals is an unnatural process. It lowers their vitality and often makes them victims of disease, while it impairs the quality of the milk. Milk and dairy products are by no means staple foods with all people. The use of milk is comparatively recent in origin in the history of the human race, and even today there are people like the Japanese who hardly take any milk."

Pasteurization is the process of heating a liquid, particularly milk, to a temperature between 131° and 158°, to destroy harmful bacteria apparently

---

* Herman Aihara, *Milk, A Myth of Civilization*, 1971.
** "Man is the only animal that ingests eggs and milk

throughout its lifetime. He is also the only animal, as far as it is known, which dies early in life." (*Consumer Bulletin*, "On Milk," November 1959.)

without materially changing the milk's nutritive value, composition or flavor. Yet pasteurized milk is subjected to two processes that alter nutritional value, composition and flavor as well. Commercial milk is first sterilized (at 140°) to destroy the coliforms, but this also in turn destroys the lactobacilli (lactobacillus acidophilus). The lactobacilli are the enzymes that inhabit our intestines, aid in the digestion of other food, protect the colon from bacteria and contribute toward proper elimination so that people do not suffer from putrefaction of food. One third to one half of the vitamin B_{12} is destroyed, vitamin C begins to be greatly reduced or destroyed and the curd is much harder and more difficult to digest.

In 1963 the FDA admitted that 67 percent of all milk shipped interstate showed pesticidal residue. In 1966 it was officially admitted that "no milk available on the market today, in any part of the U.S., is free of pesticide residues." (Hearings before Subcommittee, 89th Congress.)

Goat's milk is a much finer-quality milk to use if one feels the need for animal milk in baking or cooking. It can be found in most natural-food stores either "raw" or pasteurized. In some of the recipes that follow I have used almond milk, which not only adds an exotic flavor to desserts but additional nutritional value as well.

About Baking Powder

Some baking powders contain alum, a product of aluminum used for its gas-forming or leavening effect. Alum is a synthetic. Not only is it totally lacking in nutritional value, it may even be harmful (see p. 3). By the way, most commercially available pickles contain alum, used for a hardening effect.

2. Layer after Layer

Cakes and Petit Fours

Creating new dessert recipes is one of my greatest pleasures. Whether the occasion be a special party, a friend's birthday, a wedding celebration or a request to supply cakes to a natural-food store or restaurant, I use any occasion which pops up as a reason to experiment.

Here are some suggestions that I would like to share with you which can alter consistency, texture and taste of cakes. I hope that through these hints you can develop special techniques that work for you, so you may create and embellish imaginative recipes on your own.

Leavening

Most of these cake recipes rely on eggs and/or yeast for lightness in texture. Because the flour that is used has not been presifted, bleached, bromated or

stripped of all the bran, it reacts differently with other ingredients. Most of the cakes will not rise three or four inches; they will be lower than the normal "layer cake." If you wish a higher cake, bake several layers instead of one or two, increase the amount of yeast suggested by half, or double the amount of eggs.

Eggs

Fresh eggs have a tiny air space at either end, in between the lining and the shell. A fresh egg will sink in water, end down, and a less fresh egg will float on its side.

In all recipes eggs should be used at room temperature. If they are cold, they should be warmed as follows: Combine eggs and sweetener in a mixing bowl. Stir for 1 minute. Set the bowl over a pan of hot water on a low flame until contents are lukewarm. Stir occasionally to prevent them from cooking or sticking to the pan. Take off heat.

To use whole eggs in baking cake, beat with a rotary beater, wire whisk or electric mixer until eggs have almost doubled in volume, and are thick, fluffy and filled with air. Do not overmix when folding in with other ingredients, or you will force the air out of the eggs, and the result will be a heavy cake.

Separated Eggs

If you separate the eggs, the batter will usually be lighter.

Crack the egg and let white fall into a mixing bowl, catching yolk on half of shell. Transfer yolk to other half of shell, alternating back and forth, letting remainder of white fall from shell into bowl.

Place yolk in a separate bowl. Mix with a fork and add the other ingredients called for.

Begin to beat whites and salt together slowly, un-til whites become foamy (use rotary beater, wire whisk or electric beater). Increase the motion and beat without stopping until whites look airy and stand up in firm peaks.

Fold whites into batter by hand (pp. 4–5) or with a rubber spatula to retain as much air as possible.

Bake batter as quickly as possible without banging or opening oven door until at least half of the baking time suggested has elapsed.

Yeast

See Chapter 5, "Higher and Higher," for instructions on yeast in baking.

Moisture

Sometimes home ovens (gas or electric) tend to be too dry for certain batters. Those batters that do not have any leavening agents at all may form a hard crust on top of the cake before it is sufficiently baked on the inside. To prevent this, place a small pan of hot water in the bottom of the oven while baking unyeasted, eggless batters. This allows more moisture in the air to circulate around the pans and prevent a crust from forming. This method may also be used when baking yeasted batters, but allow more baking time.

Alternate Method

Cover baking pan and "steam" for half of the recommended baking time (use a cover that is high enough to allow for rising). Remove cover and bake until cake is done.

Sweetening

Most of the recipes call for a minimum amount of sweetener, allowing the flavor and taste of the other ingredients to come through. However, you may want to use more sweetener than is suggested for certain occasions.

Add as much concentrated sweetener (maple syrup, fruit concentrates, grain honey, sorghum molasses, barley malt syrup) as you like or supple-ment with apple butter, apple cider jelly, amasake, grain syrup or raisin purée, decreasing the amount of liquid proportionately. Oil cup before measur-ing. (See Sweetness Equivalency Chart, p. 149.)

Experimenting with different qualities and quanti-ties of sweeteners will allow you the flexibility needed in creating your own imaginative recipes.

Decorations Baked on the Cake

Some decorations can be put onto a cake before it is baked.

Nuts

Unroasted nuts are usually easy to apply before baking and look attractive on top of a cake.

For very special occasions, blanch the nuts before scattering them on top of the cake (see p. 46).

To make a glaze over the nuts, you may brush a little egg white carefully over the unroasted or blanched nuts before baking.

Rind

Plain cakes look more attractive if you sprinkle orange or lemon rind on top. If baking period is long, sprinkle the rind gently on top of the cake three quarters of the way through the baking time.

Crumb Topping

If the cake has a long baking period, sprinkle the crumb topping (p. 68) on halfway through the baking time allotted.

Meringue Topping

A meringue topping (see p. 60) gives a very pleasing look to a cake or pie as well as a special taste.

Pastry as a Decoration

Pastry can be used as a decoration, especially if you are making pastry and batter cakes on the same day. Use a lattice design of pastry (p. 73) over a fruit cake or any design you choose on top of any cake. Be sure that proper time is allotted to bake the pastry as well as the cake.

Ready or Not

Insert a thin wire cake-tester or metal skewer into the center of the cake. It will come out dry when the cake is ready.

Press a fingertip lightly in the center of the cake.
The center will spring back when cake is done.

A leavened cake will pull away from sides of pan when baked.

Cake will be sufficiently browned when baked.

Removing Cake from Pan

Place a cake rack on top of the cake in its pan. Invert rack, pan and cake simultaneously. Let stand until the cake begins to contract away from the sides of the pan. If cake does not begin to slip down out of the pan and onto the rack, take a cold damp sponge and run it over the bottom of the pan several times. Then with the handle of a wooden spoon, tap the bottom of the pan gently, in a circular motion, until the cake begins to fall.

Egg cakes should be turned out immediately after removing from the oven.

If you are using a tube form (pan with a hole in the center), set the tube on the neck of a bottle so that air can circulate around it while cooling.

When using a springform pan, place it on a cake rack and let stand until cake begins to contract away from the side of the pan. Unclip and remove the side. Allow to get cold before removing bottom.

Filling a Tube Cake

Slice tube cake across top. Cut a circle 1 inch from the outer edge, stopping 1 inch from bottom of cake. Remove excess cake by cutting diagonally, first from the inside of the outer rim to the base of the inner rim. Continue all around and through the entire cake.

Reverse and repeat the cutting, from the inside of the inner rim to the base cut of the outer rim. Remove these sections. Fill and cover with the top. Ice and serve.

FORGET ME KNOTS

1. Liquid content will vary according to the temperature of the room, the moisture in the flour and the air, and the general weather conditions of the day.

2. Preheat the oven 15 minutes before baking, using a temperature gauge inside the oven. An overheated oven may produce a cracked, heavy cake and an underheated oven will produce a soggy cake.

3. Use all ingredients at room temperature so that they will blend more evenly and easily.

4. The best oils to use for all baking unless otherwise specified are unrefined corn-germ, corn or sesame oil. Too much oil may cause the cake to be too crumbly to handle.

5. Sift flour before measuring, never shaking down the flour into the cup after sifting; sift only to get out the lumps. Do not separate the bran from the wheat except for very delicate cakes or pastries. Add the bran back to the sifted flour (or reserve for puddings, breads) before folding it into the batter.

6. Too much flour (or too little liquid) will make the cake uneven and dry.

7. Bulghur wheat or couscous adds lightness to unleavened cakes.

8. When adding eggs to an eggless recipe, decrease the amount of liquid accordingly (1 egg = ⅕ cup liquid).

9. When using fewer eggs than called for, substitute 1 teaspoon arrowroot or 2 teaspoons whole-wheat pastry flour for each omitted egg.

10. Use ½ teaspoon lemon juice to every 3 egg whites to make a stiffer white, with larger volume and greater stability.

11. When measuring liquid sweeteners, oil the measuring cup to prevent the sticky liquid from adhering to the cup.

12. Wooden utensils are preferable because metal can alter the taste.

13. When using a hand beater, extra time should be allotted for beating.

14. Overbeating will break down air bubbles after they have been formed, leaving a heavy, dry cake (yeasted batters excluded).

15. To prevent cake from sticking to the bottom of the pan, dust a little flour over the oiled pan.

16. When placing batters containing eggs in a pan, DO NOT PAT DOWN batter or bang pan; this motion will cause the air in the eggs to escape.

17. When a cake sticks to the pan, wrap a damp cloth around the pan for a few minutes, and it should come out more easily.

18. To keep cake from drying up, drop an apple or orange in the cake box and keep it in a cool place.

19. An old-fashioned way to preserve fruit cake up to one year is as follows: pour a teaspoonful of brandy over the underside of the cake, and let it soak. Wrap it up in a clean cloth which has been sprinkled with brandy. Place it in an earthenware crock with a tight lid; lay a fresh apple on top of cake, and cover. Once a week, set the crock on a range until it is warmed, taking out the apple before warming. Place a fresh apple in the crock every two weeks and renew the brandy application as well. (Hard cider may be substituted for brandy.)

Basic Cakes

The basic cake is one of the most versatile cakes to make. If you do not have an electric mixer, a hand beater or wire whisk will do very nicely.

BASIC CAKE I

3 eggs (at room temperature)
¼ cup concentrated sweetener
1½ cups sifted whole-wheat pastry flour
½ cup oil
1 teaspoon vanilla
¼ teaspoon salt
1 teaspoon orange rind

Preheat the oven to 350°. Oil and lightly flour the *bottom* of a springform pan.

Combine eggs and sweetener; beat until light and fluffy. Sift flour slowly on top of egg mixture. Fold in gently, adding the oil, vanilla, salt and orange rind. DO NOT OVERMIX.

Pour batter into prepared pans. DO NOT PAT DOWN. Bake 25 to 30 minutes. Spoon topping mixture onto the cake 10 minutes before it is done, reduce temperature to 300° and bake until brown. DO NOT OPEN THE OVEN DOOR DURING THE FIRST 15 MINUTES OF BAKING TIME.

When cake is baked, remove from oven and place on rack to cool. Air must get to cake immediately. Unclip the side of the pan after the cake contracts. Or leave cake in turned-off oven with oven door open about 15 minutes before removing sides.

BASIC CAKE II

Ingredients for Basic Cake I

Separate eggs. Add vanilla and orange rind to yolks; mix and set aside. Beat egg whites and salt, slowly dripping in sweetener and beating continuously until peaked. Fold one quarter of the egg whites into yolks. Pour this mixture over remaining egg whites and sprinkle sifted flour on top. *Fold* eggs and flour *gently*, adding oil at the same time, until the flour and oil are no longer visible. DO NOT OVERMIX.

To bake, follow directions for Basic Cake I.

Variations

Tofu Sour Creame

Combine Tofu Sour Creame I (p. 60), ½ cup apples and ½ teaspoon cinnamon or ginger. Spoon this topping over the cake 10 minutes before cake is done. Lower temperature to 300° and bake until browned.

Special Party Cake

Add to basic recipe 3 eggs and ¼ to ½ cup more flour. This will yield a larger cake or two smaller ones. See also Party Cakes, p. 27.

Vanilla

Increase vanilla to 2 tablespoons.

Tangerine, Orange or Lemon

Add 2 teaspoons more of tangerine, orange or lemon rind, and 3 tablespoons juice of fruit; or add juice and rind of half a grated tangerine, orange or lemon.

Seed

Add 2 teaspoons caraway, roasted poppy, sunflower or sesame seeds before folding in flour.

Nut

Add ½ cup roasted chopped nuts — almonds, walnuts, pecans, or cashews — before folding in flour. Or prepare ½ cup cooked chestnuts (p. 66). Add to mixture before folding in flour.

Dried Fruit

Marinate ¼ cup dried fruit in apple juice or cider to cover overnight. Squeeze out liquid; dice fruit and toss in small amount of flour. Follow recipe for basic cake, adding fruit before folding in flour.

Raisin

Substitute ½ cup raisin purée (p. 66) for sweetener, adding more flour if necessary.

Apricot

Substitute ½ cup apricot purée (p. 66) for sweetener, adding more flour if necessary.

Fruit Concentrate

Substitute strawberry, cherry or any other flavor fruit concentrate for sweetener.

Spice

Sift into the flour before adding to egg mixture 2 teaspoons cinnamon or dried mint, ¼ teaspoon cloves, ½ teaspoon ginger; *or* 1 teaspoon cloves, 1 teaspoon cinnamon.

Ginger

Sift into flour before adding to egg mixture ½ teaspoon cinnamon, ¼ teaspoon cloves, 1 teaspoon ginger.

Arrowroot

Substitute 1 cup arrowroot flour for 1 cup whole-wheat pastry flour. Combine sifted pastry flour and arrowroot flour before adding to batter. This cake will be smaller than the basic cake, so you may want to add an extra egg or two.

Coffee

Mix 4 tablespoons grain coffee (p. 9) with the yolks. Or add ½ cup grain coffee to dry ingredients before folding into eggs.

SOUR CREAME COFFEE CAKE

Follow recipe for Basic Cake I or II. Combine 1 cup Tofu Sour Creame (p. 60) and 1 to 2 tablespoons extra sweetener. Add this to eggs or egg yolks in basic recipe. Also add ½ cup grain coffee (p. 9) and ¼ cup additional whole-wheat pastry flour to dry ingredients before folding into egg mixture.

Alternate Method

Follow recipe for Basic Cake I or II, adding 1 to 2 tablespoons extra sweetener and ½ cup grain coffee to dry ingredients before folding in eggs. Prepare 1 cup Tofu Sour Creame and spoon on top of cake 10 minutes before baking time has elapsed.

Or, prepare 1 cup Crumb Topping (p. 68). Follow recipe for Basic Cake I or II. Add grain coffee and sweetener as in alternate method above. Pour half of the batter into pan, sprinkle half of topping over it and cover with remaining batter. Spoon Tofu Sour Creame on top of cake and sprinkle re-

maining Crumb Topping over it 10 minutes before baking time has elapsed.

BASIC SPONGE SHEET

This versatile recipe can be used to make jelly rolls, petit fours, or any type of cake roll desired. The filling can be anything from Chestnut Creame to apple butter.

    3 eggs
    1 teaspoon vanilla
    ¼ teaspoon salt
    ¼ cup concentrated sweetener
    1 cup sifted whole-wheat pastry flour

Preheat the oven to 375° and line the bottom of an 8 x 11 x ½-inch baking sheet with wax or brown paper. Oil the paper.

Separate the eggs. Break up yolks with a fork; add vanilla. Beat whites until they are stiff, gradually adding salt. Add sweetener, and continue beating 3 to 5 minutes longer, or until whites are peaked. Fold a quarter of the white into yolks, and add to remaining whites. Sprinkle sifted flour over mixture and fold gently. DO NOT OVERMIX.

Bake 12 to 15 minutes, or until sponge is lightly browned and pulls away from the side of the pan. Immediately remove sponge from pan, and place on a towel or cloth. Peel off the paper, trim the edges so that it will roll without splitting. Spread with filling. Roll up the sheet tightly in the towel or cloth. Let stand on a rack to cool. Glaze.

Alternate Method

After trimming, roll up sheet tightly in a towel or cloth. Cool. Unroll and spread with desired filling. Roll up again firmly, without cloth, placing it seam side down. Cover and chill until serving. You may glaze the top with any of the basic glazes (pp. 62–64) and sprinkle chopped nuts or roasted chestnut flour over the glaze before serving.

Filling Suggestions

    ½ cup Chestnut Creame I or II (pp. 57–58)
    ½ cup apricot purée (see Fruit Purée, p. 66)
    1 cup creame (pp. 55–60) or custard filling (pp. 61–62)

See variations for Basic Cakes I and II.

FOUR-LAYER SPONGE

Ingredients for 2 sponge sheets

Filling
1 tablespoon arrowroot flour
½ cup apple juice or cider
1 teaspoon lemon juice
1 recipe Chestnut Creame (p. 57)
Roasted chopped nuts

Prepare sponge sheets, and bake 10 to 15 minutes or until brown. Remove from oven, place upside-down on a rack and remove paper. Cool.

Cut into strips 4 x 11 inches. Sandwich layers together, spreading Chestnut Creame in between each layer. Keep 1 layer aside. Chill at least 1 hour.

Dilute arrowroot in apple juice. Cook, stirring constantly, until mixture boils, turns clearer and begins to thicken. Remove from heat. Stir in lemon juice.

Put top layer on cake. Cover sides with remaining Chestnut Creame. Pour arrowroot apple glaze on top of cake. Chill at least 5 hours. Just before serving, sprinkle nuts on top.

PARTY CAKES

Bake any basic cake mixture in 8- or 9-inch pans, doubling or tripling the recipe, depending on how many layers you plan to have. Cut each layer into two layers. (Before decorating, see p. 42).

Spread desired filling in between cut layers, placing first layer top side up and each succeeding layer top side down. Spread filling around side of cake.

Roll the sides in chopped nuts, orange rind, etc. (see p. 46). Decorate the top with the same filling or frosting as the layers or choose one that is complementary to the filling.

CUPCAKES

Use any cake recipe and bake at 350°. Sprinkle top with nuts or seeds. *Or*

Fill the cupcake tins half full, put 1 tablespoon purée, creame or custard filling in the center, cover with remaining batter and bake. *Or*

Cut a thin slice off the top of a baked cupcake, scoop out the center, and fill with custard, creame or purée. Replace the top, frost and serve.

See Chapter 3 for other fillings and decorations.

Petit Fours

Petit fours, or "little cakes," are made by cutting larger cakes into smaller, different-shaped cakes — diamond, square, round, triangular or rectangular. They are very delightful to serve at children's parties or as small dessert cakes for unexpected guests. It is a great way to "dress up" leftovers and serve a new dessert to friends and family. For example:

Cut cake into thirds.

Cut one part into eight squares.

Cut another section into small rectangles.

Cut remaining third into triangles and diamonds by cutting diagonally in strips, then cut again diagonally.

Dip squares into glaze (pp. 62–64), sprinkle crushed nuts on top.

Spread Nut Butter Icing (p. 54) on top of rectangles.

Decorate with raisins (features of a face), orange or tangerine or lemon rind, crushed roasted nuts, seeds, mint.

Spread creame (pp. 55–60) on top and sides of diamonds and trim the edges with seeds or crushed nuts.

Spread with Tofu Creame.

Cut cake into ¼-inch slices.

Spread 5 slices with raisin purée (p. 66).

Stack 6 slices to make 6 layers.

Cut into 1-inch slices and then cut slices into 2-inch cubes.

Top with any crushed roasted nut, seed, lemon, orange or tangerine rind or shredded coconut.

See also "Before Decorating the Cake" (p. 42). Cut finished decorated cake into 1-inch shapes.

Cakes without Icing

If a cake has an attractive appearance when baked or steamed, or has a very definite flavor, icing it may detract from both, so never decorate a cake unless it will be an advantage to do so.

APPLE-MINT VALENTINE COUSCOUS CAKE

    2 cups uncooked couscous
    4 tablespoons oil
    1 teaspoon salt
    5 cups apple juice or cider
1¼ bars kanten
    1 tablespoon dried mint
    1 recipe Chestnut Creame II (p. 57)

Couscous

Sauté couscous until well coated with oil (2 tablespoons oil for 1 cup couscous). Place in a mixing bowl and add salt and 3 cups warm juice or cider. Stir well. Set aside. Rinse kanten under cold running water quickly. Squeeze out excess liquid. Shred into small pieces and combine with remaining apple juice or cider. Bring to a boil, lower flame and cook together with mint until kanten dissolves. Add couscous to kanten mixture and stir until well combined.

Rinse a heart-shaped mold under cold running water; dry well and oil. See "Inlay" (p. 49) for various decorating ideas. Place couscous into mold *immediately* after cooking (if too much time elapses the mixture will begin to set). Cool at room temperature before chilling.

Filling

Prepare Chestnut Creame filling. Rinse another heart-shaped mold under cold running water; dry well and oil. Pour creame into mold immediately after cooking. Leave at room temperature to set.

Turn out couscous cake on platter (p. 42). Spread any filling or icing on couscous layer. Place Chestnut Creame layer on top (p. 49). Serve as is or see Chapter 3 for other ideas. Chill before serving, if desired.

STEAMED APPLE CAKE

2 cups raisins
   Apple juice or cider to cover raisins
1 cup couscous
1 cup roasted sweet brown rice flour
2 cups whole-wheat pastry flour
1 teaspoon cinnamon
½ teaspoon cloves
2 teaspoons orange, tangerine or lemon rind
½ teaspoon salt
½ cup oil
3 cups diced apples

Soak raisins in juice or cider until soft. Reserve liquid.

Combine all dry ingredients. Add oil to dry mixture, rubbing with your hands until oil is fully absorbed.

Dice apples (peel if not organic). Boil reserved juice. Add apples and raisins to the dry mixture and pour boiled juice or cider over the mixture slowly until the consistency is pancakelike — thick enough to drop from a wooden spoon. Add more boiled liquid if necessary.

Prepare steamer (see p. 5). Pour batter into pre-oiled mold, place in steamer, cover mold and steam 3 to 4 hours.

Alternate Method

Pour batter into pan, cover and steam in a preheated 350° oven for 1 hour. Remove cover and bake 15 to 20 minutes longer or until cake is set and lightly browned.

Variation

Substitute any fresh fruit in season for apples. See also variations for Basic Cakes I and II (p. 25).

APPLESAUCE CAKE

    2 cups Applesauce (p. 51)
    1 cup apple butter or apple cider jelly
    ½ cup oil
    ½ cup raisins
    ½ cup roasted chopped walnuts or sunflower
        seeds
    4 cups sifted whole-wheat pastry flour
    2 teaspoons cinnamon
    ¾ teaspoon cloves
    2 teaspoons ginger
    1 teaspoon salt

Combine Applesauce, apple butter and oil. Beat with a wooden spoon until the oil is well mixed in. Add raisins and nuts. Preheat the oven to 350°. Oil and lightly flour an 8-inch round pan.

Sift the remaining ingredients, add to the apple mixture and stir until batter is smooth and creamy. The consistency should be thick and pancakelike (p. 5). Adjust flour-liquid content accordingly.

Pour into pan and bake 40 to 50 minutes or until cake pulls away from the sides of the pan and is springy to the touch.

Variations

Substitute 2 cups roasted or unroasted chestnut flour for 2 cups of the whole-wheat pastry flour.

Substitute any fruit sauce for Applesauce.

Substitute ½ cup concentrated sweetener for ½ to 1 cup apple juice.

BARBARA'S BEAN DELIGHT

    1 cup dried chestnuts
    Apple juice or cider to cover
    1 cup uncooked azuki beans*
    1 cup raisins
    4 cups apple juice or cider
    ½ teaspoon salt
    ½ cup roasted chopped walnuts
    ¼ cup roasted chestnut flour
    1¼ teaspoons vanilla

Soak chestnuts overnight in apple juice or cider to cover. Reserve liquid. Pressure-cook beans, chest-

* Azuki beans are very small red beans which can be found in most Chinese, Japanese or natural-food stores.

nuts and ½ cup raisins together in 4 cups liquid (from soaking chestnuts) for 30 minutes. Add salt and cook 10 minutes longer on a low flame. Toss ½ cup raisins and nuts lightly in flour and set aside. Oil a 6 x 8 x 2-inch pan. Preheat the oven to 375°.

Purée half of the cooked mixture in a food mill or blender. Combine the three mixtures and add vanilla (adjust liquid-flour content to form a heavy thick mixture). Spread into pan. Bake 45 minutes or until firm.

Alternate Method

Soak chestnuts, beans and raisins together overnight in liquid to cover. Bring to a boil, lower flame, cover and cook until beans are soft. Add salt, simmer 10 minutes longer, and proceed as in above recipe.

BLUEBERRY CAKE

        2 cups fresh organic blueberries
        1 cup apple butter or apple cider jelly
    1 to 2 cups apple juice or cider
        1 teaspoon cinnamon
        ½ teaspoon salt
        Juice and rind of ½ lemon
        1 cup unprepared couscous
        1½ cups cornmeal or corn flour
        1½ cups whole-wheat pastry flour
        ½ cup oil
        ½ cup roasted chopped nuts

Combine berries with apple butter or jelly and 1 cup juice or cider. Add cinnamon, salt, lemon juice and rind. Set aside for at least 30 minutes.

Preheat the oven to 325° and oil an 8-inch round pan. Combine couscous and flour, then rub the oil into the mixture. Fold in blueberry mixture and nuts until blueberries are covered with the batter. The consistency of the batter should be pancakelike (p. 5). Add more juice or cider if necessary.

Pour into prepared pan, cover and steam about 45 minutes; remove cover and bake 15 to 20 minutes longer or until cake is browned and set. Place on a rack to cool.

Variations

Follow recipe for blueberry cake, but reserve

blueberries. Prepare a fruit glaze with blueberries (see Fresh Fruit Glaze, p. 63) and spoon over the cake after it has cooled.

Top each slice with a tablespoon of Tofu Creame (p. 59) just before serving.

See variations for Basic Cakes I and II (p. 25).

BOB'S BON VOYAGE

Crust

1¼ cups corn flour
1¼ cups whole-wheat pastry flour
¼ cup oil
   Crushed nuts
½ teaspoon salt
   Apple juice or cider

Cake Mixture I

8 cups tofu (p. 13)
½ cup tahini
2 teaspoons vanilla
¼ teaspoon salt
¼ cup oil
1 cup raisin purée

Cake Mixture II

2 cups raisin purée
¾ cup arrowroot flour
¼ teaspoon salt
2 teaspoons orange rind

Icing

Instant Tofu Creame (p. 59)
Coconut (optional)

Crust

Roast corn and whole-wheat pastry flours together in oil until lightly browned. Place in a mixing bowl and add nuts and salt. Add apple juice or cider until the dough begins to stick together. Preheat oven to 375° and oil an 8-inch springform pan. Press the crust mixture into the bottom of pan and prebake 10 minutes.

Cake Mixture I

Drop whole pieces of tofu into boiling salted water. Turn off flame and let sit 2 to 3 minutes. Drain and rinse under cold water. Combine tofu, tahini, vanilla, salt, oil and raisin purée; blend until creamy. Set aside in a bowl.

Cake Mixture II

Combine 2 cups raisin purée with the arrowroot flour, ¼ teaspoon salt and orange rind. Mix until smooth.

Putting It All Together

Remove crust from oven and pour the first mixture into it. Add the second mixture and stir gently into the first mixture until the batter is marbled.

Lower oven temperature to 350° and bake 25 to 30 minutes (see Tofu Cheesecake Pie, p. 37). Remove cake from oven and place on a rack to cool. When cake has cooled completely, remove the sides of the pan. Leave outside 3 to 6 hours longer. Chill at least 2 days uncovered to mellow. (The longer this cake is aged, the better it will taste.)

A few hours before serving, prepare the Instant Tofu Creame, blending the ingredients until smooth. Then decorate the cake with the creame, adding the coconut as trim. See Chapter 3 for decorating technique and ideas.

CARROT CAKE

Sometimes you may make a glass of carrot juice and not know what to do with the leftover pulp. May I suggest that you incorporate it into your baking. It is one of the most beneficial parts of the carrot, containing valuable nutrients, and should not be discarded.

4 cups carrot pulp or grated carrots
½ cup oil
1 cup apple butter
3 to 4 cups apple juice or cider
1 cup roasted chestnut flour
2 cups whole-wheat pastry flour
1 teaspoon cinnamon
½ teaspoon cloves
½ teaspoon salt
¼ cup tahini
2 cups raisins
2 cups roasted sunflower seeds
   Juice and grated rind of ½ orange or tangerine

Sauté carrot pulp in ½ cup oil. Preheat the oven to 350° and oil two 7-inch loaf pans.

Dilute the apple butter in 2 cups of juice or cider. Add carrot pulp, set aside. Mix all the dry ingredients together, and mix in tahini with your

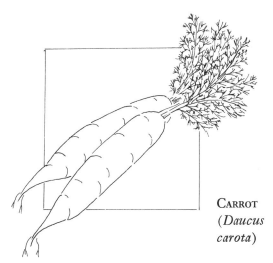

CARROT
(*Daucus
carota*)

*Carrots were known to the Romans and the Greeks
and are now cultivated in every part of the world.
They are a rich source of vitamin A and contain a
great deal of natural sugar. There is another kind of
carrot, known to many as "wild carrot," that grows
wild all over the countryside. This is also an edible
species, with a small, pale-colored root, but there are
plants resembling the carrot which are poisonous,
so be careful. Because of the high amount of sugar
that they contain, carrots are a wonderful source of
natural sweetness that can be used in any dessert.*

hands. Add the raisins and seeds and toss until well
coated. Stir in the remaining liquid, orange juice
and rind. (Adjust liquid or flour content. Batter
should be of pourable consistency, but thick enough
to drop with difficulty from a wooden spoon.)

Pour into prepared pans, and steam covered 20
minutes. Remove cover and bake 15 to 25 minutes
longer or until cake pulls away from the sides of the
pan and is springy to the touch. Remove from the
oven, and set on a rack to cool.

Prepare raisin glaze (see Fruit Glaze, p. 63), and
spoon over the loaves, or over each slice before serving.

Variations

Substitute 2 to 3 cups puréed squash for carrots
(p. 65).

Substitute ½ cup soaked poppy seeds or roasted
walnuts for sunflower seeds.

CARROT-GINGER CAKE

¾ cup bulghur
4 tablespoons oil
1 cup raisins
2 teaspoons cinnamon
2 to 3 teaspoons ginger
½ teaspoon salt
½ teaspoon cloves
3 to 4 cups boiling apple juice or cider
2 cups grated carrots
¼ cup whole-wheat pastry flour
1 cup corn flour
½ cup sweet brown rice flour
½ cup oil or ¼ cup tahini
1½ cups roasted chopped walnuts

Sauté bulghur in 2 tablespoons oil. Add raisins, cinnamon, ginger, salt, cloves and 3 cups boiling apple
juice or cider; cover and cook for 10 minutes. Sauté
carrots in 2 tablespoons oil. Combine grated carrots
and cooked bulghur. Add flour and rub oil into
the mixture.

Preheat the oven to 350°; oil and lightly flour a
7-inch cake mold.

Add the nuts and more apple juice or cider until
the batter has a heavy pancakelike consistency, thick
enough to drop from a wooden spoon.

Pour batter into pan. Cover and steam about 45
minutes; uncover and bake 15 minutes longer or
until cake pulls away from the sides of the pan. Remove from the oven and cool on a cake rack.

Variations

Prepare Orange Glaze (p. 63) and spoon over
cake or individual slices before serving.

Substitute 1 cup couscous for bulghur. Sauté
couscous in ¼ cup oil. Combine raisins, cinnamon,
salt, cloves and 2 cups warm juice or cider with
couscous mixture. Set aside for 30 minutes. Combine this mixture with 2 more cups juice or cider
and bring to a boil. Add the rest of the ingredients
and proceed as in recipe.

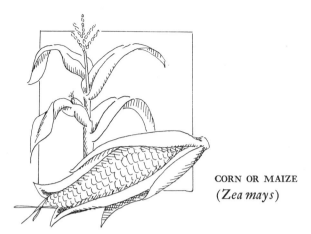

CORN OR MAIZE
(*Zea mays*)

Originally a food crop of the Western Hemisphere, corn was taken to Europe by Columbus and has spread all over the temperate zones of the world. It has long been the major staple of the American Indians and was supplemented in their diet by beans, sweet potatoes and squash.

The people of Latin America and southern and eastern Africa use ground corn or meal. In Latin America cornmeal is cooked into flat cakes called tortillas; in Africa it is boiled with water into a cereal resembling the Italian polènta.

In the United States most of the corn crop is grown for livestock feed. But white and yellow cornmeal is commonly used as a cereal, and, as corn flour, goes into breads, pancake batters and desserts.

CORN CAKE

½ cup raisins
  Apple juice, cider, mu or mint tea to cover
    raisins
½ cup sifted chestnut flour
 2 eggs
½ cup oil
  Corn from 3 ears, grated
½ teaspoon salt
½ cup sifted whole-wheat pastry flour

Soak raisins in juice or tea until soft. Roast chestnut flour until lightly browned. Set aside to cool.

Separate eggs; combine yolks, oil, corn and ¼ teaspoon salt. Mix well.

Sift pastry and chestnut flours into mixing bowl. Add yolk mixture and stir, then add raisins and mix well until all ingredients are thoroughly combined.

Beat whites, adding remaining salt gradually, until they form peaks. Preheat oven to 375°. Fold one quarter of flour mixture into whites. Pour egg-white mixture over remaining batter, and *fold* in gently until white disappears. DO NOT OVERMIX. Consistency should be that of a fluffy pancakelike batter (see p. 5).

Place batter in oiled round or square 6-inch cake pan. DO NOT PAT DOWN. Bake 40 to 45 minutes, or until lightly browned and puffy. Remove from oven and cool on a rack.

Variations

Substitute 4 grated yams for corn. Add ¼ cup roasted seeds or chopped nuts before folding in the egg whites.

Substitute 1½ to 2 cups grated squash, pumpkin, carrots, parsnips or any fresh organic fruit in season for corn.

Substitute ¼ cup barley, rice or Oat Creame (p. 55) for ¼ cup roasted chestnut flour (decrease liquid content accordingly).

Substitute 2 tablespoons of any nut butter for ¼ cup oil.

Add 1 teaspoon cinnamon when folding in flour.

CHESTNUT BROWNIE

4½ cups sifted chestnut flour
 2 cups raisins
   Apple juice or cider to cover raisins
¼ cup oil
¼ teaspoon salt
 1 teaspoon vanilla
 2 cups sifted whole-wheat pastry flour
 2 cups chopped roasted walnuts

Dry roast the chestnut flour until it is lightly browned (see p. 9). Set it aside to cool. Soak the raisins in apple juice or cider to cover until soft. Preheat oven to 325° and oil a 6 x 8-inch pan.

Add oil, salt and vanilla to the raisin-juice combination and beat until foamy. Add sifted flours and mix well. The batter should be thick and pancakelike in consistency (adjust flour-liquid content accordingly). Fold in walnuts.

Pour into prepared pan, cover and steam about 45 minutes. Remove cover and bake 15 to 20 minutes longer or until cake is set and pulls away from the sides of the pan.

Variations

Add ¼ cup pine nuts and ½ teaspoon rosemary to batter. Top each piece with Tofu Creame (p. 59) before serving.

DIANA'S DREAM

I created this recipe for one of my first cooking classes. Diana was one of the people in the class who was especially fond of this cake. Perhaps it was because of the bulghur wheat, which she said reminded her of her mother's home cooking.

This wheat has been widely used by the Persians since the fifth century B.C. Today, roasted bulghur and nuts cooked in olive oil make a favorite eggplant stuffing among Middle Eastern people.

2 cups Chestnut Purée (p. 66)
1 cup raisins
3 to 4 cups apple juice or cider
1 cup uncooked bulghur
¼ cup oil
½ teaspoon salt
1 tablespoon orange or tangerine rind
2 cups sweet brown rice flour

Prepare Chestnut Purée. Set aside. (This may be prepared several days ahead.)

Soak raisins in apple juice or cider to cover until soft. Reserve liquid. Roast bulghur in oil for a few minutes on a medium flame (see p. 9). Add raisins, salt and 2 cups boiling apple juice or cider (use juice or cider from soaking raisins); cover and cook 15 to 20 minutes on a low flame.

Preheat the oven to 325°. Oil a small round or square pan. Sprinkle pan lightly with flour. Combine orange rind and Chestnut Purée. Add the flour to the bulghur, mix in Chestnut Purée and slowly add remaining juice or cider until a thick pancakelike batter is formed (see p. 5). Mix well. Place in pan. Cover and steam about 1 hour, remove cover and bake 10 to 15 minutes longer or until firm.

Variations

Add 2 well-beaten eggs to the batter after mixing in Chestnut Purée. Decrease liquid content accordingly. DO NOT PAT DOWN IN PAN.

Substitute 2 cups apple, squash or any vegetable or fruit purée for Chestnut Purée (pp. 65–66). Adjust liquid content to allow for extra water in fruit or vegetables.

See variations for Basic Cake (pp. 25–26).

FRUIT CAKE I

½ cup dried fruit
½ cup raisins
1 cup hard cider
1 teaspoon orange, tangerine or lemon rind
1 teaspoon vanilla
¼ cup oil
¼ cup concentrated sweetener
¼ teaspoon salt
1 cup whole-wheat pastry flour
3 eggs
1 cup Almond Creame (p. 56)

Preheat oven to 350°. Oil and lightly flour the bottom of an 8-inch round pan (preferably springform).

Soak dried fruit and raisins in hard cider to cover until soft. Squeeze out excess liquid. Dice fruit. Combine fruits and rind in a bowl. Add vanilla, oil and sweetener. Let stand at least 30 minutes. Combine the salt and flour. Add the fruit to the flour mixture. Set aside. Beat the eggs until they double in volume, fold into fruit mixture until eggs are no longer visible.

Pour half of batter into cake pan. Cover with Almond Creame. Add remaining batter and bake 60 to 70 minutes or until cake is springy to the touch and pulls away from the sides of the pan. Remove from the oven and cool on a cake rack.

For storing, see p. 24, No. 19.

FRUIT CAKE II

Follow the recipe for Fruit Cake I, omitting eggs. Add 1 cup more flour and enough cider to form a pancakelike batter (p. 5). Steam covered for the first 45 minutes, remove cover and bake 20 to 30 minutes longer.

BOSTON FRUIT CAKE

One Christmas a friend and I baked 24 of these cakes, aging them for two weeks before giving them as gifts for the holiday. This recipe makes 12 cakes.

                3½   pounds dried mixed fruit
                 3   pounds raisins
                16   cups amasake (p. 82) or hard cider
                 8   cups whole-wheat pastry flour
                 7   cups rye flour
                 6   tablespoons orange or tangerine rind
                12   teaspoons cinnamon
                 6   teaspoons cloves
          2 to 3   teaspoons ginger (to taste)
                 4   cups roasted chopped almonds
                 2   teaspoons salt

Soak the dried fruits in amasake (uncooked) or cider to cover overnight. Squeeze out and reserve the excess liquid and dice fruit into bite-size pieces. Add flours to the liquid and let sit at least a few hours. Combine the fruit and flour mixtures with the rest of the ingredients and beat until batter is smooth and thick with the consistency of pancake batter (p. 5).

Oil and flour 12 to 14 small cake molds. Fill pans two-thirds full, cover and steam 1½ hours in pre-heated 300° oven. Remove cover and bake until cake pulls away from the sides of the pan and is firm. Place on cake racks to cool.

To age: When the cake has cooled completely, remove from pan; dip a piece of cheesecloth into hard cider or amasake, wrap it around the cake and cover tightly with a dry piece of cheesecloth and brown paper. If you have a tin can (an old coffee can will do nicely), place the wrapped cake in the can and store it for a few weeks in a dry cool place.

GINGER BY THE SEA

Every summer Joanne and her family go to their summer home in Nantasket, Massachusetts. Joanne not only cooks and bakes for her husband and five children but for a constant stream of friends that visit her open house daily. This is one of the many delightful treats that she serves.

                 1   cup raisins
                 2   cups corn flour
                 1   cup whole-wheat flour
                 1   cup whole-wheat pastry flour
                 1   teaspoon salt
                ½   cup oil
                 1   teaspoon ginger
                 1   cup apple cider jelly (p. 7)
       ¼ to ½   cup liquid

Soak the raisins in liquid to cover until soft. Dry-roast the flours separately until lightly brown. Set aside to cool. Preheat the oven to 350°.

Combine all the dry ingredients, including the raisins. Rub the oil into the mixture. Dissolve the apple cider jelly in ¼ cup liquid and add it to the dry mixture. Stir, adding more liquid if necessary, until a thick batter is formed.

Oil and lightly flour a 6 x 8-inch cake pan. Spoon batter into the pan. Cover pan and steam 45 minutes. Remove the cover and bake 15 to 20 minutes longer or until firm.

Alternate Methods

Place the filled cake pan or mold in a pressure cooker, on a steaming rack or inverted cake pan. (Make sure that you use a pan or mold that is at least 1 to 2 inches smaller than the pressure cooker so that it is easy to remove the pan from the pot.) Fill the pressure cooker with water three quarters of the way up the sides of the cake pan.

Bring the pressure up to 10 pounds (not full pressure) and cook 1½ hours. Remove pan and cool on a rack.

To steam cakes in oven, fill pan two-thirds full and cover with the same size baking pan.

PEACH
(*Prunus persica*)

The tree from which the peach originates is a small, deciduous type, producing small pink and sometimes white flowers from which spring forth peaches varying from greenish white to yellow. They mostly grow in a warm climate in countries like the United States, China, Japan, South Africa and Australia.

UPSIDE-DOWN PEACH DIP

        2 tablespoons oil
      ¼ cup concentrated sweetener
        4 peaches
        1 egg
   2 to 3 cups boiling apple juice or cider
        1 teaspoon vanilla
        2 cups sifted whole-wheat pastry flour
        1 tablespoon cinnamon
        1 teaspoon salt
      ½ cup roasted chopped nuts

Preheat the oven to 325°. Oil and lightly flour the bottom of a 6 x 8-inch pan or a pie pan. Heat oil and sweetener together. Core and slice peaches (peel if not organic). Mix peaches into the oil-sweetener combination. Set aside.

Beat egg, gradually adding juice or cider, and vanilla. Add sifted flour, cinnamon and salt to the egg mixture. Mix in the nuts.

Place peach mixture decoratively into the pan, pour batter over peaches and bake 20 to 30 minutes or until set. Remove from oven and place on a rack to cool. Turn upside-down, remove pan and serve.

Variations

Add 2 tablespoons orange rind to egg mixture before adding boiling juice.

Substitute for peaches 3 cups strawberries or blueberries or any fresh fruit in season.

Soak 1 cup dried fruit overnight in liquid to cover. Squeeze out excess liquid; dice and substitute for peaches.

Add ¼ teaspoon cloves, ½ teaspoon ginger and 1 teaspoon lemon, orange or tangerine rind to flour and salt before combining with egg mixture.

Substitute 1 cup chestnut flour for 1 cup pastry flour.

ORANGE-CHESTNUT CAKE

        2 cups grated oranges or tangerines
             (organic only)
        1 cup apple juice or cider
        1 teaspoon vanilla
        1 teaspoon cinnamon
      ¼ teaspoon cloves
        1 cup oil
        2 cups roasted, sifted chestnut flour
        2 cups sifted whole-wheat pastry flour
      ½ teaspoon salt

Grate the oranges and skin together. Combine apple juice or cider, vanilla, spices and grated oranges and let sit for at least 1 hour. Preheat the oven to 350°. Oil and lightly flour an 8-inch round cake pan or cupcake tin.

Add the oil to the juice mixture and beat well. Slowly add sifted flours and salt, beating until the batter is smooth, creamy and pancakelike in consistency (p. 5).

Pour into prepared pan and bake 60 minutes or until cake is lightly browned and set. Remove from the oven and set on a rack to cool.

Alternate Method

Try steaming this cake for a delightful change (p. 5).

Variations

Substitute diced strawberries or any fresh fruit in season for oranges.

Follow recipe for Basic Raisin Cake (p. 116), substituting Orange-Chestnut Cake ingredients and yeast (adjust flour-liquid content accordingly).

See variations for Basic Cakes I and II (pp. 25–26).

Prepare Orange or Tangerine Glaze (p. 63) and spoon over entire cake after cooling or over each individual serving.

RENEE'S CAKE

Several years ago in San Francisco I was served one of the most delicious Christmas cakes I have ever tasted. I asked for the recipe but was never able to get the exact ingredients. This is my version of this delightful cake.

> 3 cups raisins
> 2 to 3 cups apple juice or cider
> 3 cups whole-wheat flour
> 4 cups chopped apples
> 2 tablespoons miso (p. 10)
> ½ cup oil or ¼ cup sesame butter or tahini
> 3 tablespoons lemon juice
> 2 teaspoons lemon rind
> 2 teaspoons vanilla
> 1 cup roasted chopped walnuts

Combine the raisins and enough apple juice or cider to cover in a heavy saucepan. Bring to a boil, cover and simmer about 30 minutes or longer. Roast the flour in a dry skillet until it begins to brown lightly. Set aside to cool. Cut the apples into small pieces (peel if not organic). Toss together with flour.

Preheat the oven to 325° and oil and lightly flour a 7-inch cake mold.

Dissolve the miso in a small amount of the warm juice from the boiled raisins. Combine the miso, oil or nut butter, lemon juice and rind and vanilla. (You may boil the raisins with a vanilla bean and omit the liquid vanilla.) Add this mixture to the flour-apple combination, folding in until a thick batter is formed.

Spoon into cake pan, cover and steam 40 minutes. Remove cover and bake about 20 minutes longer or until the cake is set. Remove from the oven and place on a rack to cool.

Alternate Method

Prepare steamer (p. 5) and steam 3 to 4 hours. Remove the cake from the steamer and bake in a preheated 350° oven about 15 minutes or until cake is dry.

RUSS' SAGITTARIUS CAKE

Another excuse to bake a cake: a birthday!

> *White Layer*
> 3 eggs
> ½ cup oil
> 1 teaspoon vanilla
> ¼ teaspoon salt
> ½ teaspoon lemon juice
> ¼ cup concentrated sweetener
> ½ cup sifted whole-wheat pastry flour
>   Apple juice or cider if necessary
>
> *Black Layer*
> 3 eggs
> ½ cup oil
> 1 teaspoon orange rind
> ¼ teaspoon salt
> 1½ cups raisin purée (p. 66)
> 1 cup sifted whole-wheat pastry flour
>
> *Icing*
> 2 cups Tahini Chestnut Creame Filling
>   (p. 59)

White Layer

Separate eggs. Combine yolks, oil and vanilla. Stir and set aside. Oil and lightly flour two 7-inch round springform pans. Beat whites gradually, adding salt and lemon juice, until they are stiff. Add sweetener slowly, drop by drop, beating continuously until whites are peaked. Fold a quarter of the whites into yolks. Pour this mixture over the remaining whites. Fold in the sifted flour gently until the whites are no longer visible. DO NOT OVERMIX.

Preheat the oven to 350°

Pour into pan. Do not pat down. Bake 30 to 40 minutes at 350°, or until cake is puffy and pulls away from the sides of the pan. Place on a cake rack to cool; unclip side of pan.

Black Layer

Follow the directions for white layer, substituting in appropriate places.

Putting It All Together

When both layers have cooled, place the black layer top side down, and spread icing over it. Place the white layer on top and ice the sides of the cake (p. 43). You may wish to roll the sides in crushed nuts, rind, etc. (see p. 46 for suggestions). Cover top with icing and decorate as desired. Refer to Chapter 3, "Inside and Outside," for other decorating ideas.

Variations

Substitute 1 cup arrowroot for whole-wheat pastry flour, in black layer. Bake at 350° 10 to 12 minutes or until *almost* solid. *Overbaking* may make the cake rubbery.

CHEESECAKE TOFU PIE

This cake tends to be very light and delicate. It would be best to use a springform fan, so that it does not have to be disturbed after baking.

Crust
1 to 1½ cups Coffee Crumb Topping (p. 68)

Filling
6 cups tofu (p. 13)
¼ cup concentrated sweetener
1 teaspoon lemon juice
1 teaspoon orange rind
1 teaspoon vanilla
2 eggs
½ teaspoon salt

Crust

To topping, add enough apple juice, mu tea or mint tea to make it stick together. Oil an 8-inch springform pan, and press in crust on the bottom. Prebake 10 minutes in 350° oven. Set aside.

Filling

Squeeze out tofu to extract excess liquid. Place in blender, add the rest of the ingredients except eggs and salt, and blend until creamy and smooth. Separate eggs. Add yolks to blender and blend un-

til creamy (2 to 3 minutes). Beat egg whites and salt together until peaked. Place tofu mixture in a bowl, fold in egg whites. DO NOT OVERMIX.

Pour entire mixture into prebaked crust and bake 30 to 40 minutes. DO NOT OPEN THE OVEN DOOR DURING THE FIRST 25 MINUTES OF BAKING TIME.

After 25 minutes, shake the pan lightly. If the center is not almost firm, continue baking until almost firm. When baked, turn off the oven, and let cake sit an additional 30 minutes with the oven door open. Remove from the oven and set on a rack until completely cool.

Allow to sit at room temperature at least 4 hours. Remove from pan, chill uncovered at least 2 to 5 days before serving. (This allows the tofu to dry out more and develop a cheeselike taste.) However, it may be served after 12 hours.

Just before serving, top with any fresh fruit glaze (p. 63).

Alternate Method

Blend eggs together with the rest of the ingredients.

CANTALOUPE CHEESECAKE

Follow recipe for Cheesecake Tofu Pie. While prebaking crust, mix together 1 tablespoon arrowroot, juice of ½ lemon, ¼ cup sweetener (optional) and 1 cup crushed cantaloupe. Place in a double boiler and cook over a low heat until the mixture boils, thickens and looks clearer. Cool slightly and pour into pressed prebaked crust.

Pour tofu-cheese mixture over cantaloupe mixture. Sprinkle top with crushed nuts.

Bake at 325° for 45 to 60 minutes. Turn off heat and let stand in the oven with the oven door open for 30 minutes longer. Cool on rack, then chill several days before serving.

Variations

Substitute ½ cup Chestnut Purée (p. 66) or ½ cup raisin purée for concentrated sweetener.

Substitute any fresh or dried fruit for cantaloupe. Prepare the same way. (If using dried fruit, soak in apple juice to cover until soft; squeeze out excess liquid before adding it to double boiler.)

DANIEL'S STRAWBERRY CHEESECAKE

Filling
1 cup raisin purée or Chestnut Purée (p. 66)
4 tablespoons tahini
1 tablespoon vanilla
½ teaspoon salt
10 cups tofu (p. 13)

Topping
Strawberry Cheesecake Topping (p. 54)

Crust
1 cup whole-wheat pastry flour
1 cup corn flour
5 tablespoons oil
3 tablespoons concentrated sweetener
½ cup apple juice or water

Filling

Combine purée, tahini, vanilla and salt. Blend until creamy. Add tofu and continue to blend 3 to 5 minutes longer. (If there is not enough liquid, add enough to form a creamy consistency.)

Crust

Roast the flours separately until they begin to brown lightly. Set aside to cool.

Combine flours and salt together in a mixing bowl. Cut the oil into the flour. Add sweetener, and enough liquid to form a semimoist crust. Preheat oven to 350° and oil an 8-inch springform pan. Press crust into the bottom of the pan. Sprinkle extra crust in another pan, and bake both 10 minutes. Set extra crust aside for the sides of the cake. Pour tofu mixture into bottom crust. Bake 25 to 30 minutes or until pie is almost solid (shake pan, see following recipe). Remove from oven and place on a rack to cool. When completely cool, remove sides of pan. Cool at room temperature 3 to 6 hours longer.

Chill at least 2 to 3 days uncovered to age cake. The longer it is aged the better it will taste; try keeping it for 5 days before serving.

Prepare cake for decorating (p. 42) immediately before using. Moisten leftover baked crust. Press around the sides of cake. Spoon topping over cake a few hours before serving. Cool.

UPSIDE-DOWN TOFU CAKE

Follow recipe for Daniel's Strawberry Cheesecake. Cover bottom crust with fruit purée (pp. 66–67). Bake 10 minutes at 375°. Cover with tofu mixture and bake 25 to 30 minutes longer or until set.

SOUEN UPSIDE-DOWN CAKE

Souen is a small Japanese natural-food restaurant, located on Manhattan's upper West Side. Three years ago when my friends decided to open this restaurant, they asked me to be the baker. This was my first venture into the world of professional dessert making and this the first successful creation.

2 cups sifted whole-wheat pastry flour
2 cups sifted sweet brown rice flour (p. 8)
½ cup oil
2 to 3 cups apple juice or cider
1 teaspoon vanilla
Juice and rind of ½ grated organic lemon
½ teaspoon salt
2½ cups apricot, raisin or other fruit purée (pp. 66–67)
½ cup chopped seeds or nuts

Topping
2 cups fruit purée or glaze (pp. 62–64)

Preheat oven to 350°. Oil and lightly flour a medium-size upside-down tube pan.

Roast both of the flours in 4 tablespoons oil, until it begins to smell sweet, and to brown lightly. Combine the juice, oil, vanilla, lemon rind and salt. Beat until foamy. Sprinkle the flour over the liquid mixture. Fold in purée, reserving ½ cup.

Mix gently until the batter is smooth and thick enough to drop from a wooden spoon (adjust liquid-flour content accordingly). Sprinkle nuts or seeds on bottom of pan. Spread the remaining purée over nuts. Pour batter over purée, cover and steam 30 minutes. Remove cover, and bake 45 to 60 minutes longer, or until cake is browned and pulls away from the sides of the pan. Place it on a bottle to cool. When cool, turn upside-down on rack, with a cookie sheet underneath to catch drippings. Remove pan. Spoon glaze over top, letting it drip down the sides.

Alternate Methods

Try steaming this cake for a different flavor (see p. 5).

Reserve fruit purée, follow directions in "Filling a Tube Cake" (p. 23), filling with purée.

Variations

Substitute 3 cups of fresh fruit for fruit purée, adding less liquid.

Substitute topping from Basic Upside-down Cake (p. 116) for apricot purée.

CARROT-MINT BREAD CRUMB CAKE

        2 cups grated carrots
    ¼ cup oil
        1 cup roasted, chopped nuts
        1 cup dry bread crumbs
        1 teaspoon cloves
        1 tablespoon mint
        3 eggs
    ¼ cup concentrated sweetener
            Rind and juice of 1 organic lemon
        2 tablespoons tahini
    ¼ teaspoon salt
            Apple juice or cider

Sauté the carrots in oil.

Mix carrots, nuts, bread crumbs, cloves and mint together in a bowl. Separate eggs. Beat yolks, sweetener, lemon rind and juice and tahini together until creamy.

Oil the bottom of a 7 x 3-inch loaf pan. Beat whites and salt together until they are peaked. Stir yolk mixture into carrot mixture. Fold in egg whites gently. Add juice if necessary. DO NOT OVER-MIX. Pour into prepared pan.

Bake about 45 to 60 minutes, or until cake is browned and pulls away from sides of pan. Remove from oven, and place on a rack to cool.

Variations

Prepare Orange-Maple Sauce (p. 67) and spoon over the cake when cooled.

Substitute 2 cups squash purée for carrots (p. 65).

Substitute 1 cup Chestnut Purée (p. 66) for carrots and omit nuts and cloves. Add 1 teaspoon vanilla.

Substitute 2 tablespoons grain coffee for cloves.

Substitute 1 cup apple butter for sweetener and add ½ cup more bread crumbs.

Substitute ½ cup raisin purée (see Fruit Purée, pp. 66–67) for concentrated sweetener and add ¼ cup more bread crumbs.

Add ½ cup raisins.

Substitute roasted sesame or sunflower seeds for nuts.

NEW YEAR'S SWEET BREAD

The Italian people have known about sweet bread since it was first introduced (according to Dante) in the eastern part of Italy by a merchant named Niccolo Salimbeni. One of the most famous sweet breads known throughout the world is *Panfòrte*, originally named Honey Spiced Bread. It was a favorite among the popes and kings as early as the twelfth century, and is a traditional sweet bread for Christmas and the New Year.

    ½ pound finely diced, dried fruit
    1 to 2 cups apple juice or cider
        1 cup roasted filberts
        1 cup roasted almonds
        1 cup whole-wheat pastry flour
        1 teaspoon cinnamon
    ¼ teaspoon cloves
    ½ teaspoon ginger
    ½ teaspoon salt
    ¼ cup concentrated sweetener
    3 to 4 tablespoons grain coffee
        2 tablespoons orange rind
        2 tablespoons lemon rind
        1 teaspoon vanilla

Oil and lightly flour a round cake pan or 7 x 3-inch loaf pan.

Soak the dried fruit in juice or cider to cover until soft. Reserve juice. Squeeze out excess liquid and dice. Combine nuts, fruit, flour and spices in a large mixing bowl. Add 1 cup liquid (use the juice that the dried fruit was soaking in). Stir and set aside.

Bring the sweetener to a boil. Add grain coffee and cook on a low flame for a few minutes. Remove from heat; add vanilla and rinds.

Pour into fruit mixture, stirring rapidly until thoroughly blended, with the consistency of pancake batter (p. 5).

Place batter in pan. Cover and bake 20 minutes at 300°, remove cover, and bake 20 to 30 minutes longer, or until bread pulls away from the sides of the pan.

Glaze during or after baking. See Chapter 3, "Inside and Outside," for sauce or glaze suggestions.

3. Inside and Outside

Fillings, Toppings, Icings, Creames, Glazes, Purées

Enjoyment can be derived from making cakes, pies, pastries or whatever you have prepared pleasing to the eye as well as to the palate. Here are some ideas to help you think about making desserts just as attractive on the outside as delicious on the inside.

General Equipment for Decorating

Pastry Bags
Metal tubes in various sizes to use for piping or fluting (see p. 47)
Cake racks or drying racks
Extra cake pans or cardboard forms the same size or slightly larger than the cake being decorated

Metal and rubber spatulas
Pastry brushes
Blender
Wire whisk
Food mill
Double boiler

Electric mixer or rotary hand beater
Brown or wax paper for making cornucopias (see p. 48)

Cookie or baking sheet (to catch drippings when decorating)
Cake-decorating stand (optional)

Choosing the Decoration or Filling

There are many different kinds of decoration and filling to choose from, each with a special look and texture of its own. Choose one or more according to the type of cake or pastry, the look, shape, taste and texture you want it to have and where and when you want to serve it.

Butter Icings and Fillings

Made from a nut-butter base, and embellished with fruit and spices, this type of decoration can give a creamy effect as well as a stiff peaked look. Try it for fillings or icings, fluting or piping, using a pastry bag for added effect.

Creames

Egg-based. Made with the yolk, white, or whole egg, these are desirable for fillings as well as toppings.
Flour-based. Usually made from pastry, corn, or chestnut flour, they too are perfect for filling pies or pastries.
Grain-based. Made from rolled, steel-cut or whole oats, barley or rice, cooked, blended and flavored, they form a delicious creamy base filling or topping on the inside or outside of any kind of dessert.
Tofu. This creame can be used for any purpose, such as icings, toppings and fillings, or as a separate cold dessert.

Glazes

Give a smooth, shiny appearance for any kind of cake, pie or pastry.

Fruit or Vegetable Purée

Simple, but tasty, these blends of fruits and/or vegetables, and added flavoring, such as rinds and vanilla, can embellish any pastry or cake as a filling, topping or trim.

Syrups

Concentrated sweetener — used alone or cooked with arrowroot and flavored with nuts, rind, spices or fruit — can give cakes, pies or pastries a glowing appearance as well as a delicious taste.

Before Decorating the Cake

1. Cool cake completely.
2. Trim off the hard, crisp edges (about ⅛ inch) from the side of the cake.
3. Check to see if layers are level. If not, cut away some of top of cake, so that they are level when sandwiched together.
4. Brush away all loose crumbs.
5. Place cake (or layer) upside-down on platter.
6. Cut 4 strips of wax paper at least 4 inches wide and long enough to cover surface of the platter that the cake is being served on.

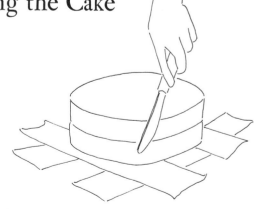

7. Lifting the cake with a spatula, place the strips

of wax paper 2 inches underneath the bottom, extending them a few inches outward.

8. After decorating cake, allow icing to dry before removing wax paper.

Finishing Touches

Before Baking

Brush or spread any glaze (pp. 62–64) on top of yeasted and unyeasted pastries, covered pies, tarts and dough cookies.

During Baking

Brush the tops with oil or concentrated sweetener or any glaze 10 minutes before removing from oven. (See "Removing Cake from Pan," p. 23.) Sprinkle unroasted chestnut flour and chopped unroasted nuts, seeds, spices or rinds on top if desired, and return to oven to finish baking.

After Baking

Brush the tops of yeasted or unyeasted pastries, covered pies, tarts, *all* cookies, cakes and petit fours with oil or concentrated sweetener or any glaze after the dessert cools. Do not pour hot glaze over warm cakes or petit fours; allow these to cool completely before glazing. Sprinkle roasted chestnut flour and/or rinds, spices, roasted seeds or chopped roasted nuts over glaze if desired. Or the nuts, seeds, etc., may be placed on the dessert before glazing and the glaze spooned or brushed carefully over them.

To prepare cakes and petit fours for glazing, follow these steps before proceeding:

Trim off hard crisp edges. Place cake on a rack. Place a pan or cookie sheet under the rack to catch the drippings. Spoon hot glaze over top of the cake, allowing it to drip down the sides. Coat sides before or after glazing.

It is good to spread a base of butter icing, creame or glaze over cakes before putting on the final icing.

Spread the icing over the top of the cake. Draw

a small knife across the icing to give a ridged effect.

Spread icing over top and sides of a cake. Mark the top with a fork, by moving it across the icing in a wavy line. Coat sides with roasted nuts or seeds, etc.

Spread a nut butter icing over the top of a cake rather thickly. (Use a cold icing that has been chilled overnight.) Sweep the point of a knife or the prongs of a fork or the back of a spoon over the icing and, at the same time, lift it in peaks. Do not try to do this evenly, since it looks more effective if it is slightly uneven.

Place a doily on top of the cake. Shake or sprinkle roasted chestnut flour, orange or lemon rind, or crushed roasted nuts or seeds on top of the doily. Lift the doily carefully, with one upward sweep.

To glaze or ice only the top of the cake, tie or pin a strong band of paper around the sides of the cake. Put the glaze or icing on top of the cake, and spread it with a palette knife. Allow to set before removing paper.

Prepare an icing or glaze that is stiffer, by using

less liquid. Spread over top and sides of cake. When the top starts to harden, take the edge of a knife and go around the rim of the cake, sweeping upward.

A broken-line effect can be gotten by spreading the butter icing roughly over the cake. It usually forms a rough-looking texture. If you want to follow a definite design, push it very gently with a knife.

Lattice design can be produced by using butter icing and different-colored jellies or fruit butters. Mark the lattice design over the top of a cake that has been given a thin layer of icing on top. Pipe either straight or slightly wavy lines following the marks. Fill the centers between lines with jelly or fruit butter. (The jelly or fruit butter can also be applied to the top of the cake using a pastry bag or cornucopia.) If the jelly or butter is too stiff, mix with a small quantity of warm liquid.

Smooth-looking nut butter icing can be made by using a knife that is long enough to cover the entire width of the cake, holding it at both ends at an angle, and pulling it toward you.

Swirl the nut butter icing using a knife and a sharp upward motion after each swirl.

To obtain a line effect with nut butter icing, use a tea knife or very thin palette knife. Make a sweep from the center of the cake to the edge and then follow this line all around. This is difficult to do around the sides of the cake, so straight or wavy lines are better there.

Hold a spatula, tea knife or very thin palette knife at the center of the cake. Turn the cake slowly, and move the spatula gradually to the outer edge of the cake or sweep the knife or spatula from the center of the cake to the edge in a semicircular motion. (Use a nut butter icing for best results.)

Stucco: Using a nut butter icing or Wedding

Threads (pp. 64–65), ice the entire cake. Place a spatula on the cake and pull it away to make a series of peaks.

Zigzag: Cut sawlike teeth along the edge of a cardboard slightly larger than the width of the cake. Holding the cardboard in both hands, and starting at the edge of the cake, move the cardboard along the top of the cake from side to side.

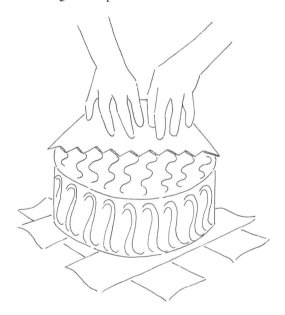

Spiral: First cover the cake with a dark- or light-colored icing, then fit a pastry bag with a small round tube and fill the pastry bag with a contrasting-color icing. Pipe a series of circles, working from the outer edge of the cake to the center. Draw a thin knife or skewer lightly over the cake, as if cutting a pie into 8 or 12 pieces.

Stencil: First ice the cake with a stiff nut butter icing. Allow the icing to dry. Cut any pattern or shape out of cardboard and place it on top of the cake. Spread icing or sprinkle roasted chestnut flour, rind, mint or cinnamon over the top of the cardboard, where the pattern has been cut out. (Use a contrasting color for best results.)

Feather Icing: Use any light-colored icing (tofu creame, oat, barley or rice creames) or light icings tinted with vegetable coloring (see p. 126) and any dark icing (nut butter base is best for piping). Place the dark icing in a decorating bag or cornucopia (use a plain round tube for the pastry bag (see p. 47). Spread light or tinted icing on cookie or cover cake with icing. Immediately pipe onto this straight lines, circles, spirals, etc., in dark icing. Use a skewer or toothpick to create design, drawing skewer either in straight lines, circles, or swirls (see illustrations).

Flowers

Choose fresh flowers that do not have poisonous properties and place them on the cake just before serving. Open-petaled flowers that have bright gay colors, arranged delicately, give an added finish to any cake.

For an added touch, use either lemon skin or orange skin, cut into different shapes (thin long strips, curves — see illustrations) and boiled until soft in mu tea, mint tea, apple juice or cider to cover. Drain immediately and keep in a bowl of cold water with a pinch of salt until using.

Lay flower down. Place strips or curves around the outside of the flower.

Decorating may be used on many different kinds of food such as cupcakes, petit fours, French pastries, molded kanten desserts, salads, cookies and pies. The same method is applied; the only change may be the icing you choose to decorate with.

Cupcakes

Here are a few ideas for cupcake decorations. An open-star tube was used for most of these designs.

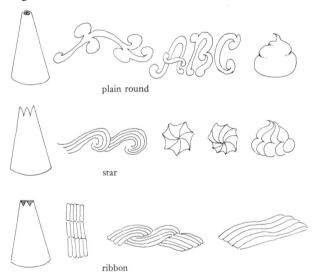

plain round

star

ribbon

This is another way of decorating a cupcake:

Cut off the top third of the cupcake. Cut this piece in half down the center.

Ice the bottom of the cupcake with a heavy nut butter icing or Wedding Threads (pp. 64–65).

Place the two halves of the top section at an angle in an upright position on top of the cupcake. Decorate with the rest of the icing, nuts and dried fruit.

Pastries, Petit Fours, Pies and Cookies

Refer to the cake-decorating section (pp. 42–50) throughout this chapter.

Nuts as a Decoration

Nuts can add an attractive appearance to any cake, pie or pastry, as well as enjoyable taste and texture.

Blanched: Blanched nuts add a certain finished look to a cake. They may be used after icing or before baking. If placing blanched nuts on top of a cake after baking, use some concentrated sweetener, nut butter icing or creame to make them adhere properly.

Whole or Halves: Good to use for border decoration.

Split: This means that the nut is split through the center. Place them around the top edge of a cake before or after baking.

Chopped: Spread the cake with sweetener, or glaze, creame or icing, and sprinkle with chopped nuts.

Shredded or Slivered: Cut into strips lengthwise, nuts (usually almonds) make a very pretty form of cake decoration.

Coating a Round Cake with Nuts or Seeds: Cover sides of cake with icing. Roll sides in crushed, sliced or ground roasted nuts, seeds, cookie crumbs, granola, orange or lemon rind.

Spread top with a base of nut butter icing, creame or glaze.

Blanching

Sometimes a recipe calls for "blanched nuts," used mainly on top of a cake for decoration, or for almond milk. Fresh fruit can also be blanched by the same method.

Drop nuts or fruit into boiling water. Turn off flame and let sit about 1 minute. Drain immediately and rinse under cold water. Peel and use as desired. (If the fruits are organic, save the skins and use them in salads or fruit compotes, or to flavor other desserts.)

Fancy Free

Necessary Items

Cake decorating is fascinating and simple to do, and is something everyone can learn, but it requires perseverance, patience and practice. Once you acquire the knack of working with a pastry bag, you will be able to serve attractive and skillfully decorated pastries, cakes, cookies and pies, which will elicit compliments not only for taste, but for looks as well.

I began to learn cake decorating when two of my friends asked me to make their wedding cake. I bought myself a pastry bag, four basic tubes and a cake-decorating book, and began to practice piping and fluting on upside-down bowls, baking pans, cookie sheets, cardboard boxes, wax paper — anything that could be decorated. In a short time, I was able to create homemade cakes that looked as lavishly glamorous as anything I had seen in a bakery store case.

My mother used to take a piece of heavy brown paper, roll it into a cone, fill it with icing, snip off the tip and squeeze. Out came "magic" flowers, spirals, borders, even words . . . Today, most stores are supplied with pastry bags and various tubes which offer a greater variety of ways to fashion pastries, cakes and pies into tantalizing desserts.

Pastry bags can also be used to accomplish the following: shaping molded cookies, creme puffs and éclair shells; filling pies, pastries, creme puffs, éclairs, jelly doughnuts and tarts; making drop cookies; decorating petit fours and centers of cookies.

In order to accomplish quick and easy decoration, the following items are necessary:

One or two 14-inch bags. These should be large enough to use for creames, cookie batters or fillings, and small enough to handle gracefully.

A plain round tube. There are several different sizes that can be advantageous, depending on what you want to do.

⅛-inch opening can be used for filling small pastries such as jelly doughnuts, creme puffs or éclairs.

¼-inch opening can be used for the same filling as the smaller tube, shaping small cookies and for lettering or decorating the top of a cake or pie.

½-inch opening can be used for making creme puffs, éclairs, cookies and for filling tart shells.

¾-inch opening can be used for any of the above if making or filling a large shell, as well as for larger cookies.

Star tube. Various sizes are also available.

Opening less than ¼-inch can be used for decorating small pastries or petit fours, or filling small pastries (creme puffs, éclairs, etc.).

Opening slightly larger than ¼-inch can be used for fillings, and borders on small cakes.

½-inch openings can be used for cake decorations, kisses, borders and fillings, as well as for shaping small molded cookies.

¾-inch opening can be used for making cookies that contain seeds, dried fruit pieces, or nuts, for cake borders or for filling large shells or pies.

Ribbon tube. Can be used for making cookies as well as cake decorating. This is a flat tube with one serrated edge having an opening about ¾ inch long. Press out dough into one long ribbon, and break into 2 to 3-inch lengths before baking.

Coupling. With this attachment, you can interchange decorating tubes without having to empty the bag. It also prevents filling from squirting out the sides of the bag.

Revolving cake-decorating stand. You will find this to be a very useful tool, when decorating and icing cakes. It allows you to remain stationary as you decorate, giving you more flexibility in your designs.

Pastry Bag and Cornucopia

Filling the Pastry Bag

1. Insert the coupling into the pastry bag, fitting it into the small end of the tube.
2. Place the tube over the coupling.
3. Screw the coupling nut onto the coupling.
4. Hold the bag in one hand, and, keeping it open, fold the top edge over the hand.

5. An alternate method for filling is to fit the pastry bag into a large jar, folding the edge over the lip of the jar.
6. Using a rubber spatula, spoon the filling into the pastry bag. Remove excess filling from spatula by pinching the bag as you withdraw the spatula.
7. Fold over the top or flap of the bag, squeeze down filling, then fold the sides of the bag near the top, and twist until a little filling is forced through the tube. NEVER PUT TOO MUCH FILLING INTO THE BAG. Leave enough room so that the top may be folded down securely to prevent any filling from oozing out at the top.

Decorating with Pastry Bag

With your dominant hand, press down on the top of the twisted bag and squeeze out the filling. Use the other hand to guide the lower end of the bag. DO NOT PRESS THE LOWER END OF THE BAG. Re-twist the top as the bag empties.

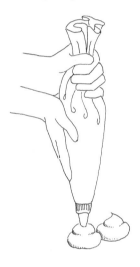

Alternate Method: Press down on the top of the twisted bag to squeeze out filling. Use the other hand to guide the dominant hand.
Cookies
For shaping round cookies, hold the pastry bag vertically above the cookie sheet with the tip about ¼ inch away from the sheet. Squeeze out the filling without moving the bag, into a 1- or 2-inch round. Pull the bag away quickly.

Try other shapes and sizes when you feel comfortable working with the bag.

Creame Puffs
For shaping creame puffs, hold vertically above the baking sheet with the tip about ¾ inch away from the sheet. Squeeze out batter, raising the bag slightly, to form a high mound about 2 inches in diameter.
Borders
For making fancy borders on cakes, use a star tube with a ¾-inch opening. Hold the pastry bag at an angle about ⅛ inch away from the cake. Squeeze out the filling by moving the bag back and forth, so that each layer of icing partly covers the previous one. Or, holding the bag vertically, squeeze out filling quickly, finishing each movement by drawing the bag away straight up, abruptly. The more you squeeze, the bigger the star.

Drop tubes into a glass of water while working, so the icing does not harden in the tubes.

Practice using a pastry bag, filled with an inexpensive ingredient (e.g., potatoes), on sheets of wax paper, upside-down bowls, pans or cardboard boxes.

Making a Paper Cornucopia

Cut out a triangle from heavy brown paper or wax paper (avoid parchment paper, as it has been treated with sulfuric acid).

Mark the center of the triangle (this will be the pointed end of the cornucopia).

Hold point A between thumb and forefinger. Grasp B with the other hand, and roll, pulling B tightly, and making A into a sharp point.

Continue to roll up the cornucopia, maintaining the point.

Fold down the two short ends to secure cornucopia. Fasten with tape.

Fill cornucopia half full.

Fold down one side of the top to enclose the filling.

Fold down the other side, and continue to fold the top, alternating sides until the filling is pressed into the tip of the cornucopia.

With scissors, cut off the tip to make an opening large enough for the filling to pass through.

Hold cornucopia. Press out filling, decorating cookies, petit fours or tops of cakes and pies. (See "Decorating with Pastry Bag," for position of hands.)

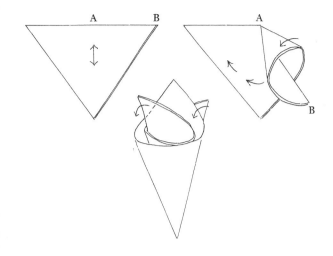

Inlay

Choose any design that you wish (fish, flower, flag). Select colorful fruits, vegetables, rinds, nuts, etc., that can be applied to form the design. Oil a shallow baking pan very well. Make the outline of the design on the baking pan using rinds, nuts, cinnamon, mint, etc. Fill in details. Carefully spoon any warm creme (such as chestnut) over the design. Allow to set at room temperature until solid.

Then, cover with paper a tray or pan as large as the cake. To unmold, place tray or pan upside-down over top of cake. Hold it fast and flip them both over at the same time. Allow the creme to fall naturally, before removing baking pan.

This cake may be used as a single layer, or as the top layer of a two-layer cake.

It is best to use another layer (such as basic cake, or yeasted cake) because the dessert will stand up better. If using a cake layer on the bottom, proceed as follows:

Remove the basic cake from pan. Trim off edges ¼ inch all around.

Spread filling on top of creme layer and place cake on top of filling.

Cover the outside of a baking pan or tray with paper.

Place covered tray on top of cake, hold fast and flip over quickly.

Allow cake to fall before taking off pan from creme layer.

Trim creme layer to size of cake.

Insert strips of wax paper underneath cake (see Before "Decorating the Cake," p. 42) and ice.

Chill before serving.

FORGET ME KNOTS

1. The amount of liquid necessary for the proper consistency of each recipe will vary according to the moisture and temperature of the flour and the room, the size of the eggs and the general weather of the day. Remain flexible and adjust liquid content accordingly.

2. Mu or mint tea (p. 10) may be substituted for liquid in any recipe. If more sweetness is desired, add a few tablespoons concentrated sweetener (see chart, p. 149), decreasing the liquid content accordingly.

3. When diluting arrowroot in liquid, stir again *immediately before* adding it to the mixture, as arrowroot tends to settle to the bottom rather quickly.

4. Kuzu may be substituted for arrowroot in any recipe.

5. Using kanten, arrowroot or kuzu with acid fruits (lemons, tangerines, oranges, strawberries) may cause the mixture to set less firmly. Add ¼ to ½ bar more kanten, or ½ tablespoon more arrowroot or kuzu, according to the amount of fruit used and the acidity of the fruit.

6. Double boilers are better to use for heating delicate icing ingredients (especially eggs), which tend to cook rather quickly and burn.

7. Never cook liquid vanilla or citrus rind, as doing so will decrease their flavor.

8. Use any creame or icing recipe for a separate dessert. Chill or freeze before serving.

Simple Fillings and Toppings

ALMOND PASTE

1 pound almonds
2 egg whites or apple juice
1 cup concentrated sweetener

Blanch almonds (p. 46) and pound with a mortar and pestle, adding a little apple juice, or egg whites.

When well pounded, place the mixture in a pan, add sweetener and cook, stirring constantly until the mixture thickens. Use for fillings.

ORANGE-APPLE FILLING

1 cup Applesauce
¼ cup oil
   Juice and grated rind of 1 orange
½ cup roasted chopped walnuts or pecans

Combine all ingredients except nuts. Blend. Add

nuts and mix well. (If you wish, omit oil and blend nuts with other ingredients.) Use to fill pies, pastries, tarts, strudel, turnovers, etc.

MINCEMEAT FILLING

1 cup chopped apples
1 cup apricot purée
½ cup orange rind
¼ cup lemon rind
1 teaspoon cinnamon
½ teaspoon cloves
½ teaspoon ginger
¼ teaspoon salt
4 cups raisins

Core and chop apples (peel if not organic). Combine apricot purée, apples, rinds, spices and salt. Add raisins and mix well. Cook about 30 to 45 minutes.

Fill prebaked pie shell. Or fill a half-baked pie shell, then bake together for 10 to 15 minutes longer.

Use in pastries, turnovers, strudel, etc., or in between layers of cakes.

Variations

Dilute 1 tablespoon arrowroot flour in ½ cup liquid for every cup of fruits, place in a saucepan and cook again until mixture boils and thickens. Add spices after cooking.

Add 1 to 2 tablespoons miso, diluted in two tablespoons apricot purée, before cooking.

APPLESAUCE

8 to 9 medium-size apples
1 teaspoon cinnamon
½ teaspoon cloves
½ teaspoon ginger
½ teaspoon salt
2 teaspoons lemon juice
½ cup raisins

Core and slice apples (peel if not organic). Place apples, spices, salt and lemon juice in a pot. Cover and cook until apples are soft. Blend sauce in a food mill or blender. (If using a blender, set at very low speed for a very short time.) Add raisins, and cool.

If desired, add arrowroot diluted in 2 tablespoons apple juice or cider to sauce after blending and return to heat. Cook, constantly stirring, until mixture begins to thicken and boil. Use 1 tablespoon arrowroot per cup applesauce.

APPLE TOPPING

2 cups Applesauce
1 egg white
Pinch of salt

Prepare Applesauce. Beat egg white and salt until peaked. Fold egg white into sauce.

Bake a cake. During the last 10 minutes of baking, place topping on cake and bake at 400°, or until browned.

The legend of Johnny Appleseed is well known in America, and is still being told in many schools today. There actually was a Johnny Appleseed, whose real name was John Chapman. He collected apple seeds from cider mills, dried them and put them into tiny bags, which he gave to every person he met who was headed west.

For more than 35 years he traveled through Indiana, Ohio, Iowa and Illinois, planting seeds in every likely location. He was known as a bearded wanderer with an obsession for planting orchards.

LEMON-APPLE FILLING

Follow the recipe for Orange-Apple Filling, substituting 1 grated lemon and juice for orange.

See variations for Oat Creame (pp. 55–56).

APPLE-APRICOT FILLING

8 apples
½ cup raisins
2 cups dried apricots
½ to 1 cup apple juice or cider
½ teaspoon salt
1 teaspoon cinnamon
½ teaspoon ginger
½ teaspoon mint
1 teaspoon vanilla

Core and chop apples (peel if not organic). Set aside. Soak raisins and apricots in juice or cider to cover until soft. Add salt, cover and simmer on a low flame about 20 minutes. Combine cooked fruit and apples with spices. Drain off excess liquid (use for cakes, pastries, etc.). Stir in vanilla. Purée whole, or purée half and combine, or use as is.

Variations

Dilute arrowroot flour in a small amount of cool liquid (1 tablespoon per cup of filling). Add to cooked fruit and bring to a boil, stirring rapidly until thickened.

Substitute any fresh or dried fruit for apples and apricots.

Add ½ cup roasted chopped nuts to fruits after cooking.

GRAIN SYRUP

Pressure cook or boil 2 cups brown rice, without salt, in 6 cups water for 45 minutes. Cool to 140° (use a candy thermometer). To the cooked rice add freshly made grain sprouts* which have been crushed or blended.

Combine the rice and sprouts. Cover, and keep in a warm place, so that temperature of the rice-sprout mixture is maintained at 130° to 140° for 4 to 5 hours. (You can place it on a warm stove, near a radiator or rest it in a pan of hot water.) Remove cover and taste. If it is not sweet enough, cover and let sit another 3 to 5 hours, tasting often until it reaches the sweet stage. Squeeze liquid through cheesecloth into pan. Reserve grain for puddings, etc. Add a pinch of salt and boil. Using candy thermometer, cook till it reaches the desired consistency.

FILLING FOR PHYLO PASTRY

1 to 2 pounds spinach
1 piece tofu
2 tablespoons oil
Salt
Phylo Dough (p. 78)

Parboil spinach in boiling salted water for about 2 minutes or just until soft. Drain and squeeze out excess liquid.

Break tofu into small pieces. Sauté in oil 2 to 3 minutes, lightly sprinkling with salt. Set aside some tofu for the top.

Filling the Pastry

Place a spoonful of spinach on dough, top with tofu; or mix spinach and tofu together before filling. Fold dough over the filling, first to the left, and then to the right, alternating until a triangle is formed.

Dot the top of the pastry with oiled fingers. Sprinkle on salted tofu or gomasio (p. 79) before baking.

This dough may also be used for Baklava (p. 80).

POPPY SEED FILLING I

⅓ cup poppy seeds
⅔ cup raisins
1 cup apple juice or cider
¼ teaspoon salt
1 teaspoon vanilla

Cook all ingredients in a saucepan or uncovered double boiler for 10 to 15 minutes, or until most of the liquid has evaporated. Blend until creamy.

Use for fillings for pastry tarts, turnovers, or in between layers of cakes.

POPPY SEED FILLING II

1 cup poppy seeds
½ cup apple butter or apple cider jelly
1 tablespoon orange, tangerine or lemon rind
½ teaspoon salt
1 teaspoon vanilla
½ cup chopped roasted almonds or walnuts

Combine poppy seeds, apple butter or jelly, rind and salt in a large mixing bowl. Add liquid to cover, and soak overnight. Blend.

Cook uncovered on a medium flame about 15 minutes, or until most of the liquid has evaporated. Stir in vanilla and nuts.

---

* Use 1 tablespoon unsprouted grain to every 1½ cups cooked rice. To make sprouts, use whole oats, barley, wheat or rice. Place grain in a glass jar, put a cheesecloth over the top of the jar and secure. Soak at least 12 hours in spring water to cover. Drain through cheesecloth, rinse with fresh water and drain again. Lay jar on its side in a warm, dark place. Rinse and drain every day to maintain moisture.

The grain will sprout in 3 to 6 days, depending upon the grain used and the temperature; the warmer the temperature, the shorter the time needed.

TAHINI-POPPY SEED FILLING

⅓ cup poppy seeds
⅔ cup raisins
¼ teaspoon salt
2 tablespoons grain coffee
1 cup apple juice or cider
½ cup tahini
1 teaspoon lemon rind
1 teaspoon cinnamon

Cook poppy seeds, raisins, salt, grain coffee and apple juice or cider together for 10 to 15 minutes, or until most of the liquid has evaporated.

Place mixture in a blender, add remaining ingredients and blend until creamy. (You may have to add more liquid to get a creamy consistency.)

Variations

Poppy Seed Glaze

Follow recipe for Poppy Seed Filling I. Combine cooked filling with 1 tablespoon arrowroot flour dissolved in ½ cup apple juice or cider (at room temperature). Cook on a medium flame, constantly stirring, until mixture boils. Spoon over cake or pastry immediately.

Lemon Poppy Seed Filling

Follow recipe for Poppy Seed Filling I. Before cooking, add 2½ tablespoons sesame butter and 2½ tablespoons grain coffee. After cooking, add the juice of ½ small lemon. Blend together until creamy. Use as filling for pastry sheets, strudels, turnovers, etc.

Spice Poppy Seed Filling

Follow recipe for Poppy Seed Filling I or II. Just before blending, add 1 teaspoon cinnamon, ¼ teaspoon cloves, pinch of ginger (for Filling I, add 2½ tablespoons of any nut butter). Blend and fill pastry or cake.

Mint Poppy Seed Filling

Follow recipe for Poppy Seed Filling I or II. While cooking add 2 to 3 teaspoons fresh or dried mint.

Nut Butter Poppy Seed Filling

Follow recipe for Mint Poppy Seed Filling. After cooking you may add 2 tablespoons of any nut butter and blend until creamy.

Coffee Poppy Seed Filling

Follow recipe for Poppy Seed Filling I, adding 2 tablespoons grain coffee to ingredients before cooking.

Cinnamon Poppy Seed Filling

Follow recipe for Poppy Seed Filling I. Stir in 1 teaspoon cinnamon after cooking.

Fruit Poppy Seed Filling

Follow recipe for Poppy Seed Filling I. Substitute 1 cup of any fresh fruit in season for raisins or ⅔ cup of any soaked dried fruit.

Tofu Poppy Seed Filling

Follow recipe for Poppy Seed Filling I or II. Stir in 1 cup Instant Tofu Creame (p. 59) to mixture.

RAISIN-PRUNE FILLING OR TOPPING

1 pound prunes
1 cup raisins
¼ teaspoon salt
Juice and rind of ½ grated orange
2 tablespoons lemon rind
½ cup chopped roasted almonds

Soak prunes and raisins in liquid to cover until soft. Add salt. Bring to a boil. Cover and simmer 30 minutes. Drain off liquid. Remove pits from prunes.

Blend rind, grated orange, prunes and raisins. Add liquid if necessary. Combine nuts with blended fruit.

Variations

Add 1 teaspoon vanilla after cooking.

Substitute ½ cup roasted sunflower seeds or sesame seeds for almonds.

Add 2 tablespoons tahini and 1 teaspoon cinnamon before blending.

Add 1 teaspoon cinnamon plus 2 tablespoons grain coffee before cooking.

See Oat Creame variations (pp. 55–56).

Dissolve 1 tablespoon arrowroot flour in each cup of filling for pies and pastries (see Fruit Purée II Variations, p. 67).

Substitute any dried fruit for prunes.

STRAWBERRY
(*Fragaria
ananassa*)

The strawberry is a perennial plant native to North America. Growing mostly in woodlands of the eastern part of the United States, it radiates stems or runners which take root and grow into new plants. It has a thick, dark foliage, bearing white or pinkish flowers. Male and female flowers are borne on separate plants, and female plants will not flower into fruit unless planted with the male. Used mainly as a dessert fruit, strawberries can also be made into jam used in pies, cakes and tarts.

STRAWBERRY CHEESECAKE TOPPING

2	tablespoons arrowroot flour
1½	cups apple juice or cider
¼	cup concentrated sweetener (optional)
¼	teaspoon salt
4	cups chopped strawberries

Dissolve the arrowroot flour in juice or cider. Add sweetener, if used, and decrease liquid content accordingly. Cook on a medium flame, stirring constantly until it boils; add salt and strawberries. Stir rapidly until mixture thickens and boils again.

Spoon over Daniel's Strawberry Cheesecake (p. 38), letting it drip down sides of cake. Cool before serving.

Nut Butter Icings

The consistency of butter icing can vary, depending upon what you want to do with it. A firm icing is necessary if you want to pipe it onto a cake for decoration (pp. 46–48). A softer icing is better to use for spreading around the sides of a cake, especially if you want to roll the sides of the cake in nuts, seeds or rind. A delicate, soft, creamy butter icing is nice to make when you are planning to fill or cover the top of a delicate cake. Then, over this delicate thin layer you can pipe fluted edges or write with a firmer nut butter icing.

Add a little extra Chestnut Purée (p. 66) or nut butter to make icing stiffer. After adding nut butter or purée, chill several hours before using (icings made with arrowroot flour, however, should be used immediately).

To soften icing, add a little warm liquid before using.

If the icing is too thick, mix with a little concentrated sweetener or juice.

Nut butter icing that is going to be used for piping or writing should be made a day or two in advance and refrigerated. This makes the icing stiffer, so that the piping will maintain its shape after decorating, especially in warm weather. If the icing becomes too stiff and tends to crack, beat in a few drops of hot liquid.

When it is difficult to obtain good-quality nut butters, roast your own nuts or seeds and blend warm until oil starts to form. Remove from blender, and using a suribachi* or a mortar and pestle, grind until butter is formed. If it is possible, use a grain mill instead of a blender, and run the nuts or seeds through when they are warm, and then grind by hand. (This will allow you to obtain a much finer nut butter.)

* A suribachi is a bowl with ridges on the inside, used to crush seeds, nuts, etc. Use it with a pestle, moving the pestle around in a counterclockwise motion, for best results.

NUT BUTTER ICING I

1 cup tahini, almond or sesame butter
½ to 1 cup Chestnut Purée (p. 66) to taste
¼ to ½ cup raisin purée (p. 66) (optional)
1 teaspoon orange or lemon rind
¼ teaspoon salt
1 teaspoon vanilla

Blend together tahini, Chestnut Purée and raisin purée. (If using raisin purée, add slowly until desired consistency is reached; use more purée for fillings and less for icing.)

Add rind, salt and vanilla. Keep blending until desired consistency is reached (the longer you blend, the thicker it becomes).

NUT BUTTER ICING II

1 tablespoon arrowroot flour
1 cup apple juice or cider
2 tablespoons any nut butter

Dissolve arrowroot flour in 2 to 3 tablespoons juice or cider. Set aside.

In a heavy saucepan, combine the rest of juice and nut butter. (For piping, use less juice.) Heat over a medium flame, stirring occasionally. When it is almost boiling, add arrowroot mixture and stir rapidly until mixture comes to a boil, thickens and turns clear. Remove from heat and ice cake immediately.

MOCHA BUTTER ICING

Follow recipe for Nut Butter Icing II. Add 2 tablespoons grain coffee to juice and nut butter. When mixture is almost boiling, add arrowroot mixture and cook another 2 minutes stirring rapidly. Remove from heat and stir in ½ teaspoon cinnamon and 1 teaspoon lemon juice. Allow icing to sit for a few minutes before using.

Creames

OAT CREAME

1 cup rolled, whole or steel-cut oats
½ cup oil
4 to 6 cups apple juice or cider
½ teaspoon salt
¼ cup concentrated sweetener (optional)
1 teaspoon cinnamon
1 teaspoon vanilla

Soak whole or steel-cut oats overnight. Roast oats in ¼ cup oil, until lightly browned. (If using rolled oats omit soaking.)

Combine juice (adjust liquid content according to texture desired) and oats in a heavy pot, and bring to a boil, stirring occasionally. Add remaining oil, salt and sweetener if desired. Lower flame, cover and simmer at least 30 minutes. Cook whole or steel-cut oats at least 1½ hours, or pressure-cook at least 45 to 60 minutes.

After cooking, add cinnamon and vanilla. Blend until creamy and smooth. This can be kept for several weeks if properly chilled.

Variations

Add 3 to 4 tablespoons grain coffee before cooking.

Substitute 3 to 4 tablespoons nut butter for ¼ cup oil; add nut butter after cooking.

Add 1 teaspoon cinnamon, ½ teaspoon ginger and 1 teaspoon orange, tangerine or lemon rind after cooking.

Add ½ cup fresh or soaked dried fruit before cooking, or cook fruit, blend creame and add fruit after blending (use a few tablespoons less liquid).

Add ½ cup Chestnut Purée (p. 66) and 1 to 2 teaspoons orange, tangerine or lemon rind after cooking and before blending.

Add ½ cup raisin purée and 3 to 4 tablespoons grain coffee before cooking.

Add 1 to 2 teaspoons mint to mixture before cooking.

Add the juice and grated rind of 1 orange, tangerine or lemon after cooking.

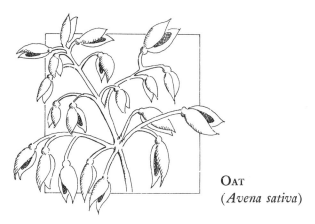

OAT
(*Avena sativa*)

The use of the oat is believed to date back to the European Bronze Age. Today, oats are usually used to feed livestock. Humans eat them in the form of breakfast cereals. Oats possess a special quality: when cooked with four to five times the amount of liquid they become glutenous, and make a fine substitute for milk and milk puddings.

Add ½ cup soaked raisins and ½ cup chopped roasted nuts after blending.

Substitute 3 to 4 tablespoons of any nut butter for ¼ cup oil in mixture. Add ½ cup Chestnut Purée and 3 tablespoons grain coffee before cooking. After cooking add 1 teaspoon orange, tangerine or lemon rind, plus 1 more teaspoon vanilla, and nut butter.

Add ½ cup cooked chestnuts (p. 66) to creame after cooking and before or after blending.

Add 1 teaspoon cinnamon and ½ teaspoon ginger to creame after cooking, and ½ cup raisins after blending.

Add ½ cup chopped roasted nuts or seeds to creame after blending.

Add 1 to 2 teaspoons more vanilla after cooking or vanilla bean before cooking.

Add vegetable and/or fruit purée to taste (pp. 65–66).

Substitute ½ to 1 cup apple butter or apple cider jelly for ½ cup juice.

Substitute mu tea or mint tea for juice, and add ½ cup concentrated sweetener before or after cooking.

Follow directions for cooking whole or steel-cut oats, substituting brown rice, sweet brown rice or barley for oats.

Substitute whole-wheat pastry flour, chestnut or corn flour for oats; omit blending.

ALMOND CREAME

    1 cup almonds
      Apple juice or cider
    2 eggs
    2 tablespoons almond butter
    1 tablespoon lemon juice
      Rind of ¼ lemon
    ¼ teaspoon salt

Blanch almonds and pound till smooth with a little apple juice. Stir in well-beaten eggs. Warm almond butter and add to eggs.

Mix in lemon juice, rind and salt.

ALMOND NUT-BUTTER CREAME

    1 cup almond butter
    ¼ cup concentrated sweetener
    1 teaspoon vanilla
    1 teaspoon lemon rind
    ¼ cup ground roasted almonds
    ½ cup Oat Creame (p. 55)
    ½ to 1 cup apple juice or cider

Combine almond butter with sweetener, mixing until a thick paste is formed. Set aside. Add vanilla, lemon rind and almonds to the Oat Creame. Mix well.

Combine Oat Creame mixture and almond paste, blending with the back of a wooden spoon, or at very low speed in a blender. You may find that this mixture is too thick for a blender because the thickness of almond butter varies, depending on the content of oil. It may sometimes be necessary to add liquid.

Use sparingly as fillings for pastry sheets, turnovers or in between layers of a cake or parfait.

Variations

Substitute 1 cup tahini or any nut butter for almond butter.

See Oat Creame variations.

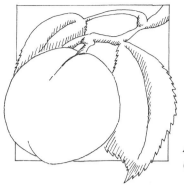

APRICOT
(Prunus armeniaca)

The apricot comes from a tree, 20 to 30 feet high, with white and sometimes pink flowers, which bloom in March or April before the leaves appear. Under proper conditions, the apricot tree can be grown from discarded pits. The trees are found mainly in warm temperate climates. Some of the fruits are pale yellow but they may range from yellow to deep-orange with a freckled skin.

APRICOT CREAME FILLING

  2 tablespoons chestnut flour
¼ cup apple juice or cider (at room
    temperature)
¼ cup concentrated sweetener
  1 cup apricot (or other fruit) purée (p. 66)
  1 teaspoon cinnamon
½ teaspoon lemon rind
½ teaspoon orange rind
  3 tablespoons lemon juice
  3 eggs
¼ teaspoon salt
¼ cup roasted almonds, pecans, filberts or
    walnuts

Roast chestnut flour until it begins to smell sweet. Set aside till cool, then sift into mixing bowl. Add juice or cider, mix and set aside.

Combine sweetener, apricot purée, cinnamon, rind and lemon juice. Set aside.

Separate eggs. Mix yolks into apricot mixture. Beat whites and salt together until peaked. Combine flour and apricot mixtures. Slowly fold in whites. Fill any tart shell, turnover or pie shell, and bake.

See Oat Creame variations (pp. 55–56).

CHESTNUT CREAME I

  1 cup sifted chestnut flour
3 to 4 cups apple cider, juice, mu tea, mint tea or
    water
3 to 4 tablespoons oil, tahini or sesame butter
  ¼ teaspoon salt
  ½ teaspoon cinnamon
  1 teaspoon vanilla

Roast flour in a dry skillet until it begins to smell sweet. Allow to cool, then sift flour into liquid. Adjust liquid content according to texture desired — the less liquid, the thicker the creame.

Cook on a medium flame, stirring constantly. Add tahini or oil, and salt. Keep stirring until mixture boils. Reduce flame and simmer 15 minutes uncovered, stirring occasionally. Add cinnamon and vanilla, and mix until spice is no longer visible.

Variations

See variations for Oat Creame (pp. 55–56).

Substitute corn, whole-wheat pastry or sweet brown rice flour for chestnut flour.

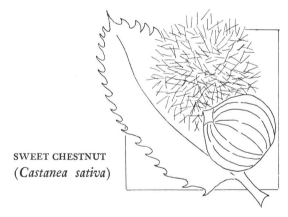

SWEET CHESTNUT
(Castanea sativa)

Originally from southern Europe, the chestnut tree has been planted in many different parts of the world.

Chestnuts grow on moderately large trees, characterized by alternate deciduous leaves with bristle-tipped margins. Their small, inconspicuous unisexual flowers are borne in catkins. The fruit, a nut, borne in clusters of two or three, is enclosed in a leathery husk, clothed with multibranched spines.

Both the wood and bark of the tree contain tannin, a chemical complex which is extracted in com-

mercial quantities and used in converting rawhides into leather.

The European or Spanish chestnut (called marron) *is probably the most important species. It grows in southern Europe as well as North Africa, southern Asia, England and India. During the nineteenth century it became widely established and is still frequently encountered in California and the Pacific Northwest.*

The largest nuts are eaten raw, boiled or roasted. Smaller ones are dried, and milled into flour. The small nuts, if and when gathered, are fed to livestock.

Chestnuts are used in soups, stuffings and desserts, as well as roasted and eaten hot from the oven.

CHESTNUT CREAME II

1 recipe Chestnut Creame I
1 bar kanten

Rinse kanten under cold running water. Squeeze out excess liquid. Shred into 1 cup juice, and bring to a boil. Reduce flame and cook until kanten dissolves, stirring occasionally. Combine flour with the rest of juice, adding oil and salt while cooking. Bring to a boil, stir in hot kanten mixture, reduce flame and simmer 15 minutes, uncovered, stirring occasionally. Add cinnamon and vanilla and stir until well combined.

Variations

Use as a separate layer for cake (see "Inlay," p. 49, Soufflé, p. 67), as a cold dessert or as a filling.

COFFEE CREAME

4 tablespoons oil
2 tablespoons concentrated sweetener
2 tablespoons grain coffee
1 teaspoon vanilla
½ teaspoon salt
1 egg
2 cups cookie, cake or bread crumbs
2 tablespoons shredded unsweetened
    coconut

Combine oil, sweetener, grain coffee, vanilla and

salt in the top of a double boiler. Cook over simmering water a few minutes. Stir in lightly beaten egg. Continue cooking, stirring constantly until mixture begins to thicken. Add crumbs and coconut.

Use as a topping for pies or cakes, or drop in the center of a cookie batter or dough before baking. Can also be used as a filling for pastries or pies.

See Oat Creame variations (p. 55–56).

LEMON-BLUEBERRY CREAME

½ bar kanten
3 cups apple juice or cider
6 tablespoons arrowroot
1½ cups blueberries
    Juice and rind of ½ lemon or orange
4 tablespoons concentrated sweetener
2 egg whites
½ teaspoon salt
            Crust
1 cup Pressed Pastry (p. 76)

Rinse kanten under cold running water; squeeze out excess liquid. Shred kanten into 1 cup juice or cider and bring to a boil. Lower flame and cook until kanten dissolves.

Combine arrowroot with 2 cups juice or cider, and add juice with kanten. Cook on a high flame, stirring constantly, until mixture boils and thickens. Add berries, rind, juice and sweetener. Beat egg whites and salt together until peaked. Fold in whites. Pour into prebaked pie crust. Cool and serve.

See variations for Oat Creame (pp. 55–56).

ORANGE CREAME

1 bar kanten
½ cup apple juice or cider
2½ cups Oat Creame (p. 55)
1 egg
2 tablespoons concentrated sweetener
1 teaspoon vanilla
    Juice and rind of ½ grated organic orange
½ teaspoon cinnamon
¼ teaspoon salt

Rinse kanten under cold running water. Squeeze

out excess liquid. Shred into ½ cup juice, bring to a boil and cook on a medium flame until kanten dissolves. Add Oat Creame, lower flame and simmer 5 minutes longer. Remove from heat. Separate egg. Combine yolk, sweetener, vanilla, orange juice and grated rind. Beat until fluffy. Combine with Oat Creame mixture and blend until smooth and creamy, adding cinnamon gradually.

Beat egg white and salt together until peaked. Fold egg white into creame gently. Place entire mixture in half-baked crust and bake until set.

You may substitute lemon juice and rind for orange juice and rind.

PASTRY CREAME

    3 tablespoons whole-wheat pastry flour
1 to 2 cups apple juice or cider
1 to 2 tablespoons concentrated sweetener
    3 egg yolks
    ¼ teaspoon salt
    ½ teaspoon orange rind
    1 tablespoon oil
    ½ teaspoon vanilla

Roast flour until lightly browned. Set aside to cool. Heat apple juice in top of double boiler or heavy saucepan. Remove from pan or boiler. Cool. Place sweetener, yolks, flour, salt and rind in pan or boiler. Pour apple juice slowly into the sweetener mixture, beating with rotary beater or wire whisk.

Cook over low flame for five minutes, stirring occasionally. Remove from heat, add oil and vanilla, mix well.

See variations for Oat Creame (pp. 55–56).

TAHINI CHESTNUT CREAME FILLING

1 recipe for Tahini Custard (p. 62)
1 cup Chestnut Pureé (p. 66)
2 cups Tofu Creame Whip (p. 60)

Combine Tahini Custard and Chestnut Purée. Chill. When firm, mix 2 cups Tofu Creame Whip into first mixture. Use as a filling for cannolis, horns or éclairs, or chill or freeze for dessert.

MOCK WHIPPED CREAME

Blanch 4 cups almonds (p. 46). Blend almonds, 1 teaspoon vanilla (add a little liquid if necessary) in a blender until creamy.

INSTANT TOFU CREAME

    2 cups tofu (p. 13)
¼ to ½ cup raisin purée (p. 66)
    3 tablespoons tahini, or almond butter
    1 teaspoon vanilla
    ¼ teaspoon salt

Drop tofu into boiling salted water. Remove from heat and let sit 2 to 3 minutes. Squeeze out excess liquid.

Combine tofu with remaining ingredients, blending until creamy. Add a few drops of sesame oil or fruit juice if difficult to blend.

See variations for Oat Creame, without cooking. (Pp. 55–56).

TOFU CREAME

    ½ cup apple cider or juice
    2 tablespoons tahini, almond butter or oil
    2 cups tofu
    ¼ teaspoon salt
 1½ tablespoons arrowroot flour
    ¼ cup concentrated sweetener
    3 tablespoons apple cider or juice
    1 teaspoon vanilla

Combine cider or juice with tahini or almond butter and cook on a medium flame until warm.

Squeeze out excess liquid from tofu. Combine with salt and apple juice mixture and blend until creamy.

Dilute arrowroot in sweetener and apple juice or cider. Set aside.

Place tofu mixture in pan, and when almost boiling, add arrowroot mixture, stirring rapidly until mixture boils and thickens. Remove from flame. Stir in vanilla. Use immediately.

See Oat Creame variations (pp. 55–56).

TOFU CREAME WHIP

    1 cup tofu
2 to 3 tablespoons concentrated sweetener
    1 tablespoon oil or nut butter
      Pinch of salt
    ½ bar kanten
    ½ cup apple juice or cider
    1 teaspoon vanilla

Drop tofu into boiling, salted water. Remove from heat and let sit 2 to 3 minutes. Squeeze out liquid.

Blend tofu, sweetener, oil or nut butter and salt together until creamy. Set aside.

Rinse the kanten under cold running water. Squeeze out excess liquid and shred into small pieces. Pour liquid over kanten and bring to a boil; lower heat and simmer until kanten dissolves. Stir occasionally. Remove from heat.

Add vanilla and tofu creame mixture. Beat with wire whisk or with electric mixer until smooth and creamy. Set aside to jell. When the mixture has almost set, beat again. Set on shelf for a few hours to mellow.

Chill if not using immediately. To freshen, beat again before using.

See variations for Oat Creame (pp. 55–56).

TOFU SOUR CREAME I

    1 cup tofu
      Juice of 1 lemon
    ½ to 1 teaspoon salt

Drop tofu into boiling salted water. Remove from heat and let sit 2 to 3 minutes. Squeeze out in your hands or cheesecloth to remove excess liquid.

Place tofu in a blender, add lemon juice and salt. Blend until creamy and taste. If it is too sour, add more salt to counteract lemon.

TOFU SOUR CREAME II

    ½ teaspoon cinnamon
    ½ to 1 teaspoon vanilla
    1 cup Tofu Sour Creame I
    ½ diced apple (peel if not organic)
    ¼ cup raisins

Blend cinnamon and vanilla with Tofu Sour Creame I; add fruit and mix together. Use as a filling or cake topping.

Variations

Use any fresh fruit in season in place of apples. Use any dried fruit; soak and dice.

Add roasted chopped nuts or seeds, before or after blending.

Add 1 to 2 teaspoons concentrated sweetener and 1 teaspoon lemon juice to fruit. Allow to marinate for several hours before mixing with creame.

Also see Oat Creame variations.

Meringues and Custards

MERINGUE

A meringue is a very delicate, light topping, using egg whites as a base. The whites are stiffly beaten, sweetened, flavored and usually baked. However, this particular meringue need not be baked. It is necessary to bake a meringue when the sweetener is not heated to 265°.

2 to 3 tablespoons concentrated sweetener
    2 egg whites
      Pinch of salt
    ½ teaspoon vanilla
    1 teaspoon lemon, orange rind or mint

Cook sweetener in a heavy saucepan or double boiler until it reaches a temperature of 265° (use a candy thermometer).

Beat egg whites and salt together. Slowly *drip* the sweetener into the whites, while beating. Beat until stiff. Add vanilla and other flavoring, and beat until peaked.

Spread on top of any baked dessert. If desired, bake at 225° for 45 minutes, at 325° for 25 minutes or at 400° for 10 minutes, on top of any prebaked or half-baked dessert.

Turn off oven, open door, and leave inside at least 15 minutes longer.

See Oat Creame variations (pp. 55–56).

APPLE CUSTARD

  3 apples
    Juice and rind of ½ lemon
  2 tablespoons concentrated sweetener
  1 tablespoon roasted whole-wheat pastry
    flour
  ½ teaspoon salt
¼ to ½ cup apple juice or cider
  2 eggs (room temperature)
  1 teaspoon vanilla
  2 tablespoons oil
  1 teaspoon cinnamon

Grate apples (peel if not organic). Combine apples, lemon juice and sweetener together. Cook on a medium flame until mixture boils. Add rind.

In a separate pan, dissolve flour and salt in apple juice. Combine with apple mixture, stirring constantly until thickened.

Separate eggs. Stir 2 to 3 tablespoons of cooked filling into egg yolks. Put this mixture back in filling, stirring rapidly. Return to heat and cook in a double boiler on a low flame, stirring constantly until mixture thickens. Remove from heat, add vanilla, spice and oil. Stir.

Variations

Substitute any fresh or dried fruit for apples.

Add 3 to 4 tablespoons grain coffee to first mixture after boiling.

Add 1 teaspoon dried mint to mixture after boiling.

Substitute any nut butter for oil.

ORANGE
(*Citrus sinensis*)

Oranges are given their color by cold weather. They have an outer skin that is green from chlorophyll. The thin membrane breaks down in cold weather, destroying the chlorophyll and turning the orange its characteristic color. The fruit is not necessarily ripe, even if it is orange.

When oranges are put into the store to be sold, they have to be orange, otherwise they will not sell. Ethylene gas is used to turn a green fruit orange, or an orange fruit brighter.

Sometimes, a wax coating is applied to the skin, to prevent the orange from shriveling up. If too much wax is applied, the orange will not be able to breathe, and will "suffocate," and lose some of its taste.

ORANGE CUSTARD

2 tablespoons whole-wheat pastry, corn or
   chestnut flour
¼ cup concentrated sweetener
  Juice and grated rind of 1 orange
1 egg
1 teaspoon lemon juice
¼ teaspoon salt

Roast flour in oil until lightly browned. Set aside to cool.

Combine the flour and sweetener together. Add juice and rind, and cook in a heavy saucepan over a medium flame, stirring constantly until mixture boils.

Beat egg slightly. Add lemon juice and salt. Combine this with the flour mixture, and cook 5 minutes on a low flame, stirring constantly, so that egg does not overcook.

TAHINI CUSTARD

2 bars kanten
3 cups cider or juice
1 cup apple juice or water
2 tablespoons tahini
1 teaspoon vanilla

Rinse kanten under cold running water. Squeeze out excess liquid. Shred into 3 cups juice or cider. Bring to boil on a medium flame. Lower flame and cook until kanten dissolves. Blend 1 cup liquid and tahini until creamy. Add to kanten mixture and cook 5 minutes on a low flame. Add vanilla.

STRAWBERRY TAHINI CUSTARD

Follow preceding recipe. Stir in 3 cups chopped strawberries and simmer 2 minutes before adding vanilla.

LEMON CUSTARD

2½ tablespoons whole-wheat pastry, corn or chestnut flour
1 tablespoon oil
1 egg
2 cups apple juice or cider
4 tablespoons lemon juice
4 tablespoons lemon rind
¼ teaspoon salt

Roast flour in oil until lightly browned. Set aside to cool.

Separate egg. Stir yolk with a fork. Combine flour with a few tablespoons apple juice and stir into a smooth and creamy batter. Remove all lumps. Combine with egg yolk and remaining juice. Cook on a medium flame, stirring constantly for 5 minutes.

Beat egg white and salt together until peaked. Add lemon juice, rind, and egg white to the cooked mixture. Fold in gently. DO NOT OVERMIX.

Variations

Add any one or a combination of the following:
Mint to taste, before or after cooking
2 to 3 tablespoons grain coffee, before cooking
1 teaspoon cinnamon, after cooking
¼ cup crushed roasted nuts or seeds before folding in egg white
½ cup fresh diced fruit to yolk mixture, after cooking
Also see variations for Oat Creme (pp. 55–56).

TOFU CUSTARD

2 cups tofu
¼ teaspoon salt
1 egg
1 teaspoon vanilla
¼ cup concentrated sweetener or ½ cup Chestnut Purée (p. 66)
Grated rind of ½ lemon or orange
½ cup raisins
¼ cup roasted chopped almonds or walnuts

Break tofu into small pieces. In a warm skillet, lightly sauté tofu and salt without oil to remove excess water. Set aside for 5 minutes to cool.

Combine lightly beaten egg, tofu, vanilla, sweetener, rind and raisins. Mix together until all ingredients are combined. Add nuts.

Fill pastry. This texture is good for strudel (pp. 87–89).

See Oat Creme variations (pp. 55–56).

Glazes

Glazes give cakes or pastries a smooth, shiny appearance. If you want the glaze to drip down the sides of the cake, thin it by adding more liquid (about 2 tablespoons). If you want to use the glaze as a filling, decrease the liquid. See Fruit Purée II Variations, p. 67, for advice on handling arrowroot flour.

Kuzu may be substituted for arrowroot, using slightly more liquid (pp. 9–10). Recipes may also be augmented with flavorings, fruit, nuts or seeds.

BASIC GLAZE I

1 cup cider or any fruit juice
Pinch of salt
1 tablespoon arrowroot flour
2 tablespoons cider or any fruit juice
¼ cup sesame seeds

Heat 1 cup juice or cider and salt together in heavy saucepan; bring it to a boil. Dissolve arrowroot flour in 2 tablespoons cider or fruit juice; add it to the boiling liquid, stirring rapidly, until it boils again, thickens and turns clear. Remove from heat immediately and stir in seeds. Pour over dessert and serve.

BASIC GLAZE II

Follow recipe for Basic Glaze I, reducing the cup of juice to ¾ cup. Substitute 2 tablespoons tangerine, orange or lemon rind for sesame seeds.

Variations for Basic Glazes

Fruit Butter or Jelly Glaze

Substitute ½ to 1 cup fruit butter or apple cider jelly for juice or cider. Stir ½ to 1 teaspoon lemon juice into glaze after removing glaze from heat.

Coffee Glaze

Bring apple juice and salt to a boil. Add 2 to 3 tablespoons grain coffee and boil until coffee dissolves, before adding arrowroot mixture.

Spice Glaze

Follow directions for Coffee Glaze, adding ½ to 1 teaspoon of cloves, ginger or cinnamon, or a combination, after cooking. Stir and let sit 2 to 3 minutes before using.

Fruit Glaze

Soak ¼ cup dried fruit in apple juice or cider to cover until soft. Drain and save liquid; add enough liquid to bring to 1 cup. Dice fruit, place back in liquid and boil 10 minutes. Add arrowroot mixture and follow Basic Glaze recipe.

Fresh Fruit Glaze

After cooking, add 1 teaspoon lemon rind and 3 cups diced strawberries, blueberries, apples, pears or other fruit. Stir well. (Decrease liquid accordingly.)

Lemon Glaze

Stir in 2 to 3 tablespoons lemon juice to taste after cooking. 1 teaspoon lemon rind may also be added if desired; decrease liquid content accordingly.

Orange or Tangerine Glaze

Add the juice and rind of ½ organic orange or 1 tangerine to glaze after cooking; decrease liquid content accordingly.

Raisin-Orange Glaze

Add ½ cup soaked raisins to orange glaze before cooking.

Mint Glaze I

Place 2 mint-tea bags in ½ cup apple juice and boil. Remove bags, add dissolved arrowroot and stir rapidly. Continue as with Basic Glaze.

Mint Glaze II

Add 1 teaspoon dried or fresh mint to ingredients before cooking.

Vanilla Glaze

Add 1 teaspoon vanilla extract (or to taste) after removing pan from heat. Or use vanilla bean (see p. 13).

Nut or Seed Glaze

Add ¼ cup roasted sesame or sunflower seeds, almonds, walnuts, pecans, peanuts or chestnuts to glaze after cooking.

Nut Butter Glaze

Blend 2 tablespoons of any nut butter into juice or cider before cooking. This glaze will not be as clear, but it will still be shiny.

Coconut Glaze

Add 1 tablespoon coconut to glaze after cooking.

SWEET ALMOND GLAZE OR FILLING

1 cup sweet almond milk (p. 12)
Pinch of salt
1¼ tablespoons arrowroot flour
1½ tablespoons concentrated sweetener
2 teaspoons lemon juice
1 to 1½ teaspoons lemon rind to taste

Heat ¾ cup almond milk and salt together in heavy saucepan over medium flame until boiling. Dilute arrowroot flour in sweetener and ¼ cup almond milk. Add this to boiling almond milk, stirring constantly, until mixture boils, thickens and turns clearer. Remove from heat, add lemon juice and rind; stir. Use immediately.

Variation

Almond Coffee Mint Glaze

Follow recipe for Sweet Almond Glaze. Add 2 to 3 tablespoons grain coffee before boiling and ¼ teaspoon dried mint to almond milk or apple juice after boiling. If you prefer, cook two mint-tea bags in juice or almond milk until liquid boils, add grain coffee and let simmer for 2 to 3 minutes. Then add other ingredients and follow recipe.

ORANGE-CHESTNUT GLAZE

        1 cup apple juice or cider
          Pinch of salt
        4 tablespoons Chestnut Purée (p. 66)
        1 tablespoon arrowroot flour
        2 tablespoons apple juice or cider
    1½ to 2 teaspoons orange rind

Heat 1 cup juice or cider, salt and Chestnut Purée in saucepan until boiling. Dissolve arrowroot flour in 2 tablespoons juice or cider. Quickly add arrowroot mixture to boiling liquid, stirring rapidly until it boils again, thickens and becomes clearer. Stir in orange rind. Remove from heat and use as desired.

Variations

Fruit-Chestnut Glaze

Substitute ¼ cup concentrated sweetener for ¼ cup apple juice. Add ¼ cup chopped apples or any fruit and ¼ cup cooked chestnuts (p. 66) to juice after boiling.

See glaze variations for additional suggestions (p. 63).

BEFORE-BAKING GLAZES

Glaze I

        4 tablespoons oil
        1 cup cake or cookie crumbs
        ½ teaspoon cinnamon

Combine ingredients and apply to dessert before baking.

Glaze II

        ¼ cup concentrated sweetener
        2 tablespoons oil
        1 unbeaten egg white
        2 tablespoons concentrated sweetener
        ½ cup crushed nuts
        ½ teaspoon cinnamon

Blend first three ingredients together. Add the rest of the ingredients and spread on top of dessert before baking.

Glaze III

        ¼ cup concentrated sweetener
        ¼ cup Oat Creame (p. 55)
        2 tablespoons oil
        ½ cup crushed nuts

Combine and spread on top of dessert before baking.

WEDDING THREADS

If you ever have an occasion to decorate a wedding cake, here is an icing that will have everyone's attention before it is eaten and will be remembered long after. It is one of Kathy's favorite ways to finish her wedding cakes and comes from a traditional Shaker recipe.

        3 cups maple syrup
        3 egg whites (room temperature)
        ¼ teaspoon salt

Place the maple syrup in a heavy saucepan (oil the rim of the pan to keep the syrup from overflowing).

Attach a candy thermometer and cook until it registers 232°, stirring occasionally. Beat the egg whites and salt together until peaked. As soon as the syrup has reached 232°, begin to drip it very slowly into the egg whites, beating with an electric mixer for best results. (A hand beater will achieve the same result but you will need assistance and more time.)

Keep beating until the icing begins to thicken. Lift a little of the icing up with a wooden spoon.

When it has a very stiff threadlike appearance it is ready.

Ice the cake immediately with a spatula, sweeping it in an upward motion around the sides and top. Decorate with real flowers, nuts, rind, etc. (see pp. 43–45).

This recipe will decorate a round four-tier cake. If you prepare a smaller amount, use 1 egg white per cup of maple syrup.

Purées

VEGETABLE PUREE I

6 to 8 cups chopped squash, carrots, parsnips, pumpkin, beets or yams
  2 tablespoons oil
  ½ teaspoon salt
  2 tablespoons concentrated sweetener (optional)

SQUASH, PUMPKIN, AND YAMS CONTAIN MORE LIQUID, SO USE A LARGER QUANTITY OF THESE VEGETABLES.

Chop vegetables into bite-size pieces. (If using squash, pumpkin or yams, remove skin before cooking). Heat oil in a heavy skillet. Sauté vegetables on a low flame for 5 minutes; stirring occasionally. Add salt, cover and cook until tender. Add sweetener if desired. Purée in food mill or blender.

Alternate Method

Cut squash, pumpkin or yams into thin strips or wedges (like melons). Baste with tamari and oil. Heat oven to 350°. Place on a baking sheet, cover and bake until tender. Uncover 5 minutes before removing from oven (to allow excess water to evaporate). These vegetables sometimes taste sweeter if baked instead of sautéed.

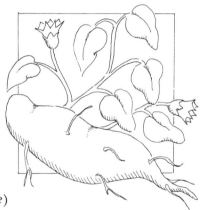

SWEET POTATO
(*Convolvulaceae*)

A vegetable of the morning glory family. Its large, fleshy roots are a popular food. Juicy sweet potatoes are often called yams, but the yam belongs to another family and grows mostly in the tropics. Sweet potatoes may be yellow or white. The yellow grows mostly in southern United States; white sweet potatoes come from Africa or Asia.

Some kinds of sweet potato plants have pale green vines with small pointed leaves. Others have purple vines with large leaves. The vines grow from the main stem and lie along the ground.

Sweet potatoes first grew in tropical regions of the western hemisphere. They were raised in colonial Virginia during the early 1600s. They are sometimes used in making alcohol and starch.

VEGETABLE PUREE II

2 cups vegetable purée
2 tablespoons tahini, sesame, almond or peanut butter
2 to 3 tablespoons arrowroot flour (see Fruit Purée II, p. 67)
¼ cup concentrated sweetener or apple juice
1 teaspoon orange or lemon rind

Prepare vegetable purée; allow to cool.

Place purée and nut butter in a saucepan, and cook on a medium flame until mixture boils. Dilute arrowroot in concentrated sweetener or juice. Add arrowroot combination to purée and stir constantly until it comes to a boil and thickens.

Remove from heat. Stir in rind.

Variations for Vegetable Purées I and II

Combine 2 different vegetables and/or fruits together in ratios such as:

carrot-beet, 3–1	beet-parsnip, 1–2
carrot-squash, 1–1	parsnip-yam, 1–2
carrot-parsnip, 3–1	squash-parsnip, 2–1
apricot-yam, 1–1	pear-parsnip, 2–1
carrot-raisin, 2–1	

See also variations for Oat Creame (pp. 55–56).

CHESTNUT PUREE

Chestnut purée is widely used in European pastries because of its delicate taste and texture.

To prepare with dried chestnuts:

Bake chestnuts in a 350° oven until lightly roasted. Soak in liquid to cover overnight. Add more liquid to cover if necessary before cooking. Bring to a boil and then simmer covered until tender. Drain off liquid, cool and purée in a food mill or blender, or mash like potatoes. Add more liquid if necessary.

To prepare with fresh chestnuts:

Cut a cross with a knife on the flat side of each chestnut. Place in a saucepan and cover with cold liquid. Bring to a boil.

Remove from heat. Take out chestnuts (a few at a time) and peel off outer and inner skins while warm.

Cover the chestnuts with liquid. Simmer until tender. Drain, reserving liquid. Cool; mash, blend or purée in a food mill. Leftover liquid can be used as flavoring in other desserts.

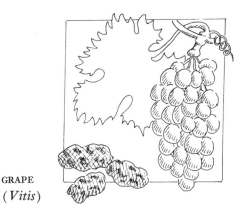

GRAPE
(*Vitis*)

The grape is one of the oldest and most important perennial fruit plants referred to in the Bible. Raisin is the commercial name for the dried or cured grape. The fruit from this species may be consumed fresh, dried for raisins or used for wines.

The important varieties differ in their versatility for these uses. Sultanini (Thompson Seedless) and Muscat are grown in large quantities for all three purposes. The Zante currant is grown only for its raisins.

California dries more than half of its grapes for raisins. Because of their high percentage of fruit sugar, sugar was manufactured from raisins in the early 1900s in practically all the countries of western Asia and southern Europe.

FRUIT PUREES (Raisin, Apricot, etc.)

FRUIT PUREE I

1 cup dried fruit
½ teaspoon lemon or orange rind
1 teaspoon vanilla
¼ teaspoon salt

Soak fruit in liquid to cover until soft. Purée all of the above ingredients together in a blender or food mill, using just enough liquid to allow ingredients to blend. Remember that each type of fruit is different; some may require more liquid, some less. Adjust accordingly.

Try making a larger quantity and keep it refrigerated until you want to use it.

FRUIT PUREE II

1½ cups dried fruit
2 tablespoons arrowroot flour (1 tablespoon per cup of the puréed fruit)
½ teaspoon salt

Soak fruit in liquid to cover until soft. Simmer in a covered pan 30 minutes. Add more liquid if necessary to cover fruit.

Strain off extra liquid and set aside. Allow liquid to cool. Purée fruit in a food mill or blender. When liquid is cool, dilute arrowroot flour in ½ cup liquid. Combine arrowroot mixture, salt and purée, adding more liquid if necessary to make 2 cups.

Place in a saucepan and cook on a medium flame, stirring constantly until mixture comes to a boil and thickens.

Variations

To use fresh fruit, follow the recipe for Vegetable Purée (p. 65), substituting fruit for vegetables. When using arrowroot flour, remember quantity needed is 1 tablespoon per cup of liquid. When you combine arrowroot flour with fruit or vegetable purée, it may be necessary to add a few more tablespoons of purée or some fruit juice per tablespoon of arrowroot flour because of the thicker consistency of the purée.

See Oat Creame variations (pp. 55–56) for other suggestions.

Apple butter may be substituted for any fruit purée.

ORANGE-MAPLE SAUCE

½ cup maple syrup
Grated juice and rind of 1½ oranges
¼ teaspoon salt

Heat maple syrup in a heavy saucepan until boiling.

Add orange juice and salt. Simmer covered for a few minutes.

Variations

Substitute any concentrated sweetener for maple syrup.

Substitute lemon or tangerine juice for orange juice.

See variations for Basic Glaze (p. 63).

SOUFFLE

3 peaches
1 bar kanten
4 cups cider or apple juice
4 tablespoons arrowroot flour
4 tablespoons apple juice or cider *or*
2 tablespoons concentrated sweetener and 2 tablespoons juice
1 cup blueberries
¼ teaspoon salt
2 teaspoons lemon juice
½ cup roasted chopped nuts

Slice the peaches into thin vertical strips (if not organic, blanch them, p. 46). Rinse kanten under cold running water. Squeeze out excess liquid. Shred into small pieces and combine it with the 4 cups cider. Cook the cider and kanten together until liquid comes to a boil. Lower flame and cook until kanten dissolves.

Dilute arrowroot in 4 tablespoons juice or juice-sweetener combination. Add this to kanten mixture and bring to a boil, stirring constantly. Then quickly add peaches, blueberries, salt, lemon juice and nuts. Bring to a boil, stirring rapidly, and cook until mixture turns clearer and thickens.

Rinse tart molds under cold running water. Dry and oil them. Immediately pour mixture into molds. Allow to cool at room temperature or chill until set. Place molds upside-down on top of a cake which has been iced already. Allow soufflé to fall before lifting off the molds.

This recipe may also be used in between layers. Use a large baking pan to mold soufflé.

Crumb Toppings and Nut Fillings

Crumbs

There are many ways to convert leftover breads, cakes or cookies into crumbs. To dry out, place them on a baking sheet in a 275° oven before making crumbs. Bake until dry, but not browned. Crush them in a hand mill, or with mortar and pestle, or chop and then roll between two sheets of paper. Substitute crumbs for flour in any of the following recipes.

Any of these crumb topping recipes may be used as fillings, pastry dough or snacks as well.

CRUMB TOPPING

      1 cup roasted whole-wheat pastry flour
     ¼ teaspoon salt
     ¼ cup oil
      1 teaspoon vanilla
 2 to 3 tablespoons concentrated sweetener
        Apple juice or cider

Mix the flour and salt together. Set aside. Combine the oil, vanilla and sweetener; stir.

Pour the liquid mixture into the dry one, and stir around with a fork until little balls begin to form (add juice or cider if too dry). Sprinkle on top of dessert and bake.

Variations

Substitute ½ cup roasted chestnut, corn or brown rice flour for ½ cup whole-wheat pastry flour.

Add ¼ cup crushed nuts or seeds to dry mixture before adding liquid.

Add small amounts of juice or cider until moist. Sprinkle topping on a cookie sheet, forming small balls. Bake at 350° until hard and browned. Store in a cool, dry place.

Add ½ to 1 teaspoon cinnamon or mint to dry mixture.

Add more liquid and use for a crust, pastry dough or cookie batter.

COFFEE CRUMB TOPPING

     ½ cup whole-wheat flour
     ½ cup sweet brown rice flour
     ½ cup rolled oats
     ¼ cup roasted sesame seeds
      2 teaspoons grain coffee
     ¼ teaspoon salt
     ¼ cup oil
 ¼ to ½ cup apple juice or cider

Roast flours separately until lightly browned. Roast rolled oats until almost burned. Combine all dry ingredients. Rub oil into dry mixture thoroughly with your hands (add more liquid if necessary).

Variations

Add ¼ cup concentrated sweetener, *or* 1 teaspoon cinnamon, *or* 1 teaspoon vanilla.

Substitute roasted brown rice flour for sweet brown rice flour.

Add 1 teaspoon orange, tangerine, or lemon rind to dry mixture before adding oil.

Substitute 1 cup roasted whole-wheat flour for sweet brown rice flour and rolled oats.

Substitute ½ cup roasted chestnut flour for sweet brown rice flour.

OAT CRUMB TOPPING

      2 cups rolled oats
     ½ cup roasted sesame or chopped sunflower
        seeds
      2 teaspoons cinnamon
      1 teaspoon orange or lemon rind
     ½ teaspoon salt
      1 teaspoon vanilla
        Apple juice or cider
     ¼ cup oil

Follow directions for Coffee Crumb Topping.

NUT FILLING I

  4 cups chopped roasted nuts
  2 teaspoons cinnamon
  1 teaspoon cloves
1½ cups oil
  ¼ teaspoon salt

Sauté the nuts and spices in oil for five minutes, stirring occasionally.

Cool and fill pastry sheets, tarts, strudels, etc.

NUT FILLING II

  ½ pound roasted sesame seeds
3 to 4 cups roasted almonds
  ½ cup concentrated sweetener
  3 tablespoons oil
  ½ teaspoon lemon rind
  1 teaspoon cinnamon
  ¼ teaspoon salt
  1 teaspoon lemon juice

Sauté all of ingredients except lemon juice for 5 minutes, mixing occasionally. Remove from heat, add lemon juice, toss lightly.

NUT FILLING III

  2 tablespoons roasted sweet brown rice flour
1½ cups roasted almonds or walnuts
  ¼ cup concentrated sweetener
  ½ cup oil
  ½ cup raisins
  1 teaspoon orange or lemon rind
  ½ teaspoon salt
  1 teaspoon vanilla

Roast flour until lightly browned. Set aside to cool. Crush the roasted nuts in a blender for 30 seconds, or with a mortar and pestle while still warm.

Combine roasted flour with concentrated sweetener, and cook for 5 minutes in a double boiler or saucepan, stirring occasionally, on a medium flame. Stir in grated nuts, oil, raisins, rind, salt and vanilla.

Use as filling for pastry sheets, tarts, strudel.

NUT FILLING IV

1½ cups roasted chopped almonds or walnuts
  ½ cup grated apple
  ½ cup oil
  ½ cup raisins
  1 teaspoon orange rind
  1 teaspoon vanilla
  ¼ teaspoon salt
  1 teaspoon cinnamon

Combine the above ingredients. Mix well. Use for pastry sheets, tarts, strudels.

Variations

See Oat Creame variations (pp. 55–56).

4. Shaping Simply

Pastries, Tarts and Pies

"Delicious . . . fragrant . . . a crust so flaky that it melts in your mouth." These and many more compliments from friends and family will surround you when you have baked pastries from among the recipes that follow.

Preparing the Dough

Methods for Adding the Oil

Drip the oil into the dry ingredients in a spiral motion. Cut into the dry mixture using two metal utensils (knives, forks or spoons). Hold one utensil in each hand and cut across and through the flour until it looks like tiny bread crumbs.

Alternate Methods

Drip oil into dry ingredients in a spiral motion.

70

Rub oil in with your hands until it looks like tiny bread crumbs.

Drip oil into dry ingredients in a spiral motion. Mix with an electric mixer, but only until the flour resembles tiny bread crumbs.

Combine liquid and oil and stir. Add to the dry ingredients slowly. Stir mixture each time you add liquid to the dry mixture because oil has a tendency to separate from any liquid.

Rolling Out

Choose a table which is comfortable for you when rolling out the dough. One that is neither too low so that you must bend over, or too high so that you cannot give the rolling pin proper weight.

Temperature of the dough: If the dough is too cold (especially oily dough), then it may be difficult to roll out because it may become too hard. If the dough is too warm, it may be difficult to roll and shape. Dough should be firm when you press your finger into it, but should not stick.

For oily dough, roll out after chilling 30 minutes, or shape, place in baking pan or form, cover and chill at least one hour before baking. For non-oily dough, cover and chill before rolling and shaping.

Pastry, Cookie and Yeasted Doughs

Cover the rolling surface with a cotton, canvas, muslin or linen cloth large enough to hang over the sides.

Flour lightly with arrowroot or whole-wheat pastry flour. (Arrowroot flour is good to use when the pastry is thin and delicate. It helps to keep the dough from tearing or splitting.) If you overflour the surface the pastry may become tough and hard to work with. If working with a cold dough, very little flour is necessary because it will rarely stick to the cloth.

Shape dough into the desired form with your hands before rolling out.

Divide dough into several pieces. Cover and set aside until ready to roll out.

Place dough in center of cloth so that there is plenty of room for expansion.

Sprinkle the top of the dough with flour.

Roll with quick, light, short strokes, not pressing too hard.

Work from the center outward, rotating the dough occasionally.

Use a pestle or light-weight rolling pin when rolling out pastry dough.

Lift the dough occasionally with a spatula or your hand and flour underneath it lightly to prevent the dough from sticking.

Roll out the dough 2 inches larger than the size of the form for pies and tarts.

Roll evenly to the desired shape and thickness.

Two-Crust Pie Shell

Divide the dough into two unequal pieces, one slightly larger than the other. Follow the above procedure.

Alternate Method

Dampen a wooden surface lightly.

Lay a piece of wax paper,* upside-down, over the surface.

Divide dough into several pieces. Cover and set aside all but the piece you are rolling out.

Place dough in the center of the paper.

Shape dough. Cover with wax paper, upside-down. Roll out into the desired shape and size.

Roll out remaining pieces of dough.

* When using wax paper, it is not necessary to sprinkle flour on surface unless you are using white flour. Excess flour will make it more difficult to reuse scraps with fresh dough.

Transferring Pastry Dough to Pie Pan

After rolling out pastry dough to desired shape and size, roll one third of it around the rolling pin and lift into the pie pan. Allow pastry dough to fall naturally. Do not stretch pastry, otherwise the dough will shrink during baking.

Be sure that the pastry dough overlaps the edge of the pie pan 1 to 2 inches to form a decorative edge (see p. 73).

Alternate Method

After rolling out pastry dough to desired shape and size between pieces of wax paper, remove the top layer of paper. Invert the piece of wax paper and dough onto the pie pan. Peel off paper and allow dough to drop naturally into the pan. Do not stretch pastry. Be sure that dough overlaps the edge of the pie form 1 to 2 inches.

Filling Pies and Tarts

Section Pie or Tart I

For 4-section pie or tart, cut a long strip of dough, and roll it into a rope.

Use this rope to divide the shell into 4 sections. Secure it to the bottom crust by brushing with cold liquid.

Chill 15 minutes.

Bake at 425° 10 minutes, and 350° 10 to 15 minutes longer.

Fill and serve, or fill after baking 10 minutes with different-colored purées and fillings, return to oven and bake 10 to 15 minutes longer at 350° or until firm and golden brown.

Section Pie or Tart II

When filling a prebaked pie shell with creame and/or fruit, reserve half of the filling for the topping.

Divide the pie into 6 or 8 slices. Do not cut through.

Place creame in a pastry bag or paper cornucopia pp. 48–49) and squeeze out design on half of every slice, leaving every other side empty.

Spoon fruit mixture on the remaining half of each slice.

Chill before serving.

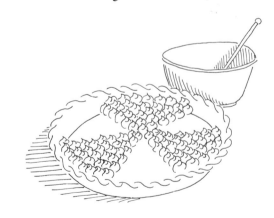

Fancy Covers for Pies and Tarts

Lattice Tops

Cut plain strips ½ inch wide and 3 to 4 inches longer than the pie shell. Roll then twist ½-inch ropelike pieces. Place them crisscross or weave them together.

Weaving

1. Place ½-inch strips or ropelike strips over the pie 1 inch apart.
2. Fold back every other strip halfway.
3. Place a strip across the unfolded strips in the center.
4. Unfold the strips.
5. Fold back the strips that have not yet been folded.
6. Place another cross strip 1-inch from the first one.
7. Continue until half of the pie is covered.
8. Repeat, beginning on the other side of the center.
9. When the whole pie is covered, moisten edges and attach strips to the pie edge loosely.
10. Cut off excess ends of strips after finishing edge.

Full Cover

Fold the top crust in half. Make fancy patterns over it with any cookie cutters. (This allows steam to escape.) Place top crust over pie, unfold, seal edges, glaze and bake.

Fancy and Free

Roll out excess pastry dough to ¼-inch thickness. With a cookie cutter, glass bowl or cup, cut out several pieces (6 to 7, depending upon the size of the cutters and pie) to cover the top of the pie. Lay the pieces over the filling touching each other (try a yeasted dough with this technique). Seal the edges.

Making Edges for Pie and Tart Crusts

Make an attractive edge by pressing the back of a spoon or fork around the edge of the pie.

Press the tines of a fork around the edge of the pie.

Fluted: Double the edge of the crust. Use your index finger or the handle of a knife to make the indentations, and the thumb and index finger of your other hand as a wedge to push against to make the scallop.

Zigzag: Double the edge of the crust, using the index finger and thumb of both hands. With a diagonal motion, bring the fingers of your left hand toward you, pushing the fingers of your right hand toward the center of the pie.

Crisscross: Trim the crust at the edge of the pan. Cut the rolled pastry into ½-inch-wide strips. Moisten the edge of the pastry in the pan. Interlace 2 strips on the edge of the pie. Keep the strips flat, do not twist, turn over or stretch them. To seal, press rounded edge on both sides of crisscrossed strip tightly against moistened edge with your finger.

Twister: Trim the crust at the edge of the pan. Cut rolled pastry into ¾-inch-wide strips. Moisten the rim of the pastry in pan with liquid or Oat Creame (p. 55). Seal one end of the strip to moistened pastry. Hold with finger of the left or right hand, twist strip with opposite hand. With the finger of one hand, seal each flattened space of the twist against the rim of pastry. Do not stretch while twisting.

The Finished Look

For added color in yeasted or unyeasted pastry, brush with egg white, yolk or whole egg, combined with 1 teaspoon of ice water, before baking.

For a hard crust and shiny look, brush with any glaze (pp. 62–64) or concentrated sweetener several times while baking; or brush with juice or concentrated sweetener immediately after removing pastry from the oven.

For a clear glaze just before the pastry has finished baking, brush with ¼ cup concentrated sweetener (dissolve in a small amount of liquid if too thick to apply).

After glazing with any of the above, decorate with nuts.

Baking a Single Unfilled Pie Crust

There are two ways to bake an unfilled pie shell:

1. Prick the pastry shell with a fork all over before baking. This allows steam to escape, and prevents the bottom from rising or buckling. The crust will be more evenly browned this way, but also may be more distorted because of the steam.

2. The second way produces a more evenly shaped pie crust, but the bottom does not brown as much as the rim. Place a large piece of brown paper on the crust. Fill the paper with enough uncooked, oiled rice or beans to hold paper in place. Bake in 375° oven 12 to 15 minutes or until crust browns lightly. This will prevent the crust from puffing up. Remove the beans or rice and paper a few minutes before the crust is done.

FORGET ME KNOTS

1. The amount of liquid and oil necessary for the proper consistency of each recipe will vary according to the moisture and temperature of the flour and the room, the size of the eggs and the general weather of the day. Remain flexible and adjust liquid and oil content accordingly.

2. When preparing an unyeasted pastry dough, handle it as delicately and as little as possible. This will inhibit the development of gluten and prevent the dough from becoming tough. Never knead it. After combining all the ingredients with a wooden spoon, lightly shape it into the desired form with your hands before rolling it out.

3. Whole-wheat pastry flour makes the most tender pastry dough.

4. Use corn or corn-germ oil for a lighter, more delicate dough.

5. For flakier pastry doughs, liquids and oils should be cold when used because cold ingredients tend to expand more quickly in the heat of the oven, helping the pastry to be light and flaky.

6. Try boiling oil and liquid together and adding it to the flour rapidly, molding it into a pie crust while still warm.

7. Mix the oil and liquid together before adding it

to the dry mixture. See "Methods for Adding the Oil," last method (p. 71).

8. Apple juice, cider, mu tea, mint tea or equal parts juice and tea may be used interchangeably for liquid in any recipe. The resulting pastry may be less sweet.

9. When rolling out a thin, delicate pastry dough, sprinkle arrowroot flour before rolling to prevent the pastry from splitting or tearing.

10. Cut pie dough 2 inches larger than pie pan to allow for shrinkage and edges.

11. Chilling dough after rolling keeps it from shrinking during baking.

12. Fill a baked shell with filling of the same temperature as the shell, or slightly warmer; otherwise the shell may crack.

13. Bake pies in oven-glass pie plates or dull metal pans for browner crusts.

14. When completely prebaking a pie shell, prick the bottom and sides with a fork before baking to allow the steam to escape, and oil the rim of the crust to prevent burning.

15. When baking a filled pie, if the filling is juicy, first brush the bottom crust lightly with an egg white or oil. This will prevent the crust from becoming soggy from the filling.

16. Roll a small tube of dough, wax paper or heavy paper and insert it into a slit in the center of the top crust of a fruit pie to carry out the steam and prevent the juices from leaking out.

17. One and one-half cups flour will make a single pie crust; three cups will make a double-crust pie.

18. Four cups of filling are necessary to fill a pie shell.

19. For a lighter-colored crust, place a sheet of paper over the pie crust the last 15 minutes of baking time.

20. Substitute any yeasted dough for unyeasted pastry dough.

21. Substitute any cookie-dough recipe for pie crusts (see item 17 above) or pastry dough.

22. To make pastry dough lighter and puffy when deep-frying, add a teaspoon or two of lemon or orange juice, rice or apple cider vinegar to the pastry dough before adding liquid.

Variations for Any Yeasted or Unyeasted Dough

Add 3 to 4 tablespoons grain coffee to dry mixture (p. 9).

Add ½ cup whole sesame or sunflower seeds.

Add ½ cup roasted crushed sesame or sunflower seeds.

Add ½ cup ground roasted nuts.

Add ½ to 1 teaspoon mint, cinnamon, ginger, cloves or any combination of these.

Add 1 teaspoon orange, tangerine or lemon rind.

Add the juice and grated rind of ½ lemon or orange.

Substitute raisin purée, apple butter or apple cider jelly for sweetener (see chart, p. 149).

Pastry Doughs

PIE OR TART DOUGH (DOUBLE CRUST)

  3 cups sifted whole-wheat pastry flour
1 to 2 teaspoons cinnamon or mint
  ½ teaspoon salt
  ¼ cup ground roasted nuts or seeds
  ½ cup oil
½ to 1 cup apple juice, cider, mu, or mint tea

Sift the flour into a mixing bowl. Add all dry ingredients and mix together. Add the oil. Cut it though the dry mixture until it looks like fine bread crumbs (see p. 70). DO NOT KNEAD OR OVERWORK THE FLOUR. Too much movement activates the gluten, resulting in a hard crust.

Add enough liquid to form a soft dough. Mix it with a wooden spoon until it begins to form into a dough.

Shape it into a ball, wrap in wax paper, cover and chill at least 30 minutes.

See p. 150 for baking temperature.

Variations

Add 1 teaspoon vanilla to flour before adding oil.

Add 2 to 3 tablespoons orange or lemon juice before adding liquid.

Add ¼ cup concentrated sweetener to dry mixture before adding liquid.

Add 3 tablespoons grain coffee to ½ cup boiling apple juice. Cool before adding it to dry mixture.

Substitute 1 cup corn flour or brown rice flour for 1 cup whole-wheat pastry flour.

Substitute ½ cup raisin purée for apple juice. Add more liquid if necessary.

EASY DOUBLE-CRUST PASTRY DOUGH

2½ cups whole-wheat pastry flour
  ½ cup brown rice flour
  ¼ teaspoon salt
  ½ teaspoon cinnamon
  1 teaspoon ginger
2 to 3 tablespoons grain coffee (or to taste)
  ½ cup cold apple juice, cider or water
  ½ cup cold oil
  ½ teaspoon vanilla

Combine pastry flour, rice flour, salt, spices and grain coffee in a mixing bowl. Set aside. Mix liquid, oil and vanilla together.

Slowly add liquid mixture to dry combination, mixing with a wooden spoon until a ball of dough begins to form. Press together with your hands. Divide dough into 2 pieces.

Cover dough with a damp cloth until it is used. Flour and roll (p. 71). Use for pastries and pie crusts.

PRESSED PASTRY (BOTTOM CRUST)

  ¾ cup whole-wheat pastry flour
  ¾ cup rolled oats
  ¼ teaspoon salt
  ¼ cup roasted sesame seeds
  1 tablespoon concentrated sweetener (optional)
¼ to ½ cup oil
  ¼ cup apple juice or cider (enough to moisten crust)

Combine pastry flour and oats in a mixing bowl. Add salt, sesame seeds and sweetener if used. Add oil slowly, rubbing it in with your hands, or cutting it in, until it looks like bread crumbs (p. 70). Put a handful of mixture in the palm of your hand, make a fist and open hand. If the mixture sticks together, then the amount of oil is sufficient.

Moisten with a little bit of juice and press into oiled pan. (Do not add more juice than necessary, otherwise the crust will not be flaky.) See Appendix (p. 150) for baking temperature.

BREAD WHEAT
(*Triticum aestivum*)

This type comprises many different kinds of wheats such as spring wheat (grown in the spring and harvested in the late summer), winter wheat (planted in the fall and harvested in early summer), hard wheats and soft wheats. They are a main source of flour for making cakes and pastry. Bread wheat is grown in many places, including America, Russia, Asia and Europe.

This particular crust takes practice, but do not be discouraged. After a few pie crusts, they will be as light and flaky as can be.

Variation

Substitute ½ cup whole-wheat pastry flour, ½ cup roasted corn or chestnut flour, ½ cup roasted rolled oats for flour-oat combination.

DOUGH FOR PASTRY AND PIE

 3 cups whole-wheat pastry flour
½ teaspoon salt
½ cup oil (cold)
 1 egg yolk (room temperature)
 1 teaspoon vanilla
 2 tablespoons concentrated sweetener
 1 teaspoon orange rind
   Apple juice to form dough

Place flour and salt in mixing bowl. Cut oil slowly into flour mixture, until it looks like bread crumbs (p. 70); set aside. Combine yolk, vanilla, concentrated sweetener and rind. Stir. Mix this mixture into flour combination. Begin to add apple juice slowly, until a ball is formed. Flour and roll out into desired shape (p. 71). Cover and chill 30 minutes before baking. See p. 150 for baking temperature.

Alternate Method

Wrap and chill dough 30 minutes before rolling out and shaping (it may be harder to work with).

YEASTED PASTRY I

 ½ tablespoon dry yeast
¾ to 1½ cups apple juice or cider
 2 to 4 tablespoons concentrated sweetener (optional)
 3½ cups whole-wheat pastry flour
 ½ teaspoon salt
 2 teaspoons cinnamon
 1 tablespoon orange, lemon rind or mint
 ½ cup oil
 1 teaspoon vanilla (optional)

Dissolve yeast in ½ cup warm apple juice or cider; add sweetener here if desired. Stir and set aside 5 minutes or until mixture bubbles.

Add enough flour to form a thin batter. Beat until smooth and not lumpy. Clean down the sides of the bowl with a rubber spatula. Cover and let rise in a warm spot until it is almost doubled in size, bubbly, and as you stir it, begins to go down. Combine the rest of the dry ingredients (reserve ½ cup of flour) cutting in the oil. Add vanilla. Combine dry mixture with yeasted batter.

Stir mixture and beat it with a wooden spoon until it is too hard to beat, adding only enough apple juice or cider to form a soft sticky dough. Knead dough on a lightly floured surface, kneading in the reserved ½ cup of flour to make the dough perfectly smooth. Place in an oiled bowl, cover and let rise in a warm spot until doubled in size. (After rising it should feel soft and puffy.)

Flatten it out on a hard surface, and flour lightly. Fold it in thirds like an envelope and pat it out again. Place it on wax paper on a board, cover with a cookie sheet or other flat surface, place a weight on it and chill at least 1 hour to firm the dough.

Roll and shape the dough into desired form. Place

it on a sheet or pan, cover with another pan and let rise until puffy, soft and swollen. Bake in a pre-heated 375° oven 25 to 30 minutes, or until browned.

For baking pies, see chart on p. 150. (Brush with an egg glaze before baking for a browner color.)

YEASTED PASTRY II

Follow the recipe for Yeasted Pastry I. Add 2 beaten eggs (at room temperature) to yeast mixture before adding flour to form a thin batter.

After the first rise add 2 more eggs and the rest of the ingredients, omitting juice or cider.

Use these doughs for coffee rings, cinnamon rolls, strudel or any shape yeasted pastry. Try Yeasted Pastry II for doughnuts.*

PHYLO DOUGH

When white flour was first introduced in Europe, it was known as a cosmetic to be used by lightly dusting it over a wig.

It was a long and tedious process to sieve the coarse part of the grain out from the flour and took the time of many servants. Owing to this labor, it became a mark of affluence and high distinction to serve pastries and bread made from the delicate and rare "white" substance. Eventually, this led to white-flour products being the accepted sign of the rich, while the coarser, dark "inferior" wheat was related to servants.

The only way that I was able to make dough thin enough for spinach pies and Baklava (p. 80) was by using unbleached white flour.

> 3 cups unbleached white flour
> ½ teaspoon salt
> 1 tablespoon oil
> 1 egg (optional)
> ½ cup cold water

Sift flour and salt into a mixing bowl or onto a flat

---

* For doughnuts cut with a doughnut cutter, or cookie cutter with a smaller cookie cutter in the center. Cover and let rise until puffy. Deep-fry about 3 to 5 minutes (p. 6). See also pp. 107–108.

---

surface covered with a pastry cloth. Rub in 1 table-spoon oil. Break egg, if used, into the center. Mix the flour and egg together with hands until well blended.

Make a well in the center of the flour and slowly begin to drip in the cold water, kneading about 10 minutes or until a soft, rubbery and smooth dough is formed.

Shape the dough into a round ball, place in an oiled bowl, cover the surface of the dough with oil and cover with a damp cloth and chill overnight. Before rolling out pastry, allow dough to reach room temperature.

Sprinkle arrowroot flour over a large wooden surface (about 4 x 5 feet). Roll out half the dough into a circle ½ inch thick. Place hands under dough and begin to stretch the dough outward over hands and arms.

Pull the periphery of the circle toward the edge of the wooden surface by holding the dough with one hand and pulling with the other, alternating movements until the dough covers the entire wooden surface, overlaps the edges and is paper thin. Cut off excess edges. Allow the dough to dry 10 to 15 minutes or until the edges begin to get slightly hard. (If the dough is allowed to dry too long, it will crack when folding.)

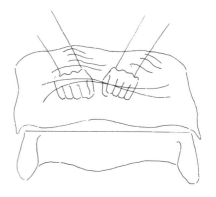

Oil the surface of the dough and cut into 4 x 10-inch rectangles. Place the filling (sautéed spinach, chopped nuts and cinnamon, cooked fruit, etc.) on the lower corner of the dough. Fold the dough over the filling into a triangle repeating until the dough is completely wrapped around the filling. Seal the edge with water and press firmly. Dot the top of the pastry with oiled fingers. Sprinkle salt or gomasio* over the top for vegetable pastries, cinnamon for fruit- or nut-filled pastries. Bake in a preheated 400° oven 15 to 20 minutes or until crisp.

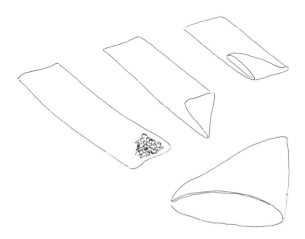

Alternate Method

Follow directions for Phylo Dough (p. 78). After kneading, cover the dough with a warm bowl and let it rest at room temperature 20 minutes. Proceed as in the above recipe.

SYRIAN PASTRY DOUGH

½ cup unrefined olive oil
¾ teaspoon salt
1 to 1½ cups apple juice or cider, mu or mint tea
4 cups whole-wheat pastry flour

Boil oil, salt and liquid together. Remove from flame and beat by hand for a few minutes. Add this to flour and knead until a soft, sticky dough is formed. Knead about 5 minutes longer, cover and set in a warm place about 2 hours.

Cut dough into pieces the size of an orange, dip in arrowroot flour, cover and let sit in a warm place another hour or two. Roll out very thin, in arrowroot flour. Fill and shape.

For a crumblier dough, substitute 1½ cups corn flour for pastry flour.

* Gomasio is made by blending 1 part salt to 8, 10 or 12 parts roasted sesame seeds in a bowl (suribachi, p. 54), using a pestle to crush the seeds until each grain of salt is coated with sesame seeds. Gomasio can be used as a condiment in place of salt and is available already prepared in most natural-food stores.

BASIC STRUDEL PASTRY

2 cups whole-wheat pastry flour
or
1 cup whole-wheat pastry flour and 1 cup sifted whole-wheat flour
½ teaspoon salt
¼ cup oil
1 tablespoon orange or lemon juice
2 egg whites
⅔ to 1 cup lukewarm apple juice, cider or water
Arrowroot flour
3 to 4 cups filling (see Chapter 3)

Place flour in a mixing bowl. Add salt. Make a well in the center of the flour, and cut in oil. Add orange or lemon juice, and egg whites, and work these ingredients into the dough gradually, adding apple juice until a very soft, sticky dough is formed (use your hands or a wooden spoon).

Knead on a floured surface about 10 minutes, or until smooth and elastic. Place in an oiled bowl, brush the top of the dough with oil. Cover and set in a warm place. If there is no warm spot, place bowl in a pan of hot water until dough becomes lukewarm (about 10 to 15 minutes).

Cover wooden surface with a pastry cloth large enough to drape over the sides. Rub arrowroot into cloth. Place dough on cloth, sprinkle with arrowroot and roll out in rectangular form till about ¼ inch thick. Brush entire surface with oil.

Cover your hands with flour and place them under the dough (palms down), make a fist and stretch the dough out from the center toward the edges, until it is as thin as possible. If it begins to break or dry in places before you have finished stretching, brush with oil in dry places and disregard holes. Allow dough to rest 5 to 10 minutes. Trim edges. Brush entire surface with oil. See "Filling the Strudel" (p. 89).

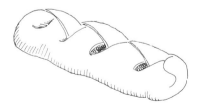

Delicate Pastries

BAKLAVA I

Baklava was created by the Persians. Originally it contained a nut filling scented with pussy-willow blossoms or jasmine. Around the sixth century, the Greeks discovered the art of making fine, thin pastry (phylo) and adopted Baklava as their traditional New Year's dessert.

1 recipe Phylo Dough (p. 78)
½ to 1 cup oil

Syrup

½ cup oil
4 to 6 tablespoons concentrated sweetener (to taste)
2 cinnamon sticks (or 2 teaspoons cinnamon)
Fresh grated rind of 1 orange
Fresh grated rind of 1 lemon
Juice of ½ lemon

Filling

5 cups crushed walnuts
1 tablespoon plus 1 teaspoon cinnamon
1 teaspoon mint

Prepare pastry. Oil an 8 x 10 x 13-inch pan. Sprinkle arrowroot flour on pastry cloth or wooden surface. Roll out the pastry to ⅛-inch thickness.

Cut pieces the size of the pan (turn pan upside-down on pastry to measure size needed). Save edges of pastry for sides. Reserve 3 pieces of pastry for the top.

Place oil in a heavy saucepan and begin to heat on a medium flame. Add sweetener, cinnamon sticks or cinnamon, and rind. Bring to a boil, turn off heat, add lemon juice, and cool.

Preheat oven to 375°. Place 1 piece of pastry in the bottom of the pan. Brush with oil. Cover with another piece and brush with oil.

Mix together walnuts, cinnamon and mint. Sprinkle walnut mixture over pastry.

Repeat procedure using the extra pieces to line the sides of the pan. Continue until all the dough has been used.

Take the 3 layers that were set aside for the top, brush oil in between each layer. Place on top of the filled pastry. With a sharp knife, cut into the Baklava at different angles. This will allow it to bake more evenly, as well as decorate the top.

Pour the cooled syrup over the pastry before or after baking. Bake about 30 to 45 minutes, or until top is golden brown. Remove from the oven, and cool on a rack. Let sit 12 to 24 hours before serving.

BAKLAVA II

1 recipe Basic Strudel Pastry (p. 79)
4 cups nut filling (p. 69)
Orange-Maple Sauce (p. 67)

Prepare pastry. Oil rectangular pan. Cut rectangles about 2 inches larger than the pan on each side.

Place pastry in pan, sprinkle some nut filling over pastry; repeat, ending with pastry.

Preheat oven to 350°. Cut pastry into diamonds before baking. Pour Orange-Maple Sauce over the top of pastry. Bake about 45 minutes, or until lightly browned.

BOWKNOTS

Pastry dough (p. 77) or yeasted dough (pp. 77–78)
Oil for deep-frying (p. 6)
Roasted chestnut flour for dusting

Deep-frying (for unyeasted or yeasted dough)

Prepare dough. Sprinkle pastry cloth or wooden surface with arrowroot flour. Divide dough into 4 parts. Roll out 1 piece of dough to ¼-inch thickness. Cover the rest of the dough with a damp cloth and set aside.

Cut into strips 6 x 1 inches. Tie in Bowknots. (See illustration.) Set aside for about 10 minutes. Repeat procedure until all the dough is shaped. (For yeasted dough, cover and let rise until almost doubled in size.)

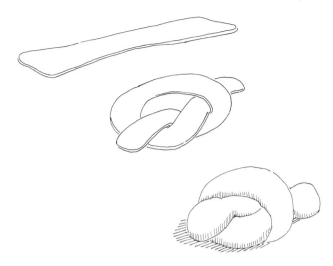

Heat oil. Deep-fry until delicately brown. Drain, dust with roasted chestnut flour immediately and cool.

Baking (for unyeasted or yeasted dough)

Roll out into desired shape. Place on an unoiled baking sheet, cover and let rise in a warm place until almost double in size. (For unyeasted dough, bake 5 to 10 minutes after shaping).

Bake at 350° 25 to 30 minutes, or until lightly browned.

Brush with concentrated sweetener or oil immediately after baking.

CANNOLI I

This is a famous old Italian delicacy passed down from generation to generation. Here is my version of this delightful dessert.

    3 cups sifted whole-wheat pastry flour
    1 teaspoon cinnamon
    ½ teaspoon salt
    2 tablespoons oil
    2 eggs
    ¼ cup concentrated sweetener
    1 teaspoon lemon or orange juice or apple
        cider vinegar*
      Oil for deep-frying (p. 6)

Sift flour, cinnamon and salt together. Place in a mixing bowl. Cut in oil. Beat eggs, add sweetener,

* Lemon juice, orange juice or vinegar makes the pastries puff up while being deep-fried.

lemon or orange juice or vinegar. Stir into dry mixture, and knead until dough is smooth (adjust flour-liquid content accordingly).

Sprinkle arrowroot flour on pastry cloth or wooden surface and roll out dough very thin. Cut into 4 to 5-inch ovals or circles.

Fold dough over 1 x 5-inch wooden or metal cylindrical form, and press the ends together in the *center only* as if sealing an envelope, but not over-lapping too far. (If ends do not stick together, brush with water or egg yolk before pressing together).

Heat oil. Deep-fry until delicately brown. (Forms may separate from cannolis. Remove them immediately from oil.) Drain and cool. Remove form, if necessary.

Fill with Tofu Creame (p. 59) or any creame desired just before serving.

Unfilled cannolis may be kept in a cool dry place for several days before using.

Variations

Substitute any yeasted or unyeasted pastry dough.

Fill with any fruit or vegetable filling. Vegetable-filled cannolis can be served as a vegetable dish for dinner.

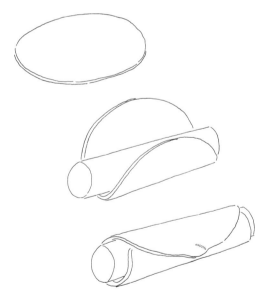

CANNOLI II

Prepare Cannoli I, omitting eggs. Add apple juice or cider to form a moist dough.

ECLAIRS

½ cup oil
1 cup apple juice or cider
1 cup sifted whole-wheat pastry flour
¼ teaspoon salt
4 eggs

Glaze
Any glaze (pp. 62–64)

Filling
2 to 3 cups Tofu Creame Whip (p. 60)

Combine oil and juice in saucepan. Cook on a medium flame until boiling. Lower flame and add sifted flour and salt constantly stirring until a ball forms in pan.

Remove from heat and add 3 eggs (one at a time), beating after each addition. Beat the last egg, and add it to the mixture slowly. Preheat oven to 425°. Oil a cookie sheet. Fill a pastry bag with batter. Squeeze out éclair shape onto cookie sheet.

Bake until brown, 20 to 25 minutes. Turn off oven, open door and leave 10 to 15 minutes longer, otherwise the change in temperature may cause them to fall and become soggy. Slit the side of the pastry open with scissors to allow steam to escape. Allow to cool.

Whip the creame filling. Fill pastry bag with creame and squeeze into éclairs just before serving (use a tube with a large opening).

Top éclairs with glaze before serving.

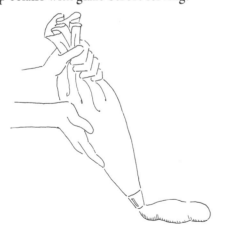

Variation

Use any filling (see Chapter 3).

APPLE TOFU DELIGHT

1 recipe Eclairs
2 to 3 cups Tofu Creame (p. 59)
1 apple, thinly sliced
2 teaspoons cinnamon
½ cup sliced almonds

Preheat oven to 375°. Oil and lightly flour a 7-inch circle on a baking sheet. Spread a thin layer of éclair pastry (about ¼ inch thick) within the outline of the circle. Spoon remaining pastry around the layer to make a border, or use a pastry bag instead of a spoon (pp. 47–48).

Pour Tofu Creame into the center of the shell. Spread over pastry. Arrange apple slices (peel if not organic) on top of creame. Sprinkle cinnamon on top of apples, and almonds on top of cinnamon.

Bake 45 to 60 minutes, or until pastry is browned.

Variation: Chestnut Creame Delight

Substitute Chestnut Creame for Tofu Creame (p. 57).

CREAME PUFFS

1 Eclair recipe
Amasake Filling
2 cups sweet brown rice
9 cups water
1 handful koji rice*

Amasake Filling

Follow recipe for grain syrup (p. 52), substituting koji rice for sprouts. Leave covered in a warm, dark place 18 to 24 hours. Remove cover and taste. If it is not sweet enough, cover and let sit another 3 to 5 hours, tasting every 3 hours until it reaches the sweet stage. Blend then boil until thick, stirring occasionally. If not using immediately, add a little salt, bring to a boil and simmer 10 to 15 minutes, to retard fermentation.

Pastry

Preheat oven to 425°. Oil a sheet or pan.

Prepare éclair batter and fill a pastry bag. Using

* Koji rice can be found in most Japanese or Chinese food stores.

a tube with a large opening, squeeze out into puffs (pp. 47–48) onto a sheet or baking pan.

Bake until brown, 20 to 25 minutes. Turn off oven, open door and leave 10 to 15 minutes longer. Cut puffs in half to allow steam to escape.

Filling the Puff

Place amasake in a pastry bag fitted with a medium-size star tube. Fill puffs just before serving, otherwise they tend to get soggy. Sprinkle roasted chestnut flour on top before serving.

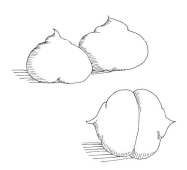

ODD BALLS

Basic Sponge Sheet batter (p. 26)
¾ to 1 cup raisin purée (p. 66)
1½ to 2 cups Chestnut Creame (p. 57)

Preheat oven to 375°. Oil cookie sheets. Shape rounds of batter with 2 spoons or pastry bag (pp. 47–48) in the manner of round drop cookies, about 2¼ inches in diameter. Place on baking sheet.

Bake in preheated oven 12 to 15 minutes, or until lightly browned.

When cakes have cooled, scoop out some of the soft inside from the flat bottom of each one. Fill pastry bag with Chestnut Creame. Brush inside of cakes with purée, and fill with Chestnut Creame. Put cakes together to form balls, and chill at least 1 hour before serving.

If desired, pour sesame glaze (see Nut or Seed Glaze, p. 63) on top of each ball before serving.

Variations

Substitute any éclair batter for sponge sheet batter (p. 82).

Fill center with Coffee-Chestnut Creame. Glaze top and sides with Cinnamon-Coffee Glaze (see Spice Glaze, p. 63).

Fill with Vanilla Oat Creame (p. 56). Prepare apricot glaze (see Fruit Glaze, p. 63) and pour over balls. Roll in crushed roasted almonds. Choose any filling and topping. Experiment for yourself.

Substitute any purée or creame for those listed above (see Chapter 3).

HORNS I

2 cups whole-wheat pastry flour
1 cup chestnut flour (or whole-wheat pastry flour)
1 cup corn flour
1 teaspoon cinnamon
½ teaspoon salt
¼ cup cold oil
    Apple juice, or any fruit juice or water to form soft, firm dough
3 to 4 cups Tofu Creame (p. 59) or any other filling (see Chapter 3)

Combine all dry ingredients. Cut oil in gradually, until mixture resembles tiny bread crumbs. Combine mixture with liquid until dough is formed.

Roll out pastry ⅛ inch thick, on arrowroot flour (p. 7).

Use horn-shaped forms. For a 5-inch form, the dough should be 4 to 5 times as long. Wind each strip around a form, starting at the narrowest end of form, slightly overlapping the edges. Wind the dough around form till it is ½ inch from the top. This space will allow you to remove the form easily after baking.

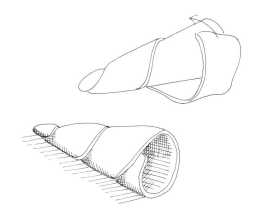

Do not stretch the pastry as you roll it around the tube; this will cause it to shrink and break while baking.

Cover and chill dough 30 minutes.

Preheat the oven to 350°. Place the horns on an oiled baking sheet. Bake 45 minutes, or until browned. Remove from oven and cool slightly before removing horns (twist to remove).

Before serving, prepare pastry bag or cornucopia with your favorite creame filling and fill (pp. 47–48).

HORNS II

Follow recipe for Horns I, substituting Yeasted Pastry I or II (p. 77). Cover and set in a warm place to rise until it is one-third larger. Wind dough around horns. Bake at 350° 30 to 40 minutes, or until lightly browned.

HORNS III

Follow recipe for Horns I. Add 2 teaspoons lemon or orange juice or vinegar to liquid before combining it with dry mixture.

Heat oil for deep-frying (p. 6). Deep-fry horns until lightly browned. Drain and cool. Remove forms.

FRIED PIES

1 recipe Yeasted Pastry (pp. 77–78)
4 cups chopped apples, peaches or pears
  Cinnamon
  Salt
  Oil for deep-frying (p. 6)
  Roasted chestnut flour or cinnamon for dusting

Chop fruit (peel if not organic). Place in a mixing bowl. Combine with cinnamon and salt and toss lightly. Set aside for 15 minutes.

Sprinkle arrowroot flour on a pastry cloth or wooden surface.

Roll out dough to ¼-inch thickness and cut out 3-inch circles.

Drain off excess liquid from fruit. Place a spoonful of filling in the center of one of the circles. Moisten the edge of the dough all around the filling with water or egg. Place another circle on top, and press edges firmly together. Repeat until all dough is used. Cover and set in a warm place for about 20 minutes. Heat oil. Deep-fry until browned on both sides. Drain, and sprinkle with roasted chestnut flour or cinnamon before cooling.

Alternate Method

Place pies on an oiled baking sheet. Cover and set in a warm place to rise until almost doubled in size. Preheat oven to 350°. Bake 30 to 40 minutes.

Variations

See Chapter 3 for more filling suggestions.

Substitute unyeasted dough for Yeasted Pastry (see Cannoli, p. 81).

CHESTNUT TWIST

  Any pastry dough, yeasted or unyeasted (pp. 76–77)
2 cups Chestnut Purée (p. 66)

Preheat the oven to 350°, and oil a baking sheet.

Roll out dough into rectangles; spread half of the filling over each rectangle. Roll up like a jelly roll.

Place rolls in a V shape, attach the ends, twist over each other. Brush with egg yolk. Bake 40 to 45 minutes, or until browned. See alternate instructions for Yeasted Pastry.

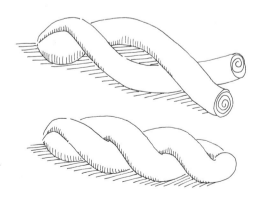

APPLE DUMPLINGS

    Easy Double Crust (p. 76)
  6 apples
  1 cup raisins
  ½ teaspoon salt
  ½ cup tahini, almond or peanut butter
  1 to 2 teaspoons cinnamon
  1 to 2 cups apple juice or cider

Prepare pastry dough; cover and set aside. Peel and core apples. Mix raisins and salt. Stuff the apples half full with raisins. Fill to the top with tahini. Sprinkle tops with cinnamon.

Roll out pastry ¼ inch thick and cut into 6 squares each large enough to cover a whole apple (pp. 70–71). Set an apple on each piece of pastry. Wrap pastry around apple, covering it completely.

Score top. Place dumplings in deep oiled pan. Cover and chill 20 minutes.

Preheat oven to 350°. Spoon a tablespoon or two of juice or cider over top of each dumpling and bake, basting every 10 minutes with apple juice or cider until browned.

Top with Tofu Creame before serving (p. 59).

Variation

Substitute peaches, pears or apricots, whole or sliced, for apples. Do not score top. Heat oil and deep-fry until browned (p. 6).

CREAME N' CRUNCH PASTRY

  1 basic pie or tart crust
  Oil for deep-frying (p. 6)
  Cinnamon
  Roasted crushed almonds
  Pastry Creame flavored with cinnamon and
    orange rind (p. 59)

Heat oil. Roll out pastry dough to ⅛-inch thickness and cut into 3 x 3-inch squares (pp. 70–71). Deep-fry until lightly browned.

Mix cinnamon and almonds together. Sprinkle on top of squares, immediately after frying. Or spread Pastry Creame on 1 square, cover with another square, sprinkle cinnamon and almonds on square and top with Pastry Creame. Repeat with as many more layers as desired, spreading creame over each layer.

Variation

Substitute Chestnut Creame (p. 57), Oat Creame (p. 55) or Tofu Creame Whip (p. 60) for Pastry Creame.

FRENCH CRULLERS

  ¼ cup concentrated sweetener
  ¼ cup oil
  ½ to ¾ cup boiling apple cider or juice
  ½ teaspoon salt
  ½ cup sifted whole-wheat pastry flour
  1 cup roasted sifted chestnut flour
  2 eggs
  1 teaspoon vanilla
  Oil for deep-frying (p. 6)

Combine sweetener, oil, juice and salt in a heavy saucepan. Bring to a boil on a medium flame, stirring occasionally. Sift flours and add to pan all at once, stirring quickly, until thickened.

Remove from heat, add eggs immediately, one at a time, beating thoroughly after each addition. Add vanilla. Consistency should be that of a very thick, heavy batter. Adjust flour-liquid content accordingly.

Fill pastry bag (p. 47). Oil wax paper. Squeeze batter onto paper in the shape of circles. Heat oil, drop crullers in by turning paper at an angle or upsidedown so that they slide off. Fry until browned, drain.

Dip into roasted chestnut flour, coconut or cinnamon after frying.

Variations

Add 1 to 2 teaspoons orange rind after cooking.

Add 1 teaspoon dried mint to oil combination.

Add 1 teaspoon cinnamon and ½ teaspoon ginger after cooking.

Spoon any glaze (pp. 62–64) over crullers after deep-frying. Then dip into roasted chestnut flour, spices or coconut.

DUMPLINGS

Yeasted or unyeasted pastry (pp. 76–78)
2 to 3 cups fruit juice or stewed fruit
1 cup crushed roasted nuts

Prepare pastry dough. Shape into little balls. Place fruit juice or stewed fruits in the bottom of a deep baking dish. Add the dumplings. (Cover, and set in a warm place to rise before baking if using yeasted pastry.) Bake 1½ to 2 hours covered, without lifting the cover off during the first hour of baking time. When all of the liquid has been absorbed, and they begin to smell sweet, remove from oven.

Garnish with nuts. Serve immediately.

SWEET BALLS

8 to 10 medium yams or sweet potatoes (4 cups cooked)
2 tablespoons tahini or sesame butter
1 teaspoon vanilla
2 tablespoons concentrated sweetener
1 teaspoon orange rind
½ teaspoon salt
Bread, cake or cookie crumbs
1 egg
Oil for deep-frying (p. 6)

Bake potatoes, peel and mash. Add tahini, vanilla, sweetener, rind and salt, and shape into balls. If balls do not stick together, add ¼ cup sifted chestnut or whole-wheat pastry flour. Chill at least 1 hour or until firm.

Roll in crumbs, dip into egg and roll in crumbs again.

Heat oil. Deep-fry until golden brown. Roll in roasted chestnut flour. Serve immediately.

Variations

Substitute squash and carrots for yams. Sauté, cover and cook until soft. Remove cover, and cook until liquid evaporates.

Roll in crushed roasted nuts or sesame seeds after deep-frying.

TEIGLACH

Adapted from a traditional Jewish recipe my mother always used.

2 cups whole-wheat pastry flour
¼ teaspoon ginger
¼ teaspoon salt
2 eggs
2 tablespoons oil
Raisins and nuts (optional)
Apple juice or cider

Syrup
1 cup concentrated sweetener
2 teaspoons ginger

Sift flour, ¼ teaspoon ginger and salt together. Place in a mixing bowl. Add eggs, oil, raisins, nuts and enough apple juice or cider to form a soft dough.

Divide dough into several pieces. Roll each piece into a rope, and cut into ½-inch pieces.

Combine sweetener and ginger in a heavy saucepan and bring to a boil. Drop pieces of dough in, cover and simmer about 30 minutes. Stir occasionally for even browning; cook until all are browned. Inside should be crisp and dry.

Remove from heat and add 2 tablespoons boiling water to pan to keep Teiglach from sticking. Remove from pan and place on a large sheet or platter so they are not touching. Roll in cinnamon, roasted chestnut flour, coconut or roasted crushed nuts or seeds.

BASIC CREPES

2 cups roasted whole-wheat pastry flour
¼ teaspoon salt
Apple juice to form batter
4 cups fruit or creame filling
Oil for pan

Combine flour and salt. Add juice to form thin pancakelike batter. Prepare any filling or creame desired.

Heat oil in skillet. When oil is very hot (test by dropping a bit of batter into skillet — when it sizzles, it is ready), using a ladle, pour just enough batter into the pan to cover the bottom. Move pan around quickly in a circular motion until the bottom of pan is completely covered with batter. Cook on a medium flame until holes begin to appear on the surface of the crêpe.

Remove crêpe by turning pan upside-down and flipping crêpe onto a cloth. Fill immediately and serve. (Place filling in center, fold both ends toward the center, overlapping, and fasten with a toothpick.)

Variations

Substitute 1 cup roasted brown rice flour or corn flour for 1 cup whole-wheat pastry flour.

FRUIT PIZZA

There are many ways to make a sweet pizza. Each province in Italy has its own specialty. This pizza has been adapted from the Sicilian "fruit pizza."

 1 recipe Yeasted Pastry (p. 77) plus
 2 tablespoons orange juice and
 1 tablespoon orange rind
   Filling
 4 medium-size apples
 2 cups apricot purée (p. 66)
   Topping
 ½ cup raisins
  Apple juice or cider to cover
  Crumb Topping (p. 68)

Oil an 8-inch round cookie sheet or shallow pie pan. Prepare dough. Roll out to ⅛-inch thickness and place on the bottom of a pan.

Soak raisins in liquid to cover until soft. Core and cut apples into ½-inch slices (peel if not organic).

Preheat oven to 350°. Prebake crust 10 minutes. Spread purée over dough, and place apples on top. Combine soaked raisins with Crumb Topping. Sprinkle over filling. Bake 15 minutes longer, or until apples are tender and dough is lightly browned.

BLUEBERRY-PEACH PIZZA

 1 recipe Yeasted Pastry plus
 2 tablespoons orange juice and
 1 tablespoon orange rind

   Filling
 5 medium-size peaches
 3 cups blueberries
 1 teaspoon cinnamon
 1 teaspoon lemon juice

   Topping
  Crumb Topping (p. 68)
 ½ cup unsweetened coconut (optional)

Blanch peaches (p. 46); slice into ¼-inch pieces. Prepare dough.

Combine peaches, blueberries, cinnamon and lemon juice in a mixing bowl. Toss lightly until fruit is coated with cinnamon and juice. Set aside for 15 minutes. Prepare topping. (Add coconut if desired.) Set aside.

Preheat oven to 350°. Oil a round 8-inch pie pan. Follow basic Fruit Pizza recipe.

See Chapter 3 for more suggestions for fillings.

Strudels

APPLE-WALNUT STRUDEL

  Any yeasted or unyeasted pastry
   Filling
 1 cup raisins
  Apple juice or cider
 2 to 3 cups chopped apples
 ½ cup chopped roasted walnuts
 3 to 4 tablespoons tahini or almond butter

Filling

Soak raisins in apple juice or cider to cover until soft. (Drain off liquid and use for dough.) Core and chop apples (peel if not organic). Chop nuts. Set aside.

Pastry

Divide dough into 2 or 3 pieces. Flour a pastry

cloth lightly. Shape piece of dough into rectangle before rolling out. Roll out to the length of your baking pan, about 12 inches wide and ½ inch thick. (If using Basic Strudel Pastry see p. 79.) Brush entire surface of dough with tahini or almond butter (if unable to spread, soften butter in a small amount of raisin water or apple juice until creamy).

Sprinkle some raisins, apples and nuts over the surface of dough (see "Filling the Strudel," p. 89).

Preheat the oven to 350°. Oil a baking sheet. Bake about 45 to 60 minutes, brushing the top and sides of strudel with oil while baking. The strudel may be glazed before or after baking (see p. 43).

BLUEBERRY STRUDEL

Any yeasted or unyeasted dough
3 to 4 cups fresh blueberries
2 cups Crumb Topping (p. 68)
1 teaspoon lemon rind
1 teaspoon cinnamon

Follow directions for Apple-Walnut Strudel, substituting blueberries for apples and Crumb Topping for walnuts.

CHESTNUT-ORANGE STRUDEL

Any yeasted or unyeasted dough
1 to 2 cups Chestnut Purée (p. 66)
1 to 2 teaspoons orange rind

Follow directions for strudel, substituting Chestnut Purée for filling. Combine orange rind with Chestnut Purée before filling. Omit tahini or almond butter.

CHERRY TOFU STRUDEL

Substitute 4 cups pitted fresh chopped cherries and 2 cups Tofu Custard (p. 62) for apple-walnut filling. Combine tofu and cherries. Fill.

MINCEMEAT STRUDEL

Substitute Mincemeat Filling (pp. 50–51) for apple-walnut filling.

POPPY SEED STRUDEL

3 to 4 cups Poppy Seed Filling (p. 52)
1 cup grated apples
1 teaspoon orange rind
1 teaspoon lemon rind

Combine ingredients. Fill any strudel dough.

APPLE BUTTER OR JELLY STRUDEL

Spread strudel with apple butter or apple cider jelly before filling.

CINNAMON-NUT STRUDEL

1 cup chopped walnuts
½ cup blanched chopped almonds
1 teaspoon cinnamon
2 recipes Syrian Pastry Dough (p. 79)
1 cup unrefined olive oil

Cinnamon Syrup
¼ cup concentrated sweetener
1 cinnamon stick or 1 teaspoon cinnamon
1 teaspoon lemon juice

Combine walnuts, almonds and cinnamon. Set aside. Prepare dough. Roll into thin sheets.

Brush half of a 7 x 12-inch pastry sheet with oil. Fold over the other half, and brush with more oil. Sprinkle with 1 tablespoon nut mixture.

Roll dough up like a strudel, very tightly (p. 89). Cut strudel in half, making 2 rolls.

Preheat oven to 350°. Oil a baking sheet lightly. Place strudel on baking sheet. Slit top. Bake 25 to 30 minutes, or until browned. Remove from oven, place on a rack with a pan underneath to catch drippings, and pour warm cinnamon syrup over pastry.

Cinnamon Syrup

Combine sweetener and cinnamon stick or cinnamon. Cook 10 minutes over a low flame. Add lemon juice and remove from heat.

Filling the Strudel

Roll out dough on floured cloth (p. 70–71).

Sprinkle and/or spread surface of dough with desired filling, leaving a 2-inch border on two ends (see illustrations).

Fold over edges that do not have any filling on them toward the center. Brush with oil.

Lift up the edge of the pastry cloth nearest you and begin to flip the dough over on the filling.

Continue until the dough is completely rolled around itself.

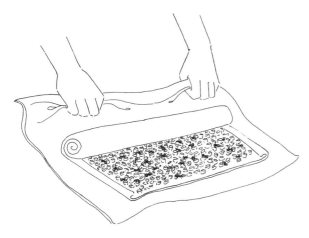

Flip the dough onto a well-oiled baking sheet.

If it is yeasted dough, slit the top diagonally about 3 inches apart, cover and set in a warm place to rise until one-third larger. Glaze immediately before or after baking (p. 43).

If it is unyeasted dough, slit the top and bake, glazing before or after baking.

Alternate Method

Roll out dough on floured cloth.

Place a 3-inch strip of filling across one end of strudel.

Fold the end of the dough to the left and right of the filling.

Brush with oil.

Lift up the end of the cloth nearest the filling, and fold the dough over onto the filling.

Raise the pastry cloth and continue until the dough is completely rolled.

Flip the dough onto a well-oiled baking sheet.

Variation

Fruit-Filled Slit Strudel

Prepare dough (p. 79).

Roll into rectangle ½-inch thick.

Place filling in the center third of dough.

Slit both sides of unfilled dough diagonally ½ inch apart, from filling to edge.

Fold strips alternately over filling, stretching and twisting slightly.

Bake (pp. 87–88).

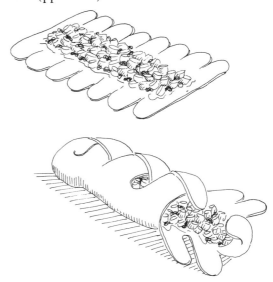

Tarts

A tart is a delicate, small open pie, made from deep-fried or baked pastry, that can be filled with cooked or raw fruit, vegetables, custards, creames, jellies or a combination of these.

Any pie filling can be used for tarts, and vice versa. Tarts can be kept for several weeks before filling.

Lining Tart Forms

Place 12 tart forms touching one another in rows of four. Roll out pastry ¼ inch thick to a size 3 to 4 inches larger than the area covered by the forms.

Fold the dough back twice, until you have a long, narrow piece of dough, which you can lift and place on top of the forms. Place dough on forms nearest you, and unfold outward to cover the others. Let

pastry stand 10 minutes to settle naturally. It will stretch and fall into the forms.

Cover pastry-lined forms with a towel or canvas cloth, and run a rolling pin over the top of the forms.

Form a small ball the size of a walnut from the leftover scraps of pastry dough. Use this to press pastry firmly into forms.

Cover and chill 30 minutes before baking.

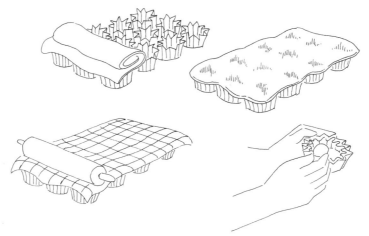

Baking or Deep-frying

To bake unfilled tarts, place them on a baking sheet and bake 10 to 15 minutes at 375°. Then fill three-quarters full and bake 15 minutes longer, or until they begin to bubble (fruit filling), get firm (creames, custards), or get dry (purées).

To bake filled, fill tart three-quarters full and place on a baking sheet on the lowest rack in the oven, so that the maximum heat will be given to the bottom of the pastry. Bake until the fruit fillings begin to rise and get juicy and bubbly, or until the creames or custards get firm, or until purées get dry.

A good technique to assure even baking is to bake the tarts on the center rack in the oven 10 minutes before filling them.

Variations

Bake or deep-fry unfilled. Cool. Place 1 tablespoon creame (pp. 55–60) in each tart. Allow to set for a few minutes. Cover with slices of cooked fruit or vegetables. Brush with apricot glaze (see Fruit Glaze, p. 63) and serve.

Line form with pastry, cover and chill 30 minutes.

Heat oil. Deep-fry pastry dough and shell together. They will separate in the hot oil. Remove form and continue frying dough until *lightly* browned, and the oil has almost completely stopped bubbling around the edges of the tart. Drain and cool.

Fill with filling the same temperature as the tart (preferably cool).

APPLE TART I

1 pastry recipe (pp. 76–78)
1 cup raisins
4 pounds apples
2 tablespoons oil
  Juice and rind of 1 lemon
¼ cup apple juice or cider
½ teaspoon salt
1 cup Crumb Topping (p. 68)
½ to 1 cup Apricot Glaze (see Fruit Glaze, p. 63)
  Cinnamon mix

Prepare pastry.

Oil a shallow 9 or 10-inch rectangular sheet or 12 tart forms.

Line the sheet or forms with pastry. Save the

extra dough for the top. Cover and chill sheet at least 30 minutes.

Soak raisins in juice to cover until soft.

Core apples (peel if not organic) and cut into eighths.

Heat oil in a heavy skillet or pan. Sauté apples for a few minutes, add lemon juice, rind, apple juice, salt. Cover and cook 2 minutes, remove cover and cook until slightly tender. Add raisins and cool.

Preheat oven to 375°. Prebake pastry 10 minutes. Fill with apple mixture.

Roll out a strip of dough 10 x 4 inches and ¼ inch thick. Brush with oil, and sprinkle with Crumb Topping. (Roll pin lightly over topping on top of dough to make it adhere better.) Cut into strips ¼ inch wide to use for lattice top. (To cut strips, use a pastry wheel to give a fluted edge.)

Lattice the pastry strips on top of the apple mix (p. 73).

Bake on lowest rack in 350° oven 1 hour or until filling begins to bubble in the center. The last 10 minutes of baking time, place the tarts on a higher rack in the oven to brown the lattice top.

Prepare apricot glaze (p. 63). Remove tart or tarts from oven, and place on rack to cool.

While still warm, brush with hot apricot glaze.

APPLE TART II

Follow directions for Apple Tart I. Soak apples in the juice of 1 lemon and 1 teaspoon vanilla. Drain off liquid (use for glazes, fillings, cake liquid). Sauté half of the apple mixture until soft. Place in tart shells.

Arrange the remaining apples overlapping each other on top of apple filling.

Bake on lowest rack in 350° oven for 1 hour. Sprinkle chopped nuts on top of tarts the last 10 minutes of baking time.

Remove from oven and cool on rack before removing from forms.

Variations

Follow Apple Tart recipe, but deep-fry pastry. Omit lattice.

Substitute any fresh fruit in season for apples.

Omit lemon juice. (Do not sauté blueberries or strawberries.)

Substitute any dried fruit. Soak in water to cover until soft. Squeeze out excess liquid. Chop fruit, place on top of apple mixture and bake.

Press ground nuts or seeds in the bottom of the pastry before adding apple mixture.

Prepare Apple Tart II using another fresh or dried fruit in place of apples for the topping. Place one layer of apples, then alternate with other fruit, topping the pastry with apple mixture.

Try using some vegetables in combination with Apple Tart II. Place a layer of apple mixture on bottom, then cover with a layer of carrot purée (p. 65). Top with a layer of apple and bake 1 hour in a 350° oven.

LATTICE CARROT TART

8 to 10 medium-size carrots
2 tablespoons oil
1 teaspoon cinnamon
½ teaspoon cloves
½ teaspoon salt
¼ cup apple juice or cider
3 tablespoons chestnut or whole-wheat pastry flour
1 pastry recipe (pp. 76–78)
½ cup Nut Filling (p. 69)
1 cup roasted, crushed nuts

Sauté carrots in oil; add spices, salt and apple juice. Cover and cook until tender. Purée.

Roast flour. Set aside to cool. Preheat oven to 375°.

Prepare pastry. Roll out dough and place in oiled forms (p. 90). Sprinkle Nut Filling and nuts in tarts.

Cut strips for lattice top (p. 73).

Combine cooled roasted flour with carrot purée. Prebake tarts 10 minutes. Pour filling into them. Place lattice strips over filling.

Brush with glaze before or after baking (p. 43).

Bake 15 to 20 minutes, or until lattice top is lightly browned.

Variations

Substitute yams, sweet potatoes or parsnips for carrots.

Substitute 1 teaspoon mint for cloves and cinnamon.

Substitute Applesauce for carrot purée (p. 51).

Use any one of the suggested creames as fillings (Chapter 3).

PUFF TART

    1 pastry recipe (pp. 76–78)
    1 cup unroasted walnuts, almonds or pecans
    1 teaspoon cinnamon
    1 cup fruit purée (p. 66)
    3 eggs
    1 teaspoon vanilla
    ½ teaspoon salt
    ¼ cup concentrated sweetener
    ¼ cup whole-wheat pastry flour
    ¼ cup arrowroot flour

Prepare pastry.

Oil a 9 or 10-inch tart pan (1 inch deep) or tart forms. Line with pastry, cover and chill at least 30 minutes (p. 90).

Preheat oven to 375°.

Roast the nuts; while they are warm, grind finely in a blender, roll in between pastry cloths or crush with mortar and pestle.

Mix with cinnamon. Press into the bottom of the chilled pastry.

Prebake 10 minutes (p. 90). Spread fruit purée on top of pastry.

Separate eggs. Set whites aside. Stir yolks lightly to break them up. Add vanilla and set aside.

Beat egg whites and salt until foamy. Slowly begin to drip in sweetener, beating continuously, until peaked. Fold one quarter of whites into yolks. Sift flours.

Combine yolk mixture and whites, and slowly fold together, sprinkling flour in as you fold. DO NOT OVERMIX. Place on top of fruit purée. Bake 10 to 15 minutes, or until lightly browned.

CHERRY
(*Prunus cerasus*)

There are many different varieties of cherries ranging from sour to sweet. Cultivated cherries are either dark red-black or pale yellow, covered with a red hue. There are beautiful white or pinkish flowers which are produced in clusters, bearing forth shiny fruit on long flower stalks. The cherry tree grows up to 75 feet in height in well-drained woodlands. Used as a fresh-fruit dessert in the summertime, the cherry is also traditionally used for cherry pie, tarts and custard.

TOFU SOUR CREAME CHERRY TART

This tart can also be made with peaches, apricots, pears or any fresh fruit in season.

    1 pastry recipe (pp. 76–78)
    3 cups pitted cherries
    2 eggs
    1 cup Tofu Sour Creame (p. 60)
    2 tablespoons concentrated sweetener
    ½ teaspoon vanilla

Prepare pastry. Oil a 9 or 10-inch pan (about 1 inch deep) or 9 to 12 tart forms. Line with pastry (see p. 90). Cover and chill 30 minutes.

Wash and pit cherries. Cut into small pieces. If using other fruit, slice, and peel if not organic.

Preheat oven to 375°. Prebake pastry 10 minutes.

Beat eggs with Tofu Sour Creame, sweetener and vanilla. Arrange fruit in tarts. Pour egg mixture over fruit, and bake 15 minutes on lowest rack in oven, or until custard is firm.

Variations

Substitute any fresh or dried fruit for cherries.

Substitute any creame for Tofu Sour Creame.

(Eggs may be omitted; use 2 more cups of creame to replace eggs.)

STRAWBERRY CUSTARD TART

1 9- or 10-inch prebaked tart (or 12 small tarts)
2 cups fresh strawberries (for garnish)
2 cups Strawberry Tahini Custard (p. 62)
4 cups Strawberry Cheesecake Topping (p. 54)
1 cup roasted ground almonds

Prebake tart at 375°.

Wash and hull strawberries. Dry well. Set aside. Prepare Strawberry Tahini Custard. Set aside to cool. Prepare Strawberry Cheesecake Topping. Allow to set, but not to completely harden.

Spread half of custard in the bottom of prebaked tart. Cover with cool strawberry topping. Top with remaining custard. Slice remaining strawberries, and arrange on top of custard. Chill.

Sprinkle ground almonds on top before serving.

Variations

Substitute any fresh or dried fruit or vegetable-fruit combination for strawberries.

Pies

BASIC FRUIT PIE

1 recipe pastry dough (pp. 76–78)
1 egg white
8 to 10 cups chopped fresh fruit
1 teaspoon cinnamon or mint
½ teaspoon salt
3 to 4 tablespoons arrowroot flour*
½ cup apple juice or cider

Prepare pastry. Preheat oven to 375°. Oil a pie pan and line with pastry; baste with egg white (p. 75, No. 15). Chop fruit (peel if not organic). Combine fruit, spice and salt. Dissolve arrowroot flour in juice or cider and stir until well combined. Pour arrowroot mixture over fruit mixture and toss. Let sit about 10 minutes. Place mixture in pie shell, piling up fruit in the shape of a pyramid. Cover with crust and secure edge. Prick top crust (p. 73). Glaze before or after baking (p. 43). Bake at 375° for 15 minutes; lower temperature to 350° and bake 40 minutes longer, or until fruit is soft (test center of pie with a toothpick).

Variations

One-half cup apple butter may be substituted for juice or cider when using fruit that contains more liquid.

* The more liquid the fruit contains, the more arrowroot flour is needed.

When using dried fruit, soak in liquid to cover until soft. Measure fruit after soaking.

Try half-and-half combinations of apple and pear, peach and blueberry, strawberry and apple, cherry and apple, peach and cherry, or raspberry and apple. Or try three quarters apple and one quarter cranberry.

Cook fruits, spice and salt together in an open pan until soft. (Use more fruit as liquid will evaporate.) Omit arrowroot flour and juice. Place fruit in pie shell. Cover with lattice crust, and bake.

CHESTNUT-APPLE PIE

1½ cups dried chestnuts
    Apple juice or cider
1 Pressed Pastry (p. 76)
8 cups sliced apples
2 tablespoons oil
½ teaspoon salt
1 teaspoon orange rind

Soak chestnuts in juice or cider to cover overnight. Bring to a boil in water to cover. Cover pot, and cook on a low flame until tender (about 1 hour).

Preheat oven to 375°. Prebake shell for 10 minutes.

Peel, core and slice apples. Heat oil in a heavy skillet. Add apples and sauté for 5 minutes on a low flame. Add salt, cover and cook until soft.

Combine chestnuts and apples. Add orange rind. Purée half of chestnut-apple mixture until creamy. Combine purée and other half of mixture. Pour into pie shell.

Bake at 350° 25 to 30 minutes longer, or until crust is golden brown.

APPLE-CRANBERRY PIE

1 Pressed Pastry recipe (p. 76)
½ cup concentrated sweetener
½ cup cranberries
¼ cup apple juice or cider
8 cups chopped apples
1 teaspoon cinnamon
3 tablespoons oil
2 tablespoons orange rind
1 tablespoon lemon juice
1 cup Oat Crumb Topping (p. 68)
¼ cup almonds, walnuts or pecans

Oil a pie pan. Press dough into pan. Preheat oven to 375°. Prebake pie shell 5 minutes.

Combine sweetener, cranberries and juice in a heavy saucepan, and cook over a medium flame until mixture boils. Lower flame, and cook until cranberries pop.

Core and chop apples (peel if not organic). Add cinnamon, oil, rind, lemon juice. Stir thoroughly; cover and cook on a low flame for 5 minutes. Combine apples and cranberries (strain off excess liquid).

Pour cranberry-apple mixture into shell, cover with Oat Crumb Topping and sprinkle extra nuts on top if desired.

Bake at 375° for 15 minutes, lower temperature to 350° and bake until lightly browned.

APRICOT CREAME PIE

1 recipe pastry dough (pp. 76–78)
2 cups Tofu Creame (p. 59) or Chestnut Creame (p. 57)
2 cups apricot purée (p. 66)
½ cup Crumb Topping (p. 68)

Preheat oven to 375°. Prepare pastry dough. Prebake shell 10 minutes.

Lower oven temperature to 350°. Pour half of

the creame into shell. Cover with half of purée. Repeat, topping with purée. Sprinkle with Crumb Topping.

Bake 15 to 20 minutes or until set.

Alternate Method

Combine purée and creame. Pour into half-baked shell. Bake until set.

CANTALOUPE CREAME PIE

1 Pressed Pastry recipe (p. 76)
Filling
4 cups diced cantaloupe
2 tablespoons oil
½ teaspoon salt
3 tablespoons tahini
4 cups apple juice or cider
1 bar kanten
1 to 2 teaspoons cinnamon
½ to 1 teaspoon ginger
4 tablespoons arrowroot flour
Topping
Tofu Creame (p. 59)
Strawberries for garnish

Prebake pie shell. Set aside to cool.

Remove skin and seeds, and dice cantaloupe. Sauté cantaloupe in oil over a medium flame for 5 minutes. Add salt and simmer uncovered about 5 minutes longer.

Blend tahini, half of cantaloupe mixture and 1 cup juice or cider together, until mixture is creamy and smooth.

Rinse kanten under cold running water. Squeeze out excess liquid. Shred into small pieces. Combine with 2 cups apple juice or cider, and heat on a medium flame until mixture begins to boil. Lower flame, and simmer until kanten dissolves. Add blended cantaloupe-tahini mixture and spices to kanten. Bring to a boil.

Dilute arrowroot in 1 cup juice or cider, and stir into mixture rapidly until it boils again and begins to thicken. Remove from heat and set aside to cool.* Prepare Tofu Creame. Set aside.

* Pie shells have a tendency to crack if they have not cooled completely before being filled; or if filling is at a different temperature from crust.

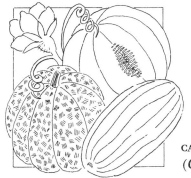

CANTALOUPE MELON
(*Cucumis melo*)

There are many kinds of melon that exist today. The flesh of a melon consists of about 90 to 95 percent water and only about 5 percent sugar. Melon plants have hairy stems, bearing many leaves which are quite large in size. An annual trailing plant, which probably originated in the tropics, it has given rise to many forms, and many cultivated varieties have been developed, varying in size, shape, color and taste. Cantaloupe melons have deep grooves on the outside running vertically around the whole melon. Mainly used as the first or last course in a meal, they can be incorporated into many different desserts.

Pour cool cantaloupe mixture into shell before it jells. Set aside to harden at room temperature (you may chill at this time, but it is advisable to wait until it is completely cool).

Spoon Tofu Creame over the top of the pie after the pie has set. Garnish with strawberries. Chill before serving.

Variations

Add 4 tablespoons grain coffee to kanten mixture before cooking.

Substitute almond butter for tahini.

Substitute 1 cup diced parsnips and 4 cups diced pears for cantaloupe. Substitute almond butter for tahini.

Substitute 3 cups diced peaches (peel if not organic) and 2 cups soaked raisins for cantaloupe.

Substitute 2 cups peeled, cored, diced pears and 3 cups peeled, cored and diced apples for cantaloupe.

Soak dried apricots in liquid to cover until soft. Substitute 4 cups diced apricots for cantaloupe.

BLUEBERRY CREAME PIE

1 9-inch pie shell (p. 74)
4 cups blueberries
2 cups Tofu Creame (p. 59)
1 bar kanten
2 cups apple juice or cider
Crushed roasted nuts

Prebake pie shell. Rinse blueberries. Allow to dry. Prepare creame.

Rinse kanten, shred into apple juice and cook until it boils. Lower flame and simmer until kanten dissolves.

Add half of blueberries and vanilla to kanten mixture. Stir well.

Fold half of creame into kanten mixture. Cook on a low flame for 3 minutes, stirring constantly. Spoon mixture into prebaked shell.

Chill until almost firm, then add remaining blueberries to remaining creame. Spread over top.

Garnish with crushed roasted nuts.

Chill until firm.

Variation

Substitute Chestnut Creame (p. 57) or Oat Creame (p. 55) for Tofu Creame.

BULGHUR PARSNIP PIE

1 cup uncooked bulghur wheat
4 tablespoons oil
3 cups apple juice or cider
½ teaspoon salt
1 cup diced parsnips
1 grated apple
1 recipe Pressed Pastry (p. 76)
Crushed roasted nuts

Roast bulghur wheat in 2 tablespoons oil until lightly browned. Boil cider. Combine bulghur with boiling cider, add salt, reduce flame, cover and cook 15 minutes.

Dice parsnips. Sauté in 2 tablespoons oil. Cover and cook until soft.

Grate 1 apple (peel if not organic). Purée parsnips and bulghur together. Add grated apple.

Prepare pie crust. Preheat oven to 375°. Oil a pie pan. Press crust into pan and prebake 10 minutes.

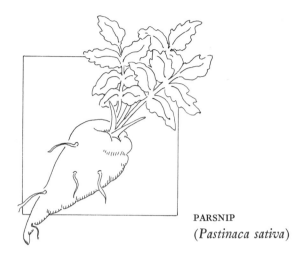

PARSNIP
(*Pastinaca sativa*)

This strong, yellowish-white root vegetable is found in most parts of the United States as well as Europe. It has been cultivated since Roman times and contains large quantities of sugar and starch used for feeding man as well as livestock. If used sparingly in desserts, it will enhance the flavor of any dish.

Spread bulghur-parsnip mixture in shell and bake 10 minutes covered. Remove cover and bake 10 minutes longer. Sprinkle crushed roasted nuts on top after baking.

Place on rack to cool before serving.

Alternate Method

Purée parsnips. Set aside. Purée cooked bulghur. Spread 1 layer of bulghur, then grated apple and cover with parsnip purée. Sprinkle on Crumb Topping (p. 68) and bake 10 to 15 minutes or until firm.

Place on a rack to cool and set before serving.

Variations

Substitute 1 cup carrot purée for parsnips (p. 65).

Substitute 1 cup half-and-half squash-carrot purée for parsnips.

Substitute ½ cup carrot purée for ½ cup parsnip purée.

Substitute 1 cup couscous (cook in 4 cups liquid; see p. 28) for bulghur.

Top with fruit purée before baking (p. 66).

To make pie more firm, add 2 tablespoons roasted pastry or chestnut flour to parsnip-bulghur mixture after blending.

Adjust liquid content accordingly.

CHIFFON PIE

  ½ bar kanten
  2 cups apple juice, mu or mint tea
  2 eggs
  1 cup Oat Creame (p. 55)
  2 tablespoons concentrated sweetener
  2 cups Tofu Creame Whip (p. 60)
  ½ cup crushed nuts
  ½ teaspoon salt
      Vanilla
  1 prebaked pie shell (p. 74)

Rinse kanten under cold running water. Squeeze out excess liquid. Shred kanten into juice or tea. Bring to a boil. Lower flame and cook until kanten is dissolved.

Separate eggs. Beat yolks lightly.

Combine Oat Creame and concentrated sweetener in a heavy saucepan. Stir until mixture boils. Reduce flame. Pour half of oat mixture over yolks. Return this mixture to pan, stir and cook until thickened. Add the kanten and stir until dissolved. Remove from heat, pour into bowl and cool. Chill until mixture begins to thicken.

Combine Tofu Creame Whip with nuts. Beat egg whites and salt together until peaked.

Fold Tofu Creame Whip and egg whites into custard. Add vanilla.

Fill prebaked pie shell. Chill until set.

Variations

Add 1 to 1½ cups cooked fruit or vegetable purée to Oat Creame combination.

Substitute 1 cup Chestnut Creame I (p. 57) for Oat Creame.

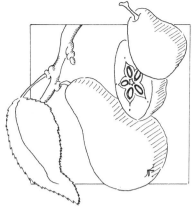

PEAR
(*Pyrus communis*)

There are many different varieties of the pear family found all over the world. They resemble the apple in many ways, but have a more elongated fruit. The tree grows wild in most parts of Europe, but more in the warmer southern parts than in the north. Many different kinds of pears are cultivated today, varying from round to top-shaped to oval shape, and red, brown, green, yellow or golden russet in color.

The fruit may be eaten raw, stewed or cooked like applesauce, or used in dessert making for pastries, pies or cakes.

LEMON MERINGUE PIE

1 recipe pastry dough (pp. 76–78)

Filling
1 bar kanten
4 cups apple juice or cider
  Pinch of salt
1 tablespoon concentrated sweetener
6 tablespoons arrowroot flour
  Juice of 1½ organic lemons or grated
    rind and juice of ½ lemon
1 teaspoon vanilla

Topping
Meringue topping (p. 60)

Prepare pastry.

Preheat oven to 375°. Bake crust 15 minutes or until lightly browned (not quite completely baked).

Wash kanten under cold running water. Squeeze out liquid and shred into apple juice. Add salt (reserve ½ cup juice for arrowroot).

Cook on a medium flame until mixture boils; reduce flame and simmer until kanten dissolves.

Dilute arrowroot in ½ cup apple juice, and sweetener.

Add arrowroot to kanten, and cook on a high flame, stirring constantly, until the mixture boils, starts to thicken and turns clear. Stir in lemon juice and vanilla, remove from heat and let sit 5 minutes.

Prepare meringue topping. Pour lemon kanten into shell. Allow to cool.

Cover with meringue and bake in a 400° oven 10 to 12 minutes or until browned. Turn oven off. Open door. Leave in oven 30 minutes before cooling on a rack.

PEAR CREAME CRISP

½ cup raisins
2 to 3 cups sweet almond milk or apple cider
14 cups sliced pears
½ cup corn flour or sweet brown rice
  flour
2 tablespoons oil
½ teaspoon salt
1 teaspoon cinnamon
1 teaspoon vanilla
1½ cups Crumb Topping (p. 68)

Soak raisins in sweet almond milk or cider to cover until soft. Squeeze out excess liquid and reserve. Set raisins aside. Core and slice pears (peel if not organic).

Roast the flour in a dry skillet until it begins to smell sweet and slightly browns. Set aside to cool.

Heat oil and sauté pears, raisins and salt together until the fruit begins to get soft.

Preheat the oven to 375° and oil a deep baking dish (11 x 7 x 2 inches). Combine the roasted flour and sweet almond milk. Add cinnamon and stir until dissolved. Add fruit and vanilla and mix gently until the fruit is coated with the liquid mixture. Place in baking dish, sprinkle on Crumb Topping, cover and steam 30 minutes. Remove cover and bake 15 to 20 minutes longer, or until fruit is soft and topping is browned.

Variations

Add 1 tablespoon orange rind.

Dilute 2 tablespoons tahini or almond butter in apple juice before adding it to flour combination.

Substitute any fresh fruit in season for pears.

POPPY SEED–APRICOT LAYER PIE

> 1 recipe Pressed Pastry (p. 76)
> 2 cups apricot purée (p. 66)
> 2 cups Poppy Seed Filling (p. 52)
> 1 cup vanilla Oat Creame, optional

Prebake pie shell 10 minutes at 375°. Fill the shell with apricot purée. Top with Poppy Seed Filling.

Bake 15 to 20 minutes longer at 350°, or until crust is browned. Top with vanilla Oat Creame before serving (see Oat Creame variations, p. 56).

Alternate Method

Prebake pie shell 15 to 20 minutes or until golden brown at 375°.

Combine apricot purée with 3 tablespoons sifted, roasted chestnut flour (p. 9). Cook, constantly stirring, until mixture begins to boil. Reduce flame, cover and simmer 20 minutes. Stir occasionally.

Pour into prebaked shell (the shell should be at the same temperature as the filling).

Top with Poppy Seed Filling (this mixture should contain almost no liquid). Allow to set. Chill before serving.

RAINBOW PIE

> 1 recipe yeasted or unyeasted pastry dough
>   (pp. 76–78)
> 1 cup raisin purée (p. 66)
> 1 cup apricot purée (p. 66)
> 1 cup Oat Creame (p. 55)
>   tinted with beet juice
> 1 cup Tofu Creame (p. 59)
>   blended with ¼ cup blueberries

Prepare purées and creames. Prepare pie crust and place in pie pan. See "Section Tart or Pie" (p. 72) for filling.

Substitute any colorful fruit glazes, custards or creames for those listed.

SQUASH
(*Cucurbitaceae*)

The squash, cucumber, melon and pumpkin are all members of the same family. They are all trailing or climbing herbs, with tendrils and large, lobed leaves. The flowers are generally yellow and the berrylike fruit is generally oval or round in shape.

The most familiar type of pumpkin grown in northern America is usually orange in color, maturing in October, just before Halloween. Another kind of pumpkin, called natawari *(from the Japanese for "split with an axe") was first grown in Hokkaido, a northern island of Japan. Unlike its relative, it is greenish-blue on the outside and deep yellow on the inside. This type of pumpkin is now grown in some parts of the eastern United States, maturing at the same time as the "Halloween pumpkin." It has a strong, sweet taste that is excellent for the traditional pumpkin pie.*

Some squash varieties that are good in desserts are butternut, buttercup, acorn and winter squash. Most of these squash are very sweet if used in season.

THANKSGIVING SQUASH-MINCEMEAT PIE

> 1 Pressed Pastry shell (p. 76)
>   *Mincemeat Filling*
> 1 cup raisins
>   Apple juice or cider to soak raisins
> 1 cup apricot purée (p. 66)
> 2 cups diced apples
>   Juice and rind of ½ lemon
>   Juice and rind of ½ orange
> 1 teaspoon cinnamon
> ¼ teaspoon cloves
> ¼ teaspoon ginger
> 1½ tablespoons miso

Mincemeat Filling

Soak raisins in apple juice or cider to cover until soft. Reserve liquid. Prepare apricot purée. Reserve excess liquid after cooking and before puréeing the apricots.

Core and dice apples (peel if not organic). Combine juice and rinds of lemon and orange, and spices with the apricot purée. Blend the miso and apricot-purée mixture together. Fold in the diced apples and raisins and enough liquid to form a thick batter (use excess apricot liquid here).

Preheat oven to 375°. Bake pie crust 10 minutes. Place mincemeat filling in the pastry shell and bake 10 minutes longer or until firm.

Squash Purée

        ¼ cup chestnut flour*
    3 to 4 cups chopped uncooked acorn, butternut, buttercup, winter squash or sweet pumpkin**
        2 tablespoons oil
        ¼ teaspoon salt
        ¼ cup concentrated sweetener
        ½ teaspoon cinnamon
        ¼ teaspoon ginger
    ½ to 1 cup apple juice or cider

Dry-roast the chestnut flour until it begins to smell sweet and is lightly brown. Set aside to cool.

Cut squash into small pieces (skin may be removed here). Heat oil in a heavy skillet, and sauté squash for a few minutes on a medium flame. Add salt, sweetener, spices and enough liquid to almost cover the squash. Cover, lower flame and cook until tender. Drain off excess liquid and remove skins from squash if not done already. Purée or blend half the squash, adding the juice from cooking until a thick purée is formed. Combine this mixture with the other half of squash. Allow to cool.

Sift and add flour here if desired and stir until smooth. Spoon squash purée on top of the mincemeat filling and bake 15 minutes longer or until squash purée is dry and firm. Cool on a rack until pie is firm enough to cut. (Refrigerate overnight before serving for a firmer filling.)

* 1 beaten egg may be substituted for flour or flour may be omitted if squash purée does not contain too much liquid.
**1 cup diced onion may be substituted for 1 cup squash or pumpkin.

YAM
Dioscorea

There are many species of yams, some of them dating back to ancient times. The air potato yam is one of the few true yams cultivated for food in the United States. Yams have thick tubers, generally a development at the base of the stem, from which protrude long, slender annual climbing stems, varying in color from white to yellowish-orange.

The thick roots of yams are a major food crop in many tropical countries. They contain mostly water. Much of the solid matter is starch and sugar. The root has less starch than the white potato, but more sugar. Some kinds of yams are not fit to eat, but they produce substances called sapogenins that can be used to make drugs such as cortisone.

In many West African countries, the consumption of yams is so great that it is regarded as a staple food. About 20 million tons of yams are grown for food each year. Half of them are grown in the countries of West Africa.

Yams are also grown in India, countries of Southeast Asia and the Caribbean Sea.

SUNSHINE PIE

    1 Pressed Pastry recipe (p. 76)
    4 cups yam or sweet potato purée
    ¼ cup roasted, sifted chestnut flour
    4 tablespoons sesame butter
    1 teaspoon ginger
    ½ teaspoon cinnamon
    ¼ cup concentrated sweetener (optional)
    ½ cup unroasted crushed pecans
       Roasted pecan halves

Preheat oven to 350°. Prepare crust; and prebake 10 minutes.

Combine purée, chestnut flour, sesame butter, ginger, cinnamon and sweetener, if used. Fill shell with mixture, and bake 20 to 25 minutes, or until crust is golden brown.

Sprinkle crushed pecans on top of pie, 10 minutes before removing from oven. Place the pecan halves on top for decoration after baking.

Variation

Substitute any fruit or vegetable-fruit purée for yams (see pp. 65–66).

CANDIED PECAN YAM PIE

Soul food developed out of the necessity of the slaves to keep alive on the meager fare allowed them by the plantation owners. They lived mainly on vegetables, and used much skill and ingenuity to turn them into the tastiest dishes possible. This is probably how they developed such delicacies as Candied Pecan Yam Pie.

1 recipe Pie Crust dough (pp. 76–78)
or
Pressed Pastry dough

Filling
Apple juice to cover yams
8 to 10 yams (6 to 7 cups chopped)
Carrots (1 to 2 cups chopped)
2 tablespoons oil
3 to 4 tablespoons concentrated sweetener
½ teaspoon salt
1 teaspoon cinnamon
½ teaspoon ginger
1 to 2 cups sweet almond milk (p. 12)
1 teaspoon vanilla

Topping
½ cup unroasted crushed pecans
Roasted pecan halves

Bring apple juice to a boil. Drop in yams, turn off heat and let sit for a few minutes. Drain; rinse under cold water immediately. Peel yams and chop (save skin for bread or soup if organic). Chop carrots. Heat oil. Sauté carrots for a few minutes. Add yams, sweetener, salt and spices. Add liquid to almost cover vegetables.

Cover pan and simmer 1 to 1½ hours, or until soft.

After cooking, drain liquid from vegetables. Reserve vegetable juice.

Prepare pie crust. Oil an 8 or 9-inch pie pan. Preheat oven to 375°.

Blend or purée half to three quarters of the yam mixture, adding just enough reserved juice to form a thick purée. Stir in vanilla.

Roast flour in a dry skillet until it browns. Set aside to cool. Sift cooled flour; combine with 2 tablespoons apple juice or reserved juice. Mix until creamy and smooth. Stir this mixture into purée and mix until there are no lumps. Combine with unpuréed vegetables.

Prebake pie crust 10 minutes. Remove from oven, fill with yam mixture and sprinkle crushed pecans on top. Return to the oven and bake 15 to 20 minutes longer at 325° or until crust is browned and filling is set and dry. Remove from oven and place roasted pecan halves on top in any design. Cool and serve.

Alternate Method

Brush yams with tamari soy sauce (p. 12) and oil (omit boiling in juice). Cover and bake in a 350° oven until soft. Remove skin. Proceed as in recipe.

THREE-PART PIE

4 fresh peaches
1 cup apricot purée (p. 66)
1 prebaked pie shell (p. 74)
1 recipe custard filling (p. 61)
1 apricot glaze (see Fruit Glaze, p. 63)

Blanch peaches (p. 46), halve, and remove pits.

Spread apricot purée in pie shell. Let set 10 to 15 minutes.

Cover with custard, and let set again for 10 to 15 minutes. Arrange peach halves on top of custard, and spoon glaze over peaches.

Let set. Chill until ready to serve.

Variations

Substitute any creame filling for custard.
Substitute any fresh or dried fruit for peaches.
Substitute any purée for apricot purée.

5. Higher and Higher

Yeasted Pastries and Cakes for Special Occasions

The fine art of baking was first enhanced by the use of yeast in Egypt around 4000 B.C. Yeast is a living bacteria which feeds on natural sugar from grain as well as from added sugar. The natural, simple sugars in the flour are usually not enough to let the yeast work quickly, so added sugar obtained from cane, honey, syrups and various fruits and juices are introduced, in order to allow the yeast to change the oxygen and sugar in the flour more rapidly into carbon dioxide and alcohol.

Beating or kneading the batter or dough activates the gluten, allowing the alcohol to evaporate and the carbon dioxide to become caught in the gluten, making the dough rise. During baking, the high oven temperature drives off the alcohol and expands the gas bubbles, enlarging the little holes in the dough and causing it to rise even more.

There is a lifelike quality to yeasted doughs which can only be felt during the transformation of a doughy mass into a finely sculptured pastry or cake. Braiding, twisting, swirling are only a few of the many ways in which you can have fun working with yeast.

Working with Yeast

There are many ways to prepare yeasted doughs or batters for pastries and cakes. The recipes in this section usually begin by first preparing a "sponge," or first-rise batter. The advantage of this method is that the yeast will get started more quickly and easily in the absence of the other ingredients, especially salt, which can delay or inhibit the yeasted batter or dough's rising action. However, if you are pressed for time, the sponge or first-rise batter may be omitted.

Sponge Preparation

Dilute the yeast (dry or cake) with a small amount (½ cup) of lukewarm (75 to 90°) apple juice or cider*. See p. 105, No. 3 and No. 4.

Stir until all the lumps and pieces have dissolved.

Set it aside about 5 minutes or until it begins to bubble.

Add enough whole-wheat flour or whole-wheat pastry flour to yeasted mixture to form a thin batter. Beat for several minutes with a wooden spoon or wire whisk.

Cover with a damp cloth and set in a warm place to rise until it is doubled in size and feels soft and puffy.

Beat down, add the rest of the ingredients and follow the recipe.

Kneading

Kneading does not refer only to bread-making. This process develops the gluten in the flour, allowing the dough to rise, forming lighter, more moist and airy cakes or pastries. This kneading technique is used when the yeasted mixture is too thick to be beaten with a wooden spoon.

If your dough is soft and sticky to the touch, you can knead it directly in the mixing bowl.

* These liquids, which contain natural sugar, help the yeast to work quickly.

Kneading Soft Dough in a Bowl

Flour your hands.

Pull the soft dough over and over from the side of the bowl to the center, holding the bowl steady as you pull.

Knead dough until it begins to pull away from the side of the bowl (10 to 15 minutes).

Kneading Heavier Dough on a Flat Surface

Flour your hands if the dough is sticky.

Knead dough on a pastry cloth or wooden board lightly dusted with flour.

Using the heels of your hands, press down firmly on the dough, folding it in half.

Press down again with the heels of your hands, rotating it slightly.

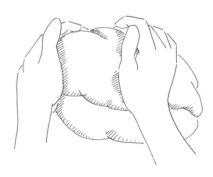

Repeat over and over again until the dough feels smooth and elastic. Do not be afraid to press firmly and punch the dough, because it is this movement that will activate the gluten in the flour, and make the dough rise.

When the dough is smooth, place it in a large oiled bowl; oil the top of the dough to prevent it from drying out. Cover and place in a warm spot to rise, until doubled in size.

Shaping Dough

TWIST

Roll dough into a large square ¼ inch thick. Brush with oil. Spread any thin filling (e.g., Orange-Maple Sauce, p. 67) over dough. Sprinkle Crumb Topping (p. 68) over filling. Roll up like a jelly roll.

Press filled dough down to a thickness of 1 inch with a rolling pin.

Divide the flattened roll lengthwise into 3 strips.

Cut each strip horizontally in half to make 6 strips.

Braid strips together to make 1 braided loaf.

Place in an oiled 9 x 5 x 3-inch loaf pan.

Cover, set in a warm place until dough doubles in size.

Sprinkle sliced almonds over top before baking.

Bake in a preheated 350° oven 45 minutes, or until browned.

Brush with glaze before or after baking (see p. 74).

JELLY ROLL

Roll out dough to ¼-inch thickness.

Spread apple cider jelly and Crumb Topping evenly over dough.

Roll up into jelly roll.

Cut roll in half.

Place each loaf in an oiled 9 x 5 x 3-inch loaf pan, or place both loaves in a slightly wider pan.

Cover, set in a warm place until dough doubles in size.

Bake in preheated 350° oven 45 minutes or until browned.

Glaze before or after baking (see p. 74).

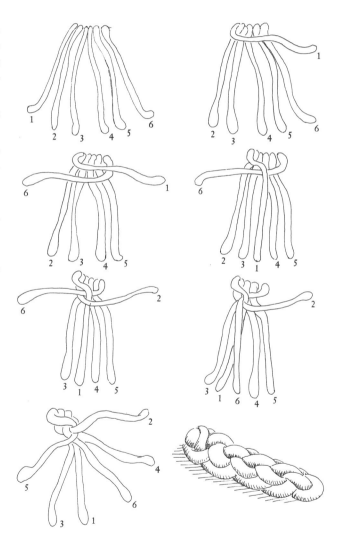

CRUMB ROLL

Roll dough into a large square ¼ inch thick.

Brush with oil and sprinkle Crumb Topping (p. 68) over dough.

Roll up like a jelly roll.

Cut roll into 6 even slices.

Place 3 slices, cut sides down, in each 7 x 5 x 3-inch loaf pan (squeeze them in if necessary).

Cover, set in a warm place until dough doubles in size.

Bake in preheated 350° oven about 45 minutes, or until lightly browned.

Glaze before or after baking (p. 74).

SCHNECKEN

Combine ¼ cup oil with 2 tablespoons maple syrup.

Oil muffin tins or cupcake tins with this mixture.

Place a few pecans in each cup.

Roll dough into a long rectangle ¼ inch thick.

Sprinkle Crumb Topping (p. 68) and raisins and nuts over dough.

Roll up dough tightly like a jelly roll, sealing the seam with water or egg.

Stretch out the roll if it is too thick for the tins, or compress it if it is too thin.

Slice into small pieces which will fill the cups half full.

Cover, set in a warm place until dough doubles in size.

Bake in preheated 350° oven about 25 to 30 minutes, or until lightly browned.

Turn pans upside-down on cake rack immediately (place cookie sheet underneath pan to catch the drippings), to remove schnecken and allow glaze to drip over the sides.

DANISH RING

Roll out dough into a rectangle approximately 6 x 20 x ¼ inches.

Spread dough with any filling (see Chapter 3).

Fold to make strip one third of its previous width.

Roll with a rolling pin to lengthen and flatten.

Cut into dough with a knife, making 3 incisions lengthwise, equally spaced apart, almost the entire length of the strip, leaving 1 inch uncut at both ends.

Take one end in each hand.

Turn and twist the ends in opposite directions to form a long twist, stretching dough slightly as you twist.

Hold ends, shaping into a ring. Cross the ends, and press them firmly together.

Press down with thumbs or hand on crossed ends, and flip over the ring to conceal the ends.

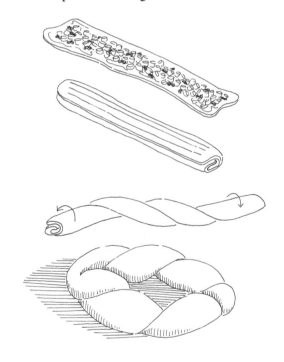

FORGET ME KNOTS

1. Rising times will vary according to the temperature and moisture of the room, the flour, the ingredients in the dough or batter, the shape of the dough and the general weather of the day.

2. The amount of liquid necessary for each dough

or batter will vary according to the temperature and moisture of the room, the flour and the general weather of the day.

3. *Compressed Yeast:*
Compressed yeast cakes contain live active yeast plants. Use lukewarm liquid to dissolve compressed yeast — a drop of liquid which feels comfortable when placed on the inside of the wrist is lukewarm.

4. *Dry Yeast:*
Dry yeast is prepared by mixing the plant with starch, pressing the mixture and then drying it at a low heat. In order to grow again, the yeast must be dissolved in warm liquid and some kind of sugar (such as apple juice).

Dry yeast, unlike fresh yeast, may be kept refrigerated in a well-sealed container for many months without losing its rising powers — it cannot decay or mold since it contains no moisture.

Use slightly warmer liquid (90 to 100°) to dissolve active dry yeast. Place your finger in the liquid; if you are able to keep your finger there without discomfort it is the right temperature.

5. A temperature of 145° will make the yeast inactive.

6. Too much salt or oil can delay the rise.

7. Place all yeasted batters or dough in a bowl for the first and second rises; cover with a damp cloth.

8. Fill pans, forms or sheets only halfway, to allow batter or dough to rise.

9. Always slit the top of a yeasted pastry before it rises, to allow for greater expansion.

10. When covering the pan containing the yeasted batter or dough for the final rise, use a glass pan as cover for best results. This will enable you to see the rate of expansion, so that the dough does not overrise.

11. Oil the rim of the pan used for covering dough or batter, so that the dough or batter does not stick to it when rising.

12. To test dough for rising: A slight impression will remain when you press the dough lightly with your fingers. To test batters for rising, touch the batter lightly with finger. If sufficiently risen, the batter should stick to your finger, and air holes should be visible when finger is removed.

13. If the dough or batter has overrisen, it will fall while baking. In this event it is best to prepare the dough or batter all over again, because the yeast has probably died (become inactive).

14. To retard rising, place the dough or batter in an oiled pan or bowl, oil the surface of the dough, cover with a damp cloth and chill until ready to use.

15. The consistency of yeasted batters should be that of thick pancake batter dropping *with difficulty* from a wooden spoon.

16. Glaze yeasted dough before rising, or before, during or after baking (p. 74). If using an egg glaze, it is best to glaze immediately before or during baking to avoid slowing down the rising process.

17. Add dried fruit, crushed nuts, seeds or extra spices to dough after the first rise.

18. Shape dough into desired form before rolling out.

19. *Ready or Not:*
Tap pastry lightly on the bottom. There will be a hollow sound when done.
Pastry will be firm but not hard.
Insert a metal skewer into cakes. Skewer should be dry when removed.
Cake will pull away from the sides of the pan when done.
Cake will spring back when pressed lightly in the center, when done.

20. The sweeter the dough, the more oil it will absorb when deep-frying.

21. Try interchanging unyeasted and yeasted pastry doughs (see Chapter 4).

22. To preserve yeasted cakes or pastries, place a small, damp paper napkin with the yeasted products. Keep container tightly sealed and in a cool place.

Puffy Pastries

<table>
<tr>
<td>

BOW TIES

1 recipe Yeasted Pastry dough I or II
    (pp. 77–78)
  Any fruit purée or Nut Butter Icing
    (pp. 54, 66)
  Nut Filling (p. 69)

Shape dough into rectangle. Roll out dough ¼ inch thick, and cut away uneven edges. Cut into 2 x 5-inch strips. Brush with purée or Nut Butter Icing, and sprinkle Nut Filling over it.

Twist each end of the strip from the center in the opposite direction so that a bow is formed and fillings are face up. Place on an oiled baking sheet. Cover and let rise until almost doubled in size.

Preheat the oven to 350°. Glaze before or after baking (p. 74). Bake 20 to 30 minutes, or until brown.

Pastry or basic strudel dough may be substituted for yeasted dough.

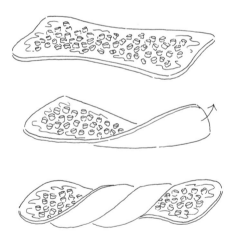

Variation

Cut into strips 2 x 10 inches. Brush with purée or Nut Butter Icing and sprinkle filling on top. Fold strips over lengthwise, making them half as long. Slit the centers. Twist each end of strip in the opposite direction until a bow is formed.

</td>
<td>

SWEET CROISSANTS

Croissants (crescent rolls) were created in Hungary about 1686, to commemorate the withdrawal of the invading Turks. Bakers, working at night, heard the Turks tunneling into the city and sounded the alarm which helped to defeat the Turkish troops. As a reward, the bakers were commissioned to produce a special pastry, shaped like a crescent, which is the emblem of Turkey.

1 recipe Yeasted Pastry dough I or II
    (pp. 77–78)
3 to 4 cups raisin purée (see Fruit Purée,
    p. 66)
1 cup concentrated sweetener
2 cups chopped almonds, walnuts, pecans
    or filberts

Prepare dough. Flour pastry cloth. Shape and roll out dough into circle or rectangle ⅛ inch thick. Cut into triangles.

Place a teaspoon or less of purée on the widest side of the triangle, or spread over the whole triangle. Roll toward the opposite end and shape into crescents.

Oil a large pan or cookie sheet. Place crescents on sheet. Cover and let rise in a warm spot until almost double in size.

Preheat the oven to 350°. Glaze with sweetener before or after baking (p. 74). Bake 25 to 35 minutes, or until browned. Sprinkle nuts on top after baking.

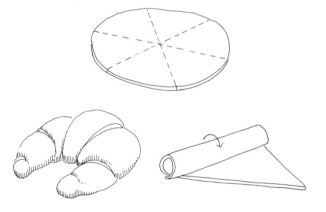

</td>
</tr>
</table>

Variations

Substitute any fruit filling or vegetable filling for raisin purée.

Roll without filling.

Alternate Method for Shaping

Roll out dough into a rectangle ⅛ inch thick. Cut the dough into 3-inch squares. Cut the squares on the bias. Roll out the triangles, beginning with the widest side, and stretch triangles slightly as you roll.

Spread filling over the whole triangle, or place a teaspoon of filling on the widest side. Roll and shape into crescents.

Alternate Method for Baking

Cover and chill 30 minutes.

Bake at 400° 10 minutes, then lower temperature to 350°, and bake about 10 to 15 minutes longer.

CINNAMON ROLLS

4 to 6 cups raisins
   1 recipe Yeasted Pastry dough I or II
      (pp. 77–78)
      Apple butter
      Cinnamon
Topping
   1 cup Tofu Sour Creame (p. 60)
   ¼ cup concentrated sweetener
   1 teaspoon vanilla

Soak raisins in apple juice to cover until soft. Squeeze out excess liquid. Divide the dough in half.

Roll out half of the dough on a *lightly* floured board or pastry cloth to a rectangle about 12 x 16 inches. Brush with oil. Spread apple butter over dough. Sprinkle cinnamon liberally over the apple butter. Cover with raisins. Roll up from the side like a jelly roll (see Basic Sponge Sheet, p. 26). Cut into 1-inch slices and place cut side up on an oiled baking sheet, or in muffin tins.

Repeat procedure with other half of the dough. Cover and let rise in a warm place until almost doubled in size.

Preheat oven to 350°. Bake 15 minutes.

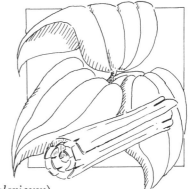

CINNAMON
(*Cinnamomum zeylanicum*)

Cinnamon is mainly used as a spice in flavoring desserts such as pies, cookies, cakes, custards and pastries. It came originally from South India and Ceylon and is cultivated only in warm tropical climates.

Planted as a seed, after two years it is ready to be harvested. The bark is removed in strips. The outer skin of the bark is scraped off, and the strips are dried very slowly. They are pale brown in color and as they dry they curl into each other forming what we know as "cinnamon sticks." There are many different grades of cinnamon, the quality depending upon where it is grown, and the various colors ranging from light to dark brown.

Combine Tofu Sour Creame with sweetener and vanilla. Spoon over the rolls. Bake 10 to 15 minutes longer.

DOUGHNUTS

Doughnuts were traditionally tossed in the air for children to catch on "Fat Tuesday" (Mardi gras), the day before Lent.

   1 recipe Yeasted Pastry dough I or II,
      substituting 2 tablespoons oil for
      ½ cup (pp. 77–78)
   ½ cup orange juice and rind
      Oil for deep-frying (p. 6)
Topping
      Any glaze (pp. 62–64)

Add orange juice and rind to spices in dough. Prepare a soft moist dough, just firm enough to handle. Knead. Cover and chill 15 minutes.

Roll out or pat dough to ½-inch thickness on a floured cloth. Cut with a well-floured doughnut cutter, or cut into rings or strips ½ inch x 4 inches. Twist the strips gently and bring the ends together.

Place on a lightly floured board or well-oiled wax paper, cover with a damp cloth and let rest 20 minutes.

Heat oil. Deep-fry about 3 minutes (1½ minutes on each side) or until lightly browned. Drain, and cool.

Glaze, dip into cinnamon, roasted chestnut flour, grated unsweetened coconut or crushed roasted seeds or nuts.

Suggestions

For more tender doughnuts, have all ingredients at room temperature.

Add dried fruits, nuts, seeds, spices to dough before resting it.

Add a few whole cloves to hot oil before deep-frying for additional flavor.

JELLY DOUGHNUTS

1 recipe Yeasted Pastry (pp. 77–78)
Apple butter, or any purée (p. 66)

Prepare dough. Cut into 3-inch rounds instead of rings.

Place 1 teaspoon apple butter or any purée into the center of one round. Brush the edge of the round with egg white. Place another round on top. Press the edges together. Repeat with the rest of the dough. Cover and set aside 30 minutes on a lightly floured board.

Deep-fry 3 to 5 minutes. Drain.

Follow directions under Doughnuts for glaze and topping.

COCONUT

The coconut, the fruit of the coconut palm (Cocos nucifera), grows in large clusters among giant, featherlike leaves. About 12 new leaves appear each year, and an equal number of compound flower stalks push out from the base of the older leaves. Thirty female flowers and 10,000 male flowers appear on each stalk, maturing at different times, thereby assuring cross-pollination. Flowering begins when the tree is about five years old, and continues thereafter.

Each coconut has a smooth light-colored rind, under which is found a one- or two-inch-thick tough husk of brownish-reddish fibers. The rind and husk surround a brown woody shell that has three soft spots or "eyes" at one end. The rind and husk are usually discarded before the coconuts are shipped to market.

The coconut seed lies inside the shell in the shape of a crisp white ball of coconut meat, surrounded by a tough brown skin. Its hollow center contains a sugary liquid referred to as coconut "milk." The coconut seed is one of the largest of all seeds, measuring 8 to 12 inches long and 6 to 10 inches across, and requiring about 1 year to ripen.

Coconut fruits float easily and have been dispersed widely by ocean currents and also by man throughout the tropics. The native home of the coconut palm is unknown. They flourish best close to the sea on low-lying areas a few feet above water where there is circulating ground water and ample rainfall.

Most of the world's coconuts are produced in the Philippines, Indonesia, India, Ceylon and Malaysia.

OLYKOECKS
(Hudson Valley Doughnuts)

Filling

4 to 6 finely chopped apples
3 tablespoons lemon rind
1½ cups raisins
2 tablespoons cinnamon
Oil for deep frying (p. 6)

Dough

1½ tablespoons dry yeast
¼ cup warm cider or juice
4 cups whole-wheat pastry flour
1 egg
½ teaspoon salt
½ teaspoon cinnamon
½ teaspoon ginger
¼ cup concentrated sweetener
2 tablespoons oil
¾ cup cold mu tea

Chop and core apples (peel if not organic). Add rind, raisins and cinnamon to apples. Mix well. Set aside.

Dilute yeast in warm liquid. Add enough flour to form a thin batter. Cover and set in a warm place to rise until doubled in size.

Beat egg. Add salt, cinnamon and ginger. Set aside.

Punch down dough. Add egg mixture, sweetener, oil and the rest of the flour. Adjust liquid-flour content accordingly. Knead until dough is smooth and elastic (p. 102). Cover and let rise in a warm place until almost double in size.

Punch down. Pinch off a small piece of dough, roll into a ball. Make a depression in the center and place some of the fruit mixture in the center of each ball; cover with dough. Roll into ball. Place on a floured board. Cover, set in a warm place to rest.

Heat oil. Remove doughnuts from board and roll again to make them round. Drop into hot oil and deep-fry about 5 minutes, rotating each ball after first 2½ minutes. Drain.

Dust with chestnut flour, or cinnamon. Serve immediately. Yield: 25 to 30.

Variation

Substitute any fresh fruit in season or any dried fruit for apples.

FANS

1 recipe Yeasted Pastry dough I or II
(pp. 77–78)
Any fruit purée or nut butter
Nut Filling (p. 69)

Prepare dough. Roll out pastry into a square about ⅛ inch thick.

Spread purée or nut butter over square. Dilute butter with a little liquid if difficult to spread. Sprinkle Nut Filling over purée or nut butter.

Cut into strips 1½ inches wide. Stack them in 6 to 8 layers; cut off pieces about 1½ inches wide with a string.

Place pieces in oiled tart forms or muffin tins (cut edges up), to rise until almost doubled in size. Preheat oven to 375°. Bake 15 to 20 minutes.

TWO FINGERS

1 recipe Yeasted Pastry dough I or II
(pp. 77–78)
Any fruit purée or Nut Butter
Icing (p. 54)
Nut Filling (p. 69)

Prepare dough. Shape and roll out into a 6 x 16 x ¼-inch strip.

Spread dough with purée or icing. Sprinkle Nut Filling over it. Fold lengthwise toward the center so that the two folded parts meet in the center. Then fold again to make a long 6-layer roll. Cut into ½ inch slices. Place on a cookie sheet.

Spread the two halves of each slice slightly so

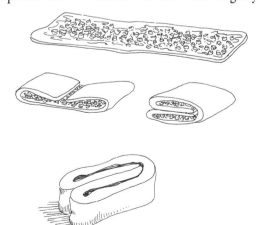

they have room to expand. Cover, and set in a warm place to rise until almost double in size.

Bake at 350° in a preheated oven for about 30 minutes (you may wish to turn the slices over after 20 minutes).

FOUR FINGERS

> 1 recipe Yeasted Pastry dough I or II
>   (pp. 77–78)
>   Any fruit purée (p. 66) or Nut Butter
>   Icing (p. 54)
>   Nut Filling (p. 69)

Prepare dough. Roll out dough into sheet ¼ inch thick. Trim and cut long strips, 6 x 16 x ¼ inches.

Spread fruit purée or Nut Butter Icing over pastry and sprinkle Nut Filling on top.

Fold each strip lengthwise toward the center so that the two folded parts meet in the center. Then fold in half, the opposite way. Fold in half lengthwise again, making a tight strip 1¼ inches wide, composed of 8 layers of dough. Slice into ½ inch slices.

Place on a cookie sheet. Cover. Set in a warm place to rise. Bake 20 minutes. Turn the slices over, and bake 10 minutes longer, or until browned.

Basic pie or tart dough (pp. 76–77) or Strudel Pastry dough (p. 79) may be substituted for Yeasted Pastry dough.

FRUITY BALLS

> 1 recipe Yeasted Pastry dough I or II
>   (pp. 77–78)
> 1 to 2 cups berries, cherries or any fresh fruit
>   ½ cup apple juice or cider
>   Few teaspoons vanilla (optional)
>   Roasted chestnut flour or roasted nuts

Shape dough into balls, and place them in an oiled pan 1 inch apart. Cover and set in warm place to rise until almost doubled in size.

Dice fruit. Combine fruits, juice and vanilla. Spoon small amounts of fruit on top of and in between the balls.

Preheat oven to 375°. Bake 20 minutes covered; remove cover and bake 20 to 30 minutes longer, or until browned. Remove from oven and cool.

Sprinkle roasted chestnut flour or nuts over top just before serving.

Variation

Substitute 2 to 3 cups fruit juice for fruit-and-juice combination.

HAMENTASCHEN

Purim celebrates the victory of the beautiful Queen Esther over the evil Haman. For me, Purim was the most exciting holiday on the Jewish calendar. It meant helping my mother bake the traditional Hamentaschen, poppy seed or prune-filled triangles of pastry, that are said to represent Haman's hat.

> 1 recipe Yeasted Pastry dough I or II
>   (pp. 77–78)
> 2 to 3 cups Poppy Seed Filling (p. 52)

Roll out dough to ¼-inch thickness. Cut into squares about 4 x 4 inches.

Make a depression in the center of each square. Fill with Poppy Seed Filling. Pinch each corner together, leaving about 1½ inches of the filling exposed.

Sprinkle with cinnamon. Place on oiled sheet, cover and set in a warm spot to rise, until pastry has almost doubled in size.

Glaze before or after baking (p. 74). Bake in a preheated 350° oven 30 to 45 minutes, or until browned.

Variations

Substitute Raisin-Prune Filling (p. 53) for Poppy Seed Filling.

Substitute Mincemeat Filling (p. 50) for Poppy Seed Filling.

See Chapter 3 for additional suggestions for fillings.

JOHN IN THE SACK

  2 cups chopped apples or any fresh fruit in
      (pp. 77–78)
  1 cup raisins
  ½ cup chopped walnuts or almonds
  2 teaspoons orange rind
  1 teaspoon cinnamon
  ½ teaspoon salt
  1 recipe Yeasted Pastry dough I or II
      (pp. 77–78)
      Apple juice for boiling pastries

Choose fruit that has little liquid content.* Combine fruit, nuts, spices and salt. Set aside.

Prepare yeasted dough. Roll out dough on a floured pastry cloth. Cut out circles or squares about 3 inches in diameter or 3 x 4 inches.

Place a tablespoon of fruit filling in the center, wrap securely (see illustration). Place on oiled baking sheet. Cover and let rise in a warm place, until almost doubled in size.

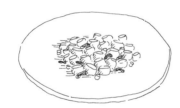

Boil juice. Drop into boiling juice and cook 20 to 30 minutes or until dough has been cooked.

Alternate Methods

Bake at 350° 35 to 45 minutes.

Deep-fry (p. 6) until brown. Drain immediately.

* To remove excess liquid from fruit, cut into small pieces and sprinkle with salt. Toss lightly, allow to sit at least 30 minutes. Pour off excess liquid.

FIRESIDE KUCHEN

  3 cups diced apples or other fruit
  ½ recipe Yeasted Pastry dough I or II
      (pp. 77–78)
  1 egg
  1 teaspoon lemon rind
  ½ cup Crumb Topping (p. 68)

Dice the apples (peel if not organic). (If using dried fruit, first soak fruit in water to cover at least 1 hour. Boil and cook until soft. Squeeze out some liquid and dice. Be sure that the fruit has enough moisture to prevent it from drying up.)

Preheat oven to 325°. Oil an 11 x 16-inch pan or cookie sheet. Roll out dough, and place on sheet or pan. Cover and let dough rise in a warm place until it becomes puffy, but not doubled in size.

Brush with a beaten egg. Arrange diced fruit on top. Combine rind and Crumb Topping, and sprinkle over fruit.

Bake in preheated oven 45 to 60 minutes, or until browned.

Variations

Brush with a layer of apple butter. Sprinkle with chopped roasted nuts or seeds and bake.

Spread with Tofu Custard (p. 62), sprinkle with cinnamon and bake. Serve warm.

TAHINI CHESTNUT KUCHEN

      1 recipe Yeasted Pastry dough (pp. 77–78)
  3 to 4 cups fruit or vegetable purée (pp. 65–66)
  2 to 3 cups Nut Butter Icing I (p. 54)
          Crumb Topping (p. 68)

Prepare dough. Oil an 11 x 16-inch pan or two smaller ones. Roll out dough to ½-inch thickness. Cover dough with purée. Spread icing on top of purée, and cover with Crumb Topping. Cover and let rise in a warm place until almost doubled in size.

Preheat oven to 350°. Bake about 30 to 45 minutes.

Variations

Prune Kuchen
        1 recipe Yeasted Pastry dough (pp. 77–78)
3 to 4 cups Raisin-Prune Filling (p. 53)
3 to 4 cups Nut Filling (p. 69)

Follow directions for Tahini Chestnut Kuchen, substituting Raisin-Prune Filling for purée. Cover with Nut Filling, spread another layer of Raisin-Prune Filling and top with Nut Filling.

Orange-Apple Kuchen
        1 recipe Yeasted Pastry dough
3 to 4 cups Orange-Apple Filling (p. 50)
2 to 3 cups Lemon Glaze (p. 63)
2 to 3 cups Crumb Topping (p. 68)

Follow recipe for Tahini Chestnut Kuchen, substituting Orange-Apple Filling for purée, and Lemon Glaze for Nut Butter Icing.

SAUCERS

    1 recipe Yeasted Pastry dough (pp. 77–78)
3 to 4 cups Chestnut Creme (p. 57)
    1 cup concentrated sweetener
2 to 3 teaspoons cinnamon

Prepare dough. Flour surface and roll out dough ¼ inch thick. Cut out circles 4 to 6 inches in diameter, using a pastry wheel if possible.

Oil a large pan or cookie sheet. Place half of the circles on sheet. Spread with filling, leaving ½ inch all around edges of circle. Using a small knife or razor blade, score remaining circles with arcs radiating from the center of the circle. Place over filling. Press edges to seal in filling.

Cover and set in a warm place to rise until almost double in size. Brush top with concentrated sweetener. Sprinkle cinnamon on top.

Preheat oven to 350°. Bake 45 to 60 minutes or until pastry is browned.

Variations

Add 2 teaspoons orange rind to dough.
Substitute any vegetable or creme filling (Chapter 3) for Chestnut Creme.

Unyeasted pastry dough may be substituted for yeasted dough (pp. 76–77).

SWEET BUNS

1 recipe Yeasted Pastry dough (pp. 77–78)
1 cup soaked raisins
½ cup concentrated sweetener

Follow directions for yeasted dough, adding raisins after first rise. Cut off small pieces of dough and shape.

Place on oiled sheet after shaping, cover and let rise until almost doubled in size.

Preheat oven to 350°. Bake 20 to 30 minutes or until browned. (Tap on bottom and top of bun, and when it sounds hollow, it is done.)

Remove from oven, brush with concentrated sweetener and *chill* immediately.

Variations

Bring apple juice to boil, add 4 tablespoons grain coffee (p. 9). Cool juice to warm before adding yeast. Add 1 teaspoon ginger to dry mixture before adding oil.

Add 1 cup roasted chopped walnuts, almonds or pecans to flour mixture.

Add juice and rind of one grated orange to flour mixture after the first rise.

UPSIDE-DOWN PECAN SWIRLS

    1 recipe Yeasted Pastry dough (pp. 77–78)
3 to 4 cups apricot purée (p. 66)
2 to 3 cups Crumb Topping (p. 68)
    1 teaspoon vanilla
½ to 1 cup sweetener
    Roasted pecan halves

Follow rolling and shaping directions for Cinnamon Rolls (p. 107).

Pour sweetener into oiled forms, baking pan or cupcake tins. Place pecans in forms or pan. Cut dough into 1-inch slices and place over pecans.

Cover, and let rise till almost double in size.

Preheat oven to 350°. Bake 25 to 30 minutes, or until brown.

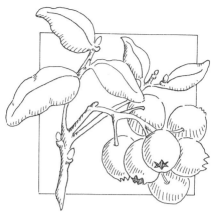

HIGH-BUSH
BLUEBERRY
(*Vaccinium
corymbosum*)

The high-bush blueberry is a native North American plant. The berries are usually eaten in the traditional form of blueberry pie or served in puddings or tarts.

In its native surroundings, it forms a bushy shrub up to 15 feet high, with pointed leaves 1 or 2 inches long, and white or pink flowers. There are about 7 different varieties that are gathered in the wild as well as about 13 cultivated ones.

BLUEBERRY-PEACH TURNOVERS

2 to 3 cups sliced peaches
2 to 3 cups blueberries
   1 teaspoon cinnamon
   1 teaspoon orange rind
  ¼ teaspoon salt
   1 recipe Yeasted Pastry dough (pp. 77–78)

Slice peaches (peel if not organic) and mix them with blueberries, cinnamon, orange rind and salt. Let sit at least 30 minutes. Prepare dough.

Flour a wooden surface or pastry cloth, sprinkling cinnamon over flour. Shape dough into square before rolling. Roll out to ¼-inch thickness. Trim edges. Cut pastry into 4 or 5-inch squares.

Drain excess liquid from fruit mixture. Place a teaspoon of filling in the center of each square. Fold over one corner of the square to make a triangle.

Press dough firmly around edges of pastry with the back or front of a fork. Oil a large pan or cookie sheet. Place pastries on sheet 2 inches apart. Slit each one diagonally twice to allow steam to escape.

Cover and set in a warm place to rise until almost double in size.

Preheat the oven to 350°. Glaze before or after baking (p. 74). Bake about 30 to 40 minutes, or until turnovers are browned.

Unyeasted pastry dough may be substituted for yeasted dough.

TWISTED LEMON RINGS

1 recipe Yeasted Pastry dough (pp. 77–78)
   Juice and rind of 1 grated lemon

Prepare dough; divide into several pieces. Cover with a damp cloth, and chill to retard rising until ready to work with.

Roll out a piece of dough with your hands on a floured cloth; shape into thin logs about 3 inches long. Holding both ends of logs, turn and twist the ends in opposite directions to form a long twist, stretching the dough slightly as you twist. See illustration for Danish Ring (p. 104).

Hold ends, shape into a ring, crossing the ends, and press them firmly together. Press down with thumbs on crossed ends, and flip over the ring to conceal the ends.

Place on an oiled cookie sheet, cover and set in a warm place to rise until doubled in size.

Preheat the oven to 350°. Glaze before or after baking (see p. 74). Bake 10 to 15 minutes or until lightly browned.

Festive Cakes

The most celebrated festival of the ancients occurred at the time of year when the sun was beginning to regain its power. Called "Yule," it was a time of mingled feasting, drinking and dancing, with sacrifices and religious rites for all. Presents were exchanged between masters and slaves, family and friends, all of whom were then considered to be on an equal basis.

At such time of thanksgiving and rejoicing, the kitchen becomes the center of all joy, radiating with restless anticipation as imaginative cooks create festive delicacies. The following recipes are offered to assist you on your way to creating glowing faces, starry songs, bright eyes and happy smiles for all special occasions.

BASIC YEASTED CAKE

This cake can be used in place of Basic Cake I or II for a change in taste and texture.

> 1 tablespoon dry yeast
> 1 to 2 cups apple cider or juice
> 2 cups whole-wheat pastry flour
> ¼ cup oil
> 2 cups soaked raisins
> 2 tablespoons orange, tangerine or lemon rind
> ½ teaspoon salt
> *Topping*
> Orange Glaze (p. 63)

Dissolve yeast in 1 cup warm apple juice or cider. Stir and set aside for a few minutes, until it bubbles. Add enough flour to form a thin batter, beating with a wooden spoon. Cover and set in a warm place to rise until doubled in size.

Combine the rest of the ingredients with the yeasted batter and beat with a wooden spoon for several minutes. The consistency should be that of a thick pancake batter (adjust flour-liquid content accordingly).

Oil an 8-inch cake mold or 2 smaller loaf pans.

Pour batter into pans. Cover and set in a warm place to rise until batter reaches the top of the pan.

Preheat the oven to 350°. Bake about 45 to 50 minutes or until the cake pulls away from the sides of the pan and is springy to the touch.

Prepare Orange Glaze.

Remove cake from oven and set on a rack to cool. After it has completely cooled, remove from pan, place on a rack with a pan underneath the rack to catch the drippings, and spoon topping over cake, letting it drip down the sides (p. 43).

Variations

See variations for Basic Cakes I and II (p. 25).

See cake decorating suggestions (pp. 42–50) for other ways to decorate.

BASIC BABKA I

> 1 recipe Yeasted Pastry dough (pp. 77–78)
>
> *Filling*
> 3 to 4 cups apple butter or raisin purée
> 2 to 3 cups Crumb Topping (p. 68)
> 2 to 3 cups crushed walnuts or almonds

Flour a wooden surface or pastry cloth. Roll out a piece of the dough ¼ inch thick. Spread apple butter or purée over entire surface of dough. Sprinkle Crumb Topping and nuts on top.

Oil tart tins. Cut off a strip of dough (size depends on tins). Fold in half lengthwise. Slit center of strip. Twist ends in opposite directions (one clockwise, one counterclockwise), stretching dough slightly in both directions as you twist.

Place in tins in a spiral motion. Keep adding strips until tins are half filled in height. Cover and place in a warm spot to rise until dough almost doubles in size.

Preheat oven to 350°. Glaze pastries before or after baking (p. 74). Bake 30 to 35 minutes or until brown. Place on cake rack for a few minutes to cool, before turning out.

Alternate Method

When making one large babka in a pan, roll out a larger piece of dough (12 x 4 inches).

Twist dough in opposite directions (counterclockwise and clockwise) about 3 times. Place in a preoiled pan until half filled in height.

Variations

Add 2 to 3 cups soaked diced fruit to dough before shaping.

Fill with any nut butter, in addition to, or in place of, apple butter or purée.

Substitute any dried fruit or fresh fruit purée for raisin purée.

BASIC BABKA II

1½ tablespoons dry yeast
1¼ cups apple juice or cider
3 cups whole-wheat pastry flour
½ cup chestnut flour
2 tablespoons oil
4 tablespoons grain coffee (p. 9)
1 tablespoon orange, tangerine or lemon rind
½ teaspoon salt
1 teaspoon vanilla
4 tablespoons concentrated sweetener
1 cup soaked raisins

Dissolve yeast in warm apple juice or cider. Set aside for a few minutes. Add enough pastry flour to form a thin batter. Cover and let rise in a warm place until double in size.

Add the rest of the ingredients, and beat with a wooden spoon until a sticky dough begins to form (adjust liquid-flour content accordingly). Knead dough on a floured cloth, adding more liquid or flour if necessary until the dough is smooth and elastic.

Oil an 8-inch round or 7-inch loaf pan. Form the dough (see Basic Babka I, p. 114). Do not fold in half. Cover with the same size pan, and let rise in a warm place until double in size.

Preheat the oven to 350°. Glaze before or after baking. Bake 30 to 40 minutes or until cake pulls away from sides of pan. Place upside down on a rack to cool.

Alternate Method

Punch down dough after second rise, place in an oiled bowl, oil the surface and cover. Chill if you do not wish to use immediately (dough can be refrigerated up to three days). Punch it down each time it rises. It will rise very often during the first 2 to 3 hours, and it should be attended to, or it can spoil, and lose its rising power. Remove from the refrigerator several hours before you need it.

Variations

Before serving babka, prepare apple, squash, carrot, peach or any fruit or vegetable purée (pp. 65–66). Spoon over babka just before serving.

Prepare coffee Instant Tofu Creame (p. 59) and spoon over babka before serving.

Prepare Tofu Sour Creame (p. 59) and spoon over babka 10 minutes before removing from oven.

BLUEBERRY-PEACH BABKA

1 recipe Pastry dough (p. 77)
Filling
6 to 8 cups fresh peaches
3 to 4 cups fresh blueberries
2 tablespoons oil
½ teaspoon salt

Blanch peaches (p. 46); cut into thin strips lengthwise. Wash and dry berries. Heat oil in skillet. Sauté peaches about 5 minutes on a low flame uncovered or until some of the liquid has evaporated. Add berries and salt, and cook 2 minutes longer. Remove from heat, and cool. Drain off excess liquid to use for dissolving yeast.

Prepare dough. Knead in fruit mixture, or roll out dough, spread filling over it, and shape (p. 103). Cover and let rise until almost doubled in size. Glaze before or after baking (p. 74). Bake in preheated oven 30 to 45 minutes, or until browned.

Variations

Follow directions for Blueberry-Peach Babka, substituting any one of the following combinations:

Pear-Parsnip   Carrot-Raisin
Apple-Raisin-Walnut   Chestnut-Orange
Apple-Apricot   Fruit-pie variations (p. 93)

BASIC RAISIN CAKE

Use this cake as the base for any special occasion cake, choosing fillings and icings to complement the theme. See Chapter 3 for decorating ideas.

> 5 cups raisins
> 2 teaspoons vanilla
> 2 teaspoons cinnamon
> ½ teaspoon cloves
> 1 tablespoon orange or tangerine rind
> ½ teaspoon salt
> ¼ cup oil
> 3 to 4 cups apple juice, cider, mu or mint tea, or water
> 1½ tablespoons dry yeast
> 6 cups sifted whole-wheat pastry flour

Combine raisins, vanilla, spices, salt, rind and oil in a large mixing bowl. Add enough liquid to cover. Set aside the night before or several hours before using.

Oil an 11 x 16 x 1½-inch cake pan, two 8-inch cake pans or 12 to 15 tart tins. Flour the bottom of forms lightly.

In a separate bowl dissolve yeast in the warm juice or tea. Set aside until it bubbles. Add enough flour to yeast mixture to form a thin batter. Beat for a few minutes. Cover and let rise in a warm place until batter doubles in size.

Blend the raisin mixture until smooth and creamy. When the batter has risen, beat it down with a wooden spoon and combine it with the raisin mixture. Stir for a few minutes until well combined. Add the rest of the sifted flour and salt to the raisin-yeast mixture. Consistency should be that of a thick pancake batter, dropping with difficulty from a wooden spoon; adjust flour-liquid content accordingly.

Fill the form one-half to two-thirds full. Cover with the same size form and let rise in a warm place until batter reaches top of form. Preheat the oven to 350°. Bake 30 to 45 minutes or until the cake is springy to the touch and pulls away from the sides of the pan.

Variations

Substitute 3 cups grated apples for 3 cups raisins.

Add 1 to 2 cups dried chopped fruit (soak before adding) to mixture after blending raisin mixture.

Substitute 3 to 4 tablespoons of any nut butter for oil.

Substitute juice and grated rind of 1 orange, tangerine or lemon for rind.

Add 1 cup chopped roasted nuts or seeds to batter after combining the two mixtures (toss lightly with flour before adding).

Set aside 1½ to 2 cups soaked raisins before blending soaked raisin mixture (squeeze out excess liquid). Toss lightly with flour and add to raisin batter before combining the two mixtures.

Add 2 to 3 teaspoons dried mint, or 1 teaspoon dried ginger, or 4 to 6 tablespoons grain coffee to raisin mixture before soaking.

See Basic Cake variations (pp. 25–26).

BASIC UPSIDE-DOWN CAKE

> 1 tablespoon dry yeast
> 1 to 2 cups apple juice or cider
> 2 cups whole-wheat pastry flour
> 2 tablespoons oil
> 1 teaspoon vanilla
> ½ teaspoon salt
> ¼ cup concentrated sweetener
>
> *Topping*
> 2 tablespoons oil
> 2 apples, sliced and cored (peel if not organic)
> ½ cup roasted chopped almonds or walnuts
> ½ cup raisins or currants
> ½ teaspoon cinnamon
> ¼ teaspoon salt

Topping

Heat oil in a skillet. When oil is hot, sauté apples lightly. Add nuts, raisins or currants, cinnamon and salt. Cook on a low flame for 5 minutes. Set aside.

Cake

Follow directions for mixing Basic Yeast Cake (p. 114).

Preheat oven to 325°. Oil and lightly flour an

8-inch cake pan or 2 small ones. After batter has doubled, add the rest of the ingredients, and beat with a wooden spoon about 10 minutes. The consistency should be that of a thick pancake batter (adjust flour-liquid content accordingly).

Place topping in the oiled cake pan. Pour batter over topping until pan is half full. Cover and let rise in a warm place, until almost double in size.

Bake about 30 to 45 minutes, or until top is slightly browned, and springy to the touch. Remove from oven and place on a rack to cool (if you bake it in a tube pan, see p. 23).

When cool, put a plate on top of cake tin, and turn the plate and pan upside-down together. If cake still sticks to the bottom of pan, run a damp cold sponge over the bottom of the tin, and tap gently in a spiral motion, until cake falls out of pan.

TANGERINE UPSIDE-DOWN CAKE

Basic Upside-Down Cake

Topping
2 cups tangerines
½ cup roasted chopped almonds
½ cup raisins
½ cup cinnamon
¼ teaspoon salt
2 tablespoons oil

Sauté topping ingredients together in 2 tablespoons oil on a low flame for 5 minutes. Substitute tangerine topping for apple topping in basic recipe.

Variations

Substitute 2 pears for apples and ½ cup parsnips for raisins in basic recipe.

See variations for Basic Cake I or II (pp. 25–26).

Combine 2 tablespoons oil and 2 tablespoons concentrated sweetener in a heavy saucepan. Cook on a low flame until mixture boils. Remove from heat and pour into oiled pan. Place fruit slices on top of mixture and sprinkle cinnamon, raisins and nuts over fruit. Pour batter on top of fruit.

MATTHEW'S CHRISTMAS TREE CAKE

5 cups raisins
3 to 4 cups apple juice, cider or any liquid (lukewarm)
1½ tablespoons dried yeast
4 cups whole-wheat pastry flour
2 cups roasted chestnut flour
1½ teaspoons cinnamon
1 teaspoon salt
¼ cup oil
2 teaspoons mint
Grated rind and juice of 1 orange
2 teaspoons vanilla

Topping
2 to 3 cups Instant Tofu Creame (p. 59)
2 to 3 teaspoons beet juice

Decorations
Orange rind
Mint (dried)
Filberts or almonds
Raisins
Sesame seeds

Soak raisins in liquid to cover (spices may be added to liquid), until soft. Set aside. Reserve juice. Blend yeast in 2 cups warm liquid; stir until dissolved. Set aside until yeast begins to bubble.

Combine dry ingredients. Sift them into a mixing bowl. Add reserved juice, oil, mint, rind and juice of orange. Mix well.

Combine dry ingredients with yeast mixture, adding soaked raisins, vanilla and enough liquid to form a thick, pancakelike batter. Beat together for a few minutes.

Oil a rectangular 11 x 16-inch pan. Pour batter into pan, cover with pan of the same size and place in a warm spot to rise until batter reaches the top of the pan.

Preheat the oven to 350°. Bake 30 to 40 minutes or until browned and springy to the touch. Remove from oven, and place on a cake rack to cool.

Variation

Substitute ¼ to ½ cup concentrated sweetener for 5 cups soaked raisins.

Making a Christmas Tree Cake

Cut a 1-inch strip from bottom of cake.

Cut cake diagonally.

Arrange cake. See illustration.

Mark sloping sides into 4 or 5 equal parts, and at each mark cut in about 1 inch.

Cut out diagonally to meet first cut. Set aside small cut-out triangles (use for Petit Fours, p. 27).

Cut 1-inch strip into thirds. Arrange to form trunk of tree. Spread a small amount of Tofu Creame in between slices to hold them together.

See "Before Decorating the Cake" (p. 42). Arrange cake for decorating. Spread a small amount of Tofu Creame in between two triangles, and put them together to form tree.

Attach trunk to tree and ice.

Topping

Prepare Instant Tofu Creame, adding beet juice to half of the Tofu Creame for coloring. Add mint to the other half. Trim the edges of the cake on all four sides before frosting.

Decorating

Spread the Tofu Creame over the entire tree, alternating the colors in four sections.

Place nuts on the tips of the branches, sprinkling orange rind and mint on the edges and the top. Place raisins and nuts on the edges.

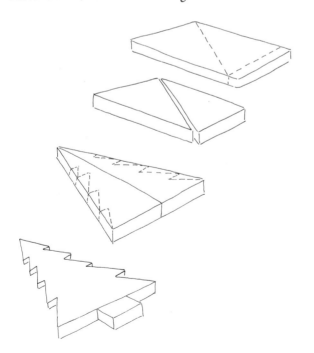

HOLIDAY FEAST

2 recipes Christmas Tree Cake

Custard Filling

2 egg yolks
1 cup hard cider or cider
2 tablespoons concentrated sweetener
3 tablespoons arrowroot flour
¼ teaspoon salt
1½ cups Oat Creame (p. 55)
¼ cup chopped apples or any fresh fruit
1 teaspoon orange rind
Cinnamon to taste
1 teaspoon vanilla

Topping

½ cup dried apricots
Apple juice to cover apricots
2 teaspoons lemon juice

Second Topping

½ cup Oat Creame
1 teaspoon vanilla
½ cup raisin purée

The day before you want to serve this cake, prepare the cake and custard filling. (Custard may be used as a separate custard dessert served warm or cold.)

Custard Filling

In a heavy saucepan or double boiler beat egg yolks, cider, sweetener, arrowroot, salt and Oat Creame together until smooth and creamy. Cook on a medium flame, stirring constantly, until mixture begins to thicken and get smooth. Remove from heat, place in a bowl and cover the top of bowl. Chill. After 1 hour, stir in chopped fruit, orange rind, cinnamon and vanilla. Cover and chill at least another 2 hours before using.

Putting It All Together

Cut each layer of the cake horizontally in half. Place layer on rack and put cookie sheet under rack to catch drippings. Drip hard cider evenly over the layers.

Place layer half on a plate, top side down, putting strips of wax paper on all four corners of the plate before setting down the layer. This enables you to decorate the cake on the same plate that you serve it on (p. 42).

Spread layer with custard filling. Repeat layering and filling, placing each layer top side down, ending with cake layer. Cover cake securely and chill overnight.

Topping

Soak apricots in apple juice or cider to cover until soft. Boil in the same liquid, covered, for 15 minutes. Purée apricots and stir in lemon juice. Set aside to cool. When cool, spread apricot mixture evenly over the top and sides of the cake. Chill about 1 hour or until set.

Second Topping

Blend together Oat Creame, vanilla and raisin purée until smooth and creamy. Frost sides and top of cake with second topping. Decorate cake with crushed nuts, orange or tangerine rind if desired. See Chapter 3, "Inside and Outside," for more decorating ideas.

JOANNE'S CRUMB CAKE

One of the nicest natural-food desserts I have ever seen was sitting on the pastry counter at *Erewhon*, a natural-foods store in Boston. I found out several days later that it was created by my friend Joanne!

    1 tablespoon dry yeast
1 to 2 cups apple juice or cider
  1½ cups whole-wheat pastry flour
    2 eggs
    ½ cup oil
    ¼ cup concentrated sweetener
    ½ teaspoon salt

Topping
1 cup Crumb Topping (p. 68)

Dissolve yeast in 1 cup warm juice or cider. Stir and set aside for a few minutes. Add enough flour to form a thin batter. Beat. Cover and let rise in a warm place until batter doubles in size.

Preheat oven to 350° and oil a 6 x 8-inch pan.

Beat eggs.

Mix in remaining ingredients, beating after each addition.

Add eggs. Mix well. Batter should have a thick pancakelike consistency.

Fill pan ½ full, cover and let rise in a warm place until cake reaches the top of the pan.

Bake about 30 to 40 minutes or until cake is springy to the touch and pulls away from the sides of the pan.

Remove from the oven and place on a rack to cool. After removing cake from the pan, brush the top with concentrated sweetener and sprinkle on topping. Allow to set before serving.

Variations

See variations for Basic Cakes I and II (pp. 25–26).

Use separated egg method (p. 21).

LIBRA DELIGHT

Judy's birthday was the following day and I wanted to bake her a cake, so I used the ingredients that happened to be in the house — and the result was a delightful surprise!

    3 cups raisins
      Apple juice or cider
    2 cups cooked soft rice or oatmeal
    ¼ cup oil
    1 teaspoon vanilla
    4 cups whole-wheat pastry flour
      Grated rind and juice of 1 orange or
      tangerine
    1 teaspoon cinnamon
    ¼ teaspoon cloves
    ½ teaspoon salt
    1 cup roasted chopped almonds
  1½ tablespoons dry yeast

Icing
2 Nut Butter Icings (p. 54)

Soak raisins in apple juice or cider to cover until soft (reserve remaining liquid for batter).

Combine rice or oatmeal, raisins, oil and vanilla. Blend until creamy. Combine all dry ingredients in a mixing bowl (reserve 1 cup flour for yeast mixture). Add blended creame and stir until well combined. Chop almonds and add to the batter. Cover the mixing bowl with a damp cloth, and let sit at room temperature overnight. (This step may be omitted if you do not have the time.)

The following day, dissolve yeast in 1 cup warm reserved juice or cider. Stir. Set aside for a few minutes. Combine yeasted mixture and enough flour to form a thin batter. Cover and let sit in a warm place until double in size. Pour yeast mixture into first mixture and beat for a few minutes with a wooden spoon. The batter should have a thick pancakelike consistency, thick enough to drop from a wooden spoon (adjust flour-liquid content accordingly).

Preheat oven to 350° and oil an 8-inch springform pan. Fill pan half full, cover and set in warm place to rise until batter reaches top of pan. Bake about 45 to 50 minutes, or until cake pulls away from sides of pan and is springy to the touch. Remove from the oven and place on a rack to cool.

See pp. 43–44 for icing techniques.

LIGHT LEMON CAKE

1½ tablespoons dry yeast
1 to 2 cups apple juice or cider
3 cups sifted whole-wheat pastry flour
1 cup arrowroot flour
¼ cup oil
Juice and grated rind of 1 lemon
1 teaspoon vanilla
¼ teaspoon salt

Dilute yeast in 1 cup warm apple juice or cider and let sit for a few minutes.

Add enough pastry flour to form a thin batter. Cover and let rise in a warm place until it doubles in size.

Add the rest of the ingredients and beat well. In consistency it should resemble a thick pancake batter, thick enough to drop from a wooden spoon (adjust flour-liquid content accordingly).

Preheat the oven to 350° and oil a small round or square cake pan. Place batter in pan, cover and let rise in a warm place until batter reaches the top of the pan.

Bake about 30 to 40 minutes, or until cake is springy to the touch and pulls away from the side of the pan. Remove from oven and place on a rack to cool.

Variations

Remove cooled cake from pan. Place it right

LEMON TREE
(*Citrus limonia*)

The lemon tree (Citrus limonia) *is native to southeastern Asia, but it is grown commercially in the countries around the Mediterranean Sea and in southern California. The tree is a small evergreen with spreading branches that give it an irregular shape. It has long, pointed, pale green leaves and large fragrant flowers that usually grow in clusters. The buds tend to be reddish purple, but the flower petals are white.*

side up on a cake rack. Place a cookie sheet or baking pan underneath rack to catch the drippings. Prepare Lemon Glaze (p. 63) and spoon the warm glaze over the top of the cake, letting it drip down the sides. Sprinkle crushed roasted nuts or seeds over top after glazing. Cool before serving.

Follow variations for Basic Cakes I and II (pp. 25–26).

LOTUS FLOWER

John and Diana asked me to prepare their wedding cake. Baking this cake for my dearest friends was one of my greatest pleasures.

2 recipes Raisin Cake (p. 116)
2 to 3 Nut Butter Icing recipes (p. 54)
Beet juice for coloring icing
1 recipe Oat Creame (p. 55)
Lemon rind
4 lemons
¼ teaspoon salt

Preheat the oven to 350°. Oil and lightly flour 4 round cake pans, approximately 8, 7, 6 and 5-inch-size. The layers may be baked in the same-size pans and trimmed down to size after baking. Spoon batter into pans and bake 30 to 45 minutes or until springy to the touch and cake pulls away from the sides of the pan.

This cake may be baked one day in advance and stored tightly sealed in a cool place until ready to use (p. 105, No. 22).

Decorations

Prepare Nut Butter Icing. Tint two thirds of the icing with the beet juice while blending. Prepare Oat Creme, adding lemon rind to taste after cooking.

Cut the peel of 2 lemons into long, thin vertical strips, ⅛ inch thick. Combine 2 cups water and salt in a pot and bring to a boil. Add lemon peel, lower flame, cover and cook until soft. Drain and rinse under cold running water immediately. Grate the rind of the other 2 lemons. Set aside.

Putting It All Together

Trim the sides of the layers and prepare the cake for decorating (p. 42). Place the layers on top of each other to make sure that they decrease in size proportionately. Spread Oat Creme between the layers and place them upside-down on top of each other. If the layers are too thick, cut them in half horizontally and spread Oat Creme between the cut layers first.

Spread a thin layer of untinted Nut Butter Icing over the entire cake. Fill a pastry bag, fitted with a medium-size star tube (p. 47), with tinted icing and decorate around the edge of each layer.

Flower Shaping

Draw a petal, 1 inch smaller than half the width of the top layer, on a heavy piece of paper. Cut it out, and place it on top of the cake, marking the design on the icing in the shape of a 6- or 8-petal lotus. Remove the pattern and place the lemon peel on the lines forming the lotus. Sprinkle the grated lemon rind inside the petal.

Finishing Touches

Holding the pastry bag vertically, finish decorating around the edge of the top layer, and the center of the flower.

Sprinkle coconut between the lotus and the edge

of the cake. Allow the icing to set before serving. Pink icing tends to darken slightly when it is exposed to the air, so do not decorate too far in advance.

M'S SPECIAL

2 cups raisins
1½ tablespoons dry yeast
½ cup apple butter
½ to 1 cup apple juice or cider
2 cups whole-wheat pastry flour
1 cup roasted corn flour
4 diced peaches
1 cup Oat Creme (p. 55)
½ teaspoon salt
4 tablespoons tahini
1 tablespoon vanilla
1 teaspoon orange rind

Topping
Mint Glaze (p. 63)

Soak only 1 cup raisins in liquid to cover until soft. Set aside. Oil and lightly flour an 8-inch springform pan.

Dissolve yeast in apple butter and ½ cup warm apple juice or cider. Set aside for a few minutes until it bubbles. Add enough flour to form a thin batter. Cover and let rise in a warm place until double in size.

Dice peaches (peel if not organic) and combine with soaked raisins. (Squeeze out excess liquid, reserve for batter.) Toss lightly in flour. Set aside. Blend Oat Creme, unsoaked raisins, salt, tahini, vanilla, orange rind and extra liquid if necessary until mixture is smooth and creamy.

When batter has risen, beat down, add diced peaches, soaked raisins and the rest of the flour. Beat with a wooden spoon for a few minutes. Consistency should be that of a thick pancake batter (adjust flour-liquid content accordingly).

Pour batter into cakepan, cover and let rise in a warm place until batter reaches the top of the pan.

Preheat the oven to 350°. Bake 45 to 60 minutes, or until cake pulls away from the sides of the pan and is springy to the touch. Remove cake from oven and place on a rack to cool. After a few minutes turn cake upside-down on rack until completely cool. Prepare Mint Glaze and spoon over the cake before serving.

Variation

Substitute pears and/or parsnips, strawberries, blueberries or any fresh fruit or vegetable-fruit combination in season for peaches.

SOUTH AMERICAN FIESTA

Before a friend of mine left for South America, a group of us got together for dinner, and shared this cake for dessert.

　4 cups soaked raisins
　1 cup dried chestnuts
　2 cups sifted whole-wheat pastry flour
　4 cups sifted chestnut flour
　½ cup oil
　1 tablespoon orange or tangerine rind
　1 tablespoon vanilla
　1 tablespoon cinnamon
　1 teaspoon salt
　2 grated apples
　1½ tablespoons dry yeast
　4 to 5 cups apple cider or juice

Center Layer
　2 bars kanten
　5 cups apple juice or cider
　½ cup Chestnut Purée (p. 66)

Topping
　5 to 6 tablespoons tahini
　2 to 3 cups raisin purée
　½ cup cooked chestnuts (p. 66)
　1 teaspoon vanilla
　½ teaspoon salt

Soak raisins in water to cover until soft (reserve liquid). Soak chestnuts overnight in water to cover. Bring to a boil and simmer on a low flame until soft.

Roast the pastry flour in 2 tablespoons oil until it begins to brown lightly. Set aside to cool. Roast the chestnut flour in 4 tablespoons oil until it begins to smell sweet. Set aside to cool.

Blend together raisins, soaking liquid, remaining oil, rind, vanilla, cinnamon and salt, until smooth and creamy. Core and grate apples (peel if not organic). Set aside. Dissolve yeast in 1 cup warm apple juice or cider. Let sit for a few minutes, until

it bubbles. Combine yeasted mixture with raisin blend. Stir well. Gradually add sifted flours, juice or cider, and grated apples to the raisin-yeast mixture. Beat with a wooden spoon until the batter has a thick pancakelike consistency (adjust flour-liquid content accordingly).

Oil an 11 x 17-inch baking pan or two small ones. Pour batter into pan. Cover and set in a warm place to rise until the batter reaches the top of the pan.

Preheat the oven to 350°. Bake 35 to 45 minutes, or until cake is springy to the touch and pulls away from the sides of the pan. Remove from the oven and set on a rack to cool.

Center Layer

Rinse kanten under cold running water. Squeeze out excess liquid. Shred into apple juice or cider and cook on a medium flame, stirring occasionally until mixture boils. Reduce heat, add blended chestnuts and cook 5 minutes longer. Rinse a baking pan (the same size as the cake pan) with cold water. Oil well and pour kanten into pan. Allow to cool at room temperature. Chill if not using immediately.

Topping

Blend all topping ingredients until creamy and thick.

Decorating

See "Before Decorating the Cake" (pp. 42–43). Before decorating, trace or draw a picture of the country or continent desired (I used South America). Place the outline on top of the layers and mark. Cut cake out into shape, or outline with contrasting-color nuts, seeds or rind after icing.

SWEET AVELINE

It was just the beginning of Pisces, and Aveline's birthday. I thought it would be appropriate to make the symbol of Pisces — two fish — to decorate the cake.

> 3 recipes (10 cups) Chestnut Creame II
>   (p. 58)
> 2 Basic Raisin Cakes (p. 116)
> 2 cups Nut Butter Icing I (p. 54)
> *Inlay*
> Pine nuts
> Orange rind
> Lemon, tangerine or orange skins
> Raisins
> Mint

Prepare cake one day in advance. Wrap securely in paper and set in a cool place to mellow. (This cake improves with age.)

Prepare Chestnut Creame.

Oil an 11 x 16-inch baking sheet very well. Lay down design. (See "Inlay," p. 49.)

Outline of the fish — pine nuts

Scales — small pieces of orange skin and rind

Tail — thin strips of lemon skin

Mouth — thin strip of lemon skin

Eye — raisin

String attaching two fish — mint

Spoon Chestnut Creame over the design carefully, covering the entire pan evenly. Allow to cool at room temperature overnight.

Prepare Nut Butter Icing. Chill before using.

Putting It All Together

See "Inlay."

Place Nut Butter Icing in pastry bag and decorate around the edges before serving (p. 47–48).

FRUIT STOLLEN

I baked four of these for a Christmas dinner, and never even tasted a crumb.

> 1 cup mixed dried fruit
> ¼ cup raisins
> 1 cup warm apple juice or cider
> 1½ tablespoons dry yeast
> ¼ cup concentrated sweetener
> 3½ cups whole-wheat pastry flour
> ½ cup oil
> ½ cup pecans or other chopped nuts
> 1 teaspoon cinnamon
> ½ teaspoon salt

Soak dried fruit and raisins overnight in apple juice or cider to cover. Squeeze out liquid and dice (set aside liquid for batter).

Dissolve yeast in warm fruit juice. Combine with sweetener.

Add enough flour to form a thin batter. Cover and let rise in a warm spot until doubled in size. Add rest of flour to form a soft dough. Adjust flour-liquid content accordingly. Place in oiled bowl, cover and let rise in a warm place until doubled in size.

Knead in other ingredients — about 5 to 10 minutes. Punch down, and roll into an oval about 12 x 8 inches. Fold over lengthwise, and place on an oiled sheet.

Preheat oven to 400°. Glaze before or after baking. Bake 10 minutes, turn down to 350°, and bake 25 to 30 minutes longer. Remove from oven and place on a rack to cool.

6. Little Nibbles

Cookies and Bars

Fill the cookie jar with a variety of shapes that complement each other in texture and flavor. You may want to experiment using various-shaped cookie cutters, natural colorings, flavorings and techniques as well as combining different flours to make rolled, chewy, nut, drop, icebox cookies or bars. If so, see the information on flour (p. 8). It is always a good idea to sample the cookie batter or dough before baking, and adjust the seasoning to taste.

Bake extra-special cookies for the holidays, and keep the jar filled with tasty treats all year round, satisfying everyone's sweet tooth.

Shades of Things to Come

BULL'S EYE

Prepare two doughs, one plain, one dark (add grain coffee or raisin purée for dark color). Form a quarter of the dark dough into a log 1 inch thick and 6 inches long. Wrap in wax paper and chill 2 hours.

Roll three quarters of the plain dough into a 4 x

6-inch rectangle, ¼ inch thick. Brush with warm Oat Creame (p. 55), and roll around dark dough. Reverse with the remaining dough. Wrap in paper and chill at least 2 hours.

Slice into ½-inch pieces and bake at 350° 12 to 15 minutes.

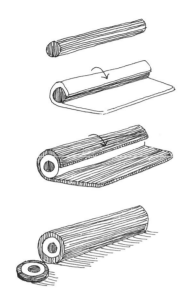

HALF AND HALF

Prepare two logs, one plain, one dark (see Bull's Eye, above). Wrap in wax paper and chill overnight.

Cut lengthwise through the center of each log. Brush cut surfaces with Oat Creame (p. 55) and press together, the plain against the dark. Wrap in wax paper and chill at least 2 hours.

Slice ¼ to ½ inch thick and bake at 350° 12 to 15 minutes (see Rolled Cookies I, p. 128).

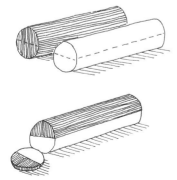

CRISSCROSS

Prepare Half and Half cookie logs. Cut lengthwise through the center. Brush cut surfaces with Oat Creame (p. 55). Turn one of the halves around and place it end to end with the other half. Press together. Wrap and chill at least 2 hours.

Slice ¼ to ½ inch thick and bake at 350° 12 to 15 minutes (see Rolled Cookies, p. 128).

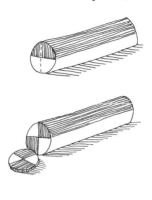

MARBLE EFFECT

Prepare a few logs of different colors. Wrap and chill. Take off small pieces from each log, and roll them out together in one large circle. Cut with cookie cutter.

Or, combine a few pieces from each color dough, shape into one log, wrap and chill at least 4 hours. Slice into ¼-inch cookies. Place on an unoiled sheet, and bake at 375° 10 to 12 minutes.

PINWHEELS

1½ cups whole-wheat pastry flour
1½ cups chestnut, sweet brown rice or
        brown rice flour
  1 tablespoon orange rind or mint
  ½ teaspoon salt
  ½ cup oil
  ¼ cup concentrated sweetener
  3 teaspoons vanilla
  1 egg (optional)
     Apple juice or cider if necessary
¾ to 1 cup grain coffee*

* 1 teaspoon cloves plus ¾ cup flour may be substituted for grain coffee.

Combine dry ingredients, except grain coffee. Cut oil in until mixture resembles tiny bread crumbs. Add sweetener, vanilla and beaten egg. Mix with a wooden spoon, adding apple juice if needed to form dough.

Divide mixture in half. Add grain coffee to one half. Add juice or cider to each mixture until 2 doughs are formed. Wrap in wax paper separately and chill at least 60 minutes.

Roll out light dough into a large rectangle between two sheets of wax paper (see p. 71). Roll dark rectangle the same way. Remove wax paper, and place dark dough on light dough. Roll up like a jelly roll. Wrap in wax paper, sealing the ends well. Chill overnight.

Preheat oven to 350°. Slice ½-inch thick. Bake 10 to 12 minutes, or until lightly browned.

Variation

Substitute ingredients for Rolled Cookies (p. 128). Follow directions for Pinwheels.

PLAINLY SIMPLE RAINBOWS

One Thanksgiving I was invited to a friend's house for dinner. I baked an assortment of cookies (Half and Half, Crisscross and Rainbows), placed them individually in a cookie box and gave them to the lady of the house.

> 2 cups whole-wheat pastry flour
> 1 cup chestnut flour
> 1 teaspoon salt
> ½ cup oil
> 2 teaspoons vanilla
> ¼ cup beet juice
> ¼ cup carrot purée
> ¼ cup squash purée
> ¼ cup raisin purée

Sift flour. Place flour and salt in a mixing bowl. Cut oil into flour mixture until it looks like tiny bread crumbs. Add vanilla. Divide mixture into 4 equal portions and place in separate mixing bowls.

Add one purée or juice to each bowl, mixing with a wooden spoon until a ball of dough begins to form (add apple juice or cider if the mixture is too dry).

Roll out each piece of dough between 2 sheets of wax paper into a rectangle. Chill at least 2 hours.

Cut each piece of dough in half lengthwise, cutting through the wax paper. Peel off the top sheets. Brush the top of one strip with Oat Creame (p. 55). Place another strip, paper side up, on top. Peel off paper. Repeat procedure with the remaining dough strips, alternating colors, to make 8 layers. Press lightly together. Cut stack lengthwise to make 2 narrow stacks. Wrap in wax paper and chill at least 60 minutes.

Preheat the oven to 350°. Cut dough into 1-inch slices. Bake 10 to 15 minutes, or until browned.

Variations

Substitute roasted chestnut flour for unroasted chestnut flour in the dark raisin-purée log. Raisin purée may be omitted here and apple juice or cider may be used instead. DO NOT COMBINE WITH OTHER FLOUR. PREPARE SEPARATELY.

Use any fruit or vegetable or juice of any fruit for coloring.

Color Variations

Add carrot or squash purée for orange or yellow color (¼ to ½ cup). Decrease liquid content accordingly. Add beet juice for rose color (p. 7). Decrease liquid content accordingly. For brown, substitute roasted, sifted chestnut flour (allow to cool before using) for brown rice flour, or add a few tablespoons grain coffee (p. 9) or about ¼ cup raisin purée.

FORGET ME KNOTS

1. The amount of liquid necessary for each recipe will differ each time, according to the moisture in the flour and the room, the size of eggs and the general weather of the day.

2. Always preheat the oven.

3. Use unrefined corn-germ or corn oil for light, flaky cookies.

4. In making any kind of cookie, never beat or knead the dough after the flour has been added or the cookies may be tough. Eggs used in dough should be at room temperature.

5. Do not roll dough in excessive amounts of flour. Roll out cookie dough on a lightly floured board, or between 2 sheets of wax paper, which are placed on a lightly floured board. This technique usually produces more tender cookies (p. 71).

6. Keep the dough chilled until you roll it.

7. Dust cookie cutters with flour, cinnamon or chestnut flour before using them. Use glasses, bowls, cups, etc., for unusual designs.

8. Usually, cookie sheets do not have to be oiled, unless specified.

9. Cookie sheets may be oiled with beeswax or used deep-frying oil in place of corn or sesame oil.

10. Use a flat baking sheet or the bottom of a reversed baking pan for best results, so that the heat can circulate directly and evenly over the cookie tops.

11. Dark cookie sheets absorb heat, and cookies may brown more on the bottom. Good cookie sheets have shiny baking surfaces, and specially dulled bottoms to produce more even browning.

12. A pan with high sides will deflect the heat, and make the cookies difficult to remove after baking.

13. A baking or cookie sheet should be at least 2 inches shorter and narrower than the oven rack, so that the air can circulate around it.

14. Cookie sheets should always be cold when you put the cookies on them so cookies will not lose their shape.

15. Transfer rolled or molded cookies from rolling surface to cookie sheet with a spatula.

16. Drop cookies tend to spread more than other cookies, so leave 2 inches between them. Try to make them the same size, so they will be done at the same time.

17. Watch cookies carefully, because ovens tend to overheat. The later batches tend to cook more quickly.

18. When a cookie sheet is partially filled, the heat is drawn to the area where the cookies lie, and the cookies may burn on the bottom before they are baked. If there is not enough batter or dough to fill a cookie sheet, use a reversed pie pan or small baking tin instead.

19. When baking cookies, place sheet on only 1 rack. If 2 racks are used, the heat circulates unevenly so that the bottoms of the cookies on the lower rack and the tops of the cookies on the upper rack brown too quickly.

20. During baking, turn the cookie sheets around for a more even baking.

21. After baking, remove cookies from the sheet immediately, or they will continue to cook.

22. Always cool cookies on a rack, not overlapping.

23. When deep-frying cookies, seeds and nuts have a tendency to separate from the batter or dough unless finely ground.

24. DO NOT STORE CRISP AND SOFT COOKIES TOGETHER.

25. Store crisp cookies in a jar with a loose-fitting cover in a cool place. If they soften, put them in a slow oven for five minutes before serving.

26. Keep soft cookies moist by storing them in a cool place in a covered jar. If cookies tend to dry out, put a piece of bread, an apple, an orange or a clove-studded lemon in the jar with them to help maintain the moisture.

Rolled Cookies

Holiday cookies usually take a shape associated with the occasion being celebrated: Christmas trees for Christmas, rabbits for Easter, hearts for Valentine's Day. By using special cookie cutters to form such shapes as these, any holiday cookies can be made.

The trick to making successful cookies is simple. The dough must not be too soft. Excess flour must not be added. Too much flour can make the cookie too tough to eat.

Divide large amounts of dough into a few pieces.

Cookie doughs that contain neither sweeteners nor eggs may be less firm than sweetened dough. Wrap and chill overnight, and roll out dough on a cloth, lightly dusted with arrowroot flour, making it firmer and easier to handle. Substituting chestnut flour for half of the whole-wheat pastry flour will also produce a firmer, as well as sweeter, dough.

Cookie dough that contains sweeteners should be chilled 1 to 2 hours. Extra-long chilling can make this dough too firm, and difficult to roll out (cookie dough that contains both sweeteners and eggs can be chilled longer). If dough becomes too firm, unwrap and let sit at room temperature until easier to work with (about 1 hour).

Roll out on a floured cloth or between 2 sheets of wax paper (see p. 71). Cut out cookie shapes as close to each other as possible. Flour cookie cutters only if the dough is soft and sticky.

If the dough is not too floury, reroll and use the scraps.

ROLLED COOKIES I

½ cup cold oil
1 teaspoon vanilla
¼ cup concentrated sweetener
¾ to 1 cup cold liquid
¾ teaspoon salt
1 teaspoon cinnamon
¾ teaspoon dry ginger
1 cup brown rice flour
2 cups whole-wheat pastry flour
1 egg (for glazing)

Mix together oil, vanilla, sweetener and liquid, and stir until smooth. Sift dry ingredients together and add the liquid mixture, mixing with a wooden spoon until a ball of dough begins to form. Divide into 3 pieces. Cover and chill at least 60 minutes before rolling. While shaping, keep unused dough covered with a damp cloth until ready to use.

Preheat oven to 375°.

Roll out dough to ¼-inch thickness (p. 71). Cut the cookies with any shape cutters, brush with beaten egg and sprinkle with one of the following: chopped nuts, cinnamon, poppy seeds or chestnut flour. Place cookies on a sheet and bake 10 to 15 minutes, or until crisp. Place on a rack to cool.

If dough becomes too soft and warm after cutting, cover sheet and chill about 30 minutes before baking; this will make the cookies more crisp.

ROLLED COOKIES II

Ingredients for Rolled Cookies I,
omitting sweetener

Follow recipe for Rolled Cookies I. Wrap dough, chill overnight. Roll out, cut and bake.

Alternate Method

Follow directions for Rolled Cookies. Experiment by shaping the dough into different forms—logs, squares, balls, etc.

Heat oil in a deep skillet (p. 6). Deep-fry cookies, until lightly browned. Drain on paper towels or paper bags before serving.

Variations for Rolled Cookies

Lemon-Walnut Cookies

Add grated rind, juice of ½ lemon and ½ cup crushed walnuts to dry ingredients.

Orange-Almond Cookies

Add grated rind and juice of ½ orange and ½ cup crushed almonds.

Poppy Seed-Lemon Cookies

Add 1 cup poppy seeds to mixing bowl before

adding flour. Add grated rind and juice of ½ lemon to liquid mixture.

Lemon-Walnut Mint Cookies

Follow directions for Lemon-Walnut Cookies, adding 2 to 3 teaspoons mint to dry mixture before combining with liquid.

Mint-Walnut Cookies

Follow directions for Rolled Cookies. Add 1 teaspoon mint to dry ingredients, and press in crushed walnuts.

Sweet Orange-Mint Cookies

Follow directions for Rolled Cookies, substituting 1 tablespoon mint for ginger, and adding orange rind to taste to dry ingredients.

Sesame-Mint Cookies

Add 1 tablespoon mint and ½ cup roasted sesame seeds to oil mixture before adding dry ingredients.

Sweet Mint Drops

Substitute 1 tablespoon mint for ginger, and add enough apple juice or cider to form a stiff batter. Drop onto cookie sheet, and bake 10 to 15 minutes, or until brown.

Wafers

Dip a piece of cheesecloth in water, wring it out and wrap it around the bottom of a glass. Tie it securely and press into any cookie dough.

ANIMAL CRACKERS

      2 cups whole-wheat pastry flour
      ½ teaspoon salt
      3 tablespoons oil
      1 teaspoon cinnamon
      2 tablespoons concentrated sweetener
      1 tablespoon lemon juice
        Apple juice, cider, mu or mint tea
        Oil for deep-frying (p. 6)

Combine flour and salt in a mixing bowl. Add oil and cut into flour until mixture looks like bread crumbs. Add cinnamon, sweetener and lemon juice. Stir lightly with a wooden spoon. Add liquid slowly until a soft dough is formed (adjust liquid-flour content accordingly). Wrap in wax paper and chill 1 hour.

Heat oil. Roll out dough to ¼-inch thickness

(p. 71). Cut into animal shapes with cookie cutters.

Deep-fry until lightly browned. Dip into roasted chestnut flour or cinnamon immediately after frying. Drain.

Variations

Add 2 teaspoons dry ginger before adding liquid.

Add 2 teaspoons orange rind and substitute orange juice for lemon juice.

Add 2 teaspoons vanilla to pastry, before adding liquid.

Add a few cloves to the oil, before deep-frying.

See variations for Rolled Cookies (p. 128).

COOKIE CANES

. . . a nice thing to see hanging on the Christmas tree . . .

      2 cups sifted whole-wheat pastry
        flour *plus*
      1 cup roasted chestnut flour
        or
      1 recipe Yeasted Pastry dough (p. 77)
      ½ teaspoon salt
      2 teaspoons mint
      2 tablespoons concentrated sweetener
      2 teaspoons vanilla
      ½ cup oil
      1 egg (optional)
  ¼ to ½ cup beet juice
        Apple juice or cider to form dough

Sift flour. Add salt and mint, and place in a mixing bowl.

Combine sweetener, vanilla and oil together. Beat in egg if desired.

Place half of dry mixture in another bowl; tint half with beet juice, leave the other half plain. Add juice or cider to each mixture with a wooden spoon until a soft dough is formed. Adjust flour-liquid content accordingly.

Pinch off a piece of dough from each mixture. Roll each piece of dough separately with your hands into a thin strip about 6 inches long. Place strips side by side, pressing ends together; twist. Place on unoiled cookie sheets, about 1 inch apart, bending the tops of the twists into a cane shape.

Preheat the oven to 350°, and bake about 10 to 15 minutes, or until firm and lightly brown. Glaze with concentrated sweetener immediately after baking. For yeasted dough, after shaping, cover and let rise until double in size.

DIAMONDS

¼ cup concentrated sweetener
¼ cup oil
    Juice and rind of ½ lemon
    Juice and rind of ½ orange
1 cup slivered almonds
1 tablespoon cinnamon
1 teaspoon cloves
½ teaspoon salt
1½ cups sifted whole-wheat pastry flour
½ cup sifted, roasted chestnut flour
    Apple juice or cider to form dough

Place sweetener and oil together in a mixing bowl, beating with a wooden spoon or wire whisk until well combined. Mix in rinds, juices and almonds.

Sift dry ingredients. Combine with sweetener-oil mixture. Add enough apple juice to form dough. Shape into rectangle. Roll out to ½-inch thickness (see p. 71). Place sheet of wax or brown paper in 10 x 15-inch baking sheet. Oil sheet and place dough on sheet. Cut halfway into dough, forming diamonds.

Preheat oven to 325°. Bake 20 to 25 minutes, or until crisp and browned. Remove from pan, and place upside-down on rack. Peel off wax paper. Cool. Cut or break diamonds apart.

Glaze with concentrated sweetener or oil.

Variations

Substitute Yeasted Pastry (p. 77) for whole-wheat pastry flour and chestnut flour.

See variations for Rolled Cookies (p. 128).

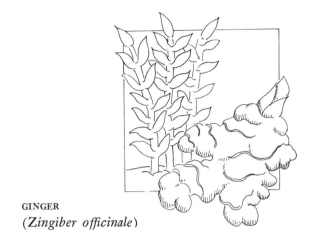

GINGER
(*Zingiber officinale*)

Ginger is a tropical plant, native to Asia, where it has been cultivated since ancient times. The roots, or rhizomes, *are dug up when the plant is about 10 months old.*

The Chinese traditionally use ginger as an external remedy for cataracts, to cure dyspepsia or settle a nauseous stomach; also as a tonic to strengthen the heart, and as a sedative.

Dried ginger is made by a complicated process of washing, soaking or boiling, peeling and drying. Fresh, unprocessed ginger is also available.

Ginger is grown throughout the tropics for local consumption, and is exported from West Africa, Jamaica and India. It is widely used all over the world for its pungent flavor, and is a major ingredient in curry powders. Ginger root or powder is also used in making ginger beer and gingerbread.

Dried ginger is very concentrated, and should be used sparingly in all baking.

GINGER COOKIES

1 recipe for Rolled Cookies (p. 128)

Substitute 1 tablespoon dry ginger for ½ teaspoon.

Roll dough into logs 1½ to 2 inches in diameter. Wrap in wax paper, cover with foil and chill overnight.

Preheat oven to 350°.

Slice into ¼-inch cookies, and bake on an unoiled sheet at 350° for 8 to 12 minutes, or until lightly browned. Remove from sheet immediately, and place on rack to cool.

GOLDEN NUGGETS

3 tablespoons concentrated sweetener
2 tablespoons oil
2 tablespoons lemon juice
2 cups whole-wheat pastry flour
½ teaspoon salt
  Apple juice or cider to form dough
  Oil for deep-frying (p. 6)

Combine sweetener, oil and lemon juice. Stir well.

Place flour and salt in a mixing bowl, add liquid mixture and add juice slowly until dough is formed. Roll out dough, and shape into nuggets.

Heat oil. Deep-fry until lightly browned. Drain well. Roll in cinnamon or roasted chestnut flour while still warm.

Alternate Method

Roll dough into log, wrap in wax paper and chill at least 60 minutes. Remove from refrigerator, cut into ¼-inch pieces and bake at 350° 8 to 10 minutes or deep-fry.

Variation

Add 2 teaspoons mint or any flavoring to dry ingredients before adding liquid.

JOE FROGGERS

Joe Froggers is the name of a cookie that the fishermen of Marblehead took with them on their long trips. These big, fat cookies are named after the big, fat frogs that sit on top of lily pads in New England ponds.

4 cups whole-wheat pastry flour
2 cups chestnut flour, brown rice or sweet brown rice flour
1 cup corn flour
1 tablespoon cinnamon
½ to 1 teaspoon ginger
1 teaspoon cloves
1 teaspoon salt
¾ cup oil
½ cup concentrated sweetener
1 tablespoon vanilla
½ cup grain coffee
1 to 2 cups apple juice or cider

Combine all dry ingredients in a mixing bowl. Set aside. Combine all liquid ingredients. Mix well with a wire whisk.

Sift dry ingredients, add liquid until a soft dough is formed (adjust liquid-flour content accordingly). Wrap in wax paper and chill overnight.

Roll out ½ inch thick. Cut cookies with a 4-inch cookie cutter.

Preheat oven to 375°. Oil cookie sheets. Place cookies on sheets, and bake 12 to 15 minutes, or until crisp and browned.

Alternate Method

Roll into a log or two. Wrap and chill overnight. Slice off into ¼-inch cookies and bake at 375° 10 to 12 minutes or until brown.

CHRISTMAS FEATHERS

1 cup sifted chestnut flour
¾ cup oil
¼ cup concentrated sweetener
1 teaspoon vanilla
3 eggs
¾ teaspoon salt
3 cups sifted whole-wheat pastry flour
1 teaspoon cinnamon

Roast chestnut flour in ¼ cup oil until lightly browned. Set aside to cool.

Combine remaining oil with sweetener and vanilla. Add eggs and beat well.

Sift together salt, both flours and cinnamon. Add dry ingredients to egg mixture. Mix well until soft dough is formed (adjust flour-liquid content accordingly). Cover and chill at least 30 minutes.

Preheat the oven to 350°. Oil cookie sheet. Roll out the dough to ¼-inch thickness (see p. 71). Cut out cookies with a cookie cutter. Bake 15 to 20 minutes or until the bottom is brown. Place on rack to cool.

Variations

Add 2 tablespoons grain coffee to eggs before beating. Press centers of cookies with your thumbs. Place apple butter in the center of each cookie before baking.

Substitute 1 cup brown rice flour for chestnut flour.

SANDWICH COOKIES I

1 recipe Rolled Cookies (p. 128)
2 to 3 cups filling (see Chapter 3)

Cut out the dough with a 3 to 4-inch round cookie cutter.

With a slightly smaller cutter (1 to 2-inch), cut out the centers of half of the cookies (use the small rounds from the centers as extra cookies or reroll).

Place cookies on a sheet, and bake at 375° 10 to 15 minutes, or until cookies are crisp. Place on rack to cool. When cookies have cooled, sandwich them together with any purée or creame, placing the ring-shaped cookie on top.

SANDWICH COOKIES II

1 recipe Rolled Cookies (p. 128)
Filling
2 tablespoons whole-wheat pastry flour
1 cup raisin purée
1 tablespoon lemon juice

Prepare dough. Wrap and chill at least 60 minutes.

Prepare purée. Combine flour and purée. Cook, constantly stirring, until mixture boils and thickens. Add lemon juice. Cool.

Roll out dough to ⅛-inch thickness (p. 71). Cut with any shape cookie cutter. Spread purée between 2 thinly rolled cookies.

Bake 15 to 20 minutes, or until lightly browned.

Variations

Follow directions for sandwich cookies, substituting any filling for raisin purée.

Suggestions

Squash and Beets	Yam Purée
Carrot-Raisin	Peach-Blueberry
Apricot Purée	Tahini-Raisin
Applesauce	Chestnut Creame
Vanilla Oat Creame	

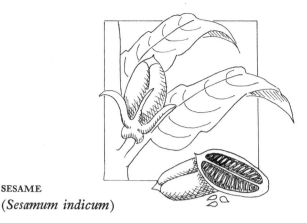

SESAME
(*Sesamum indicum*)

The sesame was originally from Africa, although today it is grown in Mexico, California and tropical and subtropical climates.

The plant grows up to 6 feet high, taking three to five months to mature. There are many flowers in different varieties such as white, pink or mauve. When harvested, the whole plants are cut and stacked upright to dry. As they dry, the seed capsules split open and the plants are usually turned upside-down and shaken out onto a cloth. These seeds contain 45 to 50 percent oil, which is used in various ways in desserts. Seeds can be used for nut butters and for decoration in cooking and baking.

SESAME SEED COOKIES

½ cup chestnut flour
2 tablespoons plus ½ cup cold oil
2 tablespoons tahini or sesame butter
½ to 1 cup cold apple juice or cider
1 teaspoon cinnamon
1 teaspoon vanilla
1½ cups whole-wheat pastry flour
½ teaspoon salt
1 cup rolled oats
½ to 1 cup roasted sesame seeds

Roast chestnut flour in 2 tablespoons oil, until it begins to smell sweet. Set aside to cool; sift.

Combine remaining oil, tahini or sesame butter, juice or cider, cinnamon and vanilla, and blend until creamy. Combine flour, salt, oats and seeds. Gradually begin to add blended liquid to dry mixture, stirring constantly until a ball of dough forms (adjust liquid-flour content accordingly).

Divide dough into small sections. Wrap in wax paper and chill at least 60 minutes.

Preheat oven to 400°, oil cookie sheets. Roll out dough to ¼-inch thickness (see p. 71). Cut out cookies with any shape or size cookie cutter. If dough becomes warm, cover and chill cookies 15 to 30 minutes before baking.

Bake 10 to 15 minutes (depending on size) or until cookie is slightly browned and crispy. Remove from pan immediately, and place on rack to cool.

Alternate Method

Heat oil for deep-frying (see p. 6). Deep-fry until golden brown. Drain well before serving.

Some seeds may not deep-fry well, so they can be omitted.

Variations

Substitute sunflower seeds for sesame seeds. Add ½ teaspoon ginger to spices.

Substitute ½ cup poppy seeds for sesame seeds.

Substitute ½ to 1 cup ground walnuts for sesame seeds. Add ½ cup soaked raisins.

See variations for Rolled Cookies (p. 128).

SWEET MINT COOKIES

¼ to ½ cup apple juice or cider
2 tablespoons almond butter
¼ cup concentrated sweetener
1 teaspoon orange rind
1 teaspoon lemon rind
1 tablespoon mint
½ teaspoon ginger
1 teaspoon cinnamon
1 cup roasted slivered almonds
2½ cups whole-wheat pastry flour
½ teaspoon salt

Combine juice or cider and almond butter. Blend until smooth. In a heavy saucepan, heat the concentrated sweetener and juice mixture together. Stir in orange, lemon rind, mint and spices. Cool.

Add nuts to cool liquid, then begin to add liquid to sifted flour and salt, stirring with a wooden spoon until a ball begins to form (adjust liquid-flour content accordingly).

Wrap and chill dough.

Preheat oven to 350°. Oil a cookie sheet. Roll

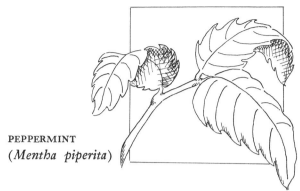

PEPPERMINT
(*Mentha piperita*)

This herb is mainly used for its essential oil, obtained by distilling the fresh plants. The oil is secreted by glands which are often visible to the eye as translucent dots on the leaf of the plant. Also used to make tea, it can be found growing wild in most parts of the United States in the late spring and summer. If used in jelly-type desserts, puddings or custards, it can enhance the flavor of any sweet.

out dough to ½-inch thickness (see p. 71). Cut into any shape. Place on sheets, and bake about 25 to 30 minutes, or until lightly browned. Remove from pan immediately, brush with oil or concentrated sweetener.

When completely cool, they can be stored for a few weeks to mellow before serving (see "Forget Me Knots," p. 127, nos. 24–26).

Variation

Substitute 1½ cups roasted chestnut flour for 1½ cups pastry flour.

CRACKERS

Use any leftover pie dough (see pp. 75–77).

Roll out dough. Place in well-oiled pan. Cut into squares, triangles, circles or any shape.

Preheat oven to 350°. Bake 10 to 15 minutes, or until browned. Spread tamari on when baking is half done (p. 12).

Suggestion

Oil a cake mold. Cool crackers and place in mold around the sides. Fill mold with Chestnut Creame II (p. 58). Chill before serving. Tamari may be omitted here.

Drop Cookies

Many drop cookies are made by the teaspoon method. Some fall easily from the spoon, and flatten while baking. When chilled before baking, some of these batters can be formed into balls and baked as is, or flattened with a lightly oiled glass, or with one dusted with chestnut flour or cinnamon.

Stiffer doughs can be formed with a pastry bag, fitted with a large, plain star or ribbon-type tube (pp. 46–47). The tube should be large enough to allow chopped fruits and nuts to pass through easily.

Fill a pastry bag half full of batter.
Seal in the batter by twisting the top of the bag (p. 48).
Line the baking sheets with wax or brown paper.
Oil the paper.
Hold the bag vertically with the tip of the tube ½ inch away from the baking sheet, and press out rounds, kisses or strips of batter onto paper.

Press out the remaining cookie batter onto prepared paper liners.
Bake cookies, then remove paper liner with cookies.
Remove baked cookies immediately from liner.
Place a new paper liner with prepared unbaked cookies on a sheet and bake.

ALMOND KISSES

3	egg whites
¼	teaspoon salt
1	teaspoon lemon juice
3 to 4	tablespoons concentrated sweetener
1	teaspoon lemon rind
½	teaspoon cinnamon
1½	cups roasted ground almonds

Separate eggs. Beat whites until foamy. Add salt and lemon juice. Gradually begin to drip in sweetener and rind. Beat until peaked. Fold in cinnamon and nuts.

Preheat oven to 325°. Oil a baking sheet. Use a pastry bag and a medium-size tube. Fill the bag with cookie dough, and press out 1-inch-wide kisses (p. 47).

Bake 10 to 15 minutes or until browned.

Alternate Method

Drop by teaspoons onto sheet.

Variations

Substitute any ground roasted nut or seed for almonds.

Add 1 teaspoon vanilla to egg whites after eggs are foamy.

Add 1 teaspoon mint to egg whites after eggs are foamy.

Add 1 teaspoon more lemon rind.

Substitute orange juice and rind for lemon.

Add 3 to 4 tablespoons grain coffee (p. 9) to egg whites after they become foamy. Substitute ground roasted walnuts or pecans for almonds.

JUMBLES

¼ cup dried fruit
   Apple juice or other juice
¼ cup oil
¼ cup concentrated sweetener
1 cup corn flour or brown rice flour
1 cup whole-wheat pastry flour
1 teaspoon cinnamon
½ teaspoon ginger
1 tablespoon mint or orange rind
½ teaspoon salt
3 to 4 tablespoons grain coffee
1 teaspoon vanilla

Soak dried fruit in juice to cover until soft. Drain, squeeze out excess liquid and reserve juice. Dice fruit.

Combine oil, sweetener, vanilla and diced fruit in a mixing bowl.

Sift dry ingredients and combine with fruit mixture. Add enough reserved juice to form a very thick batter.

Preheat oven to 325°. Oil cookie sheets.

Drop onto sheets and bake 15 to 35 minutes or until edges and bottom are lightly browned.

Variations

Substitute 1 cup brown rice flour for corn flour.

Substitute 1 cup crushed or chopped walnuts for dried fruit.

Substitute 4 tablespoons any nut butter for oil.

OATMEAL COOKIES

½ cup raisins
   Apple juice or cider
1 cup rolled oats
½ cup oil
½ cup whole-wheat pastry flour
½ cup brown rice flour
¼ cup roasted sesame seeds
¼ cup roasted sunflower seeds
1 tablespoon orange rind
2 teaspoons cinnamon
¼ teaspoon salt

Soak raisins in juice to cover until soft. Reserve juice. Drain and let sit for 1 hour. Roast oats in oil, until they are very dark brown (almost burnt). Combine all dry ingredients and raisins.

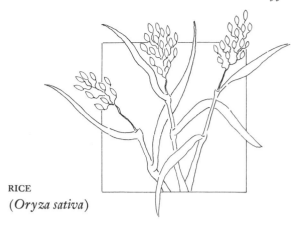

RICE
(*Oryza sativa*)

Rice was a staple food of China as early as 2800 B.C. The majority of rice is produced and used in Asia, and grown from the equator to as far north as Japan. Rice, usually grown in water, forms a hollow stem that lets oxygen pass downward and reach the roots in the wetted soil. In the milling process, the inedible outer husk is first removed.

This leaves brown rice, containing the bran, where all of the essential vitamins and minerals are stored. It is an excellent nutritious food that can be cooked easily by simply boiling. Another variety, known as "glutinous" or sweet brown rice, is sweeter and stickier than brown rice. It is used in Japan and China mainly for festive occasions, in the form of sweet white rice.

"White" rice is brown rice with the most valuable part of the grain — bran — removed. Milled to remove the bran, the rice is then subjected to a process known as pearling, leaving a white grain, then coated with glucose and talc to preserve the whiteness, and finally marketed.

Rice, whether it be boiled, steamed, baked or fried, is a basic dish of many countries. Served in Asia with vegetables, India with curry, and Spain with fish, rice also provides the Japanese with their staple grain, saki (rice wine) made from fermented grains, and rice paper from the stems.

Add reserved juice or cider until mixture resembles a very thick pancake batter.

Preheat oven to 350°. Oil cookie sheet. Drop cookies onto sheet, and press each cookie down lightly with a fork.

Bake 15 to 20 minutes, or until crisp. Place on rack to cool.

TANGERINE COOKIES

      2 cups raisins
         Apple juice or cider
      3 cups sweet brown rice flour
     ½ teaspoon salt
 2 to 3 tablespoons dried tangerine rind
         Concentrated sweetener (optional)
     ½ cup oil
    1¼ cups rolled oats
    1¼ cups roasted sesame seeds
      1 teaspoon cinnamon
         Juice and grated rind of fresh tangerine
      1 teaspoon vanilla

Soak raisins in juice to cover until soft. Drain and reserve juice.

Preheat oven to 350°. Oil cookie sheets.

Combine flour, salt, tangerine rind and sweetener if used. Cut oil into dry mixture until it looks like bread crumbs.

Stir in the rest of the dry ingredients, add fresh tangerine and juice, and vanilla, then slowly add reserved juice or cider to mixture until batter has a thick pancakelike consistency. Add raisins. Drop on cookie sheet and press down with fork. Bake 15 to 20 minutes or until browned. Remove from oven and place on rack to cool.

Variations

See variations for Rolled Cookies (pp. 128–129).

Place in a cake pan and bake covered 20 minutes, remove cover and bake until browned and set.

PEANUT COOKIES

      2 cups brown rice flour
     ¼ teaspoon salt
 2 to 3 tablespoons peanut butter
      1 cup apple juice or cider
      2 teaspoons cinnamon
     ¼ cup concentrated sweetener (optional)
      1 cup raisins
      1 cup roasted chopped peanuts
      1 teaspoon vanilla or orange rind

Combine flour and salt. Blend peanut butter, 1 cup juice or cider, cinnamon and sweetener together until smooth and creamy. Soak raisins until soft in blended liquid.

Combine mixture with flour, adding more liquid if necessary, to form a very thick batter. Fold in peanuts; add vanilla or orange rind.

Preheat oven to 350°. Oil cookie sheets. Drop cookies on sheet, and press down with fork. Bake 15 to 20 minutes, or until golden brown. Place on rack to cool.

Variations

Substitute any nut for peanuts. Also substitute any nut butter for peanut butter.

Substitute 1 cup chestnut flour for 1 cup brown rice flour.

POPPY SEED COOKIES

     ½ cup raisins
     ½ cup apple juice or cider
     ½ cup roasted poppy seeds
      1 teaspoon cinnamon
     ½ teaspoon cloves or ginger
      1 grated apple
     ½ teaspoon salt
     ¼ cup oil or 2 tablespoons tahini
     ½ cup whole-wheat pastry flour
     ½ cup brown rice flour
      1 tablespoon lemon juice

Soak raisins in liquid to cover until soft. Reserve liquid. Roast poppy seeds on a medium flame in a dry skillet until they begin to pop. Combine spices, grated apple, salt and poppy seeds with soaked raisins and liquid. Let sit 20 minutes. Add oil or tahini and lemon juice to poppy seed mixture and stir well until creamy.

Sift flour. Stir into mixture. Add more juice if necessary to form a stiff batter.

Preheat oven to 375°. Oil cookie sheets. Drop batter from teaspoon onto cookie sheet and press down with a fork. Bake 25 to 30 minutes, or until edges are browned.

Alternate Method

Combine raisins, poppy seeds and apple juice in a heavy saucepan, and cook on a medium flame until juice evaporates and mixture is almost dry. Add ½ cup more juice and the rest of the ingredients and blend or use as is, following directions for Poppy Seed Cookies.

CLOVES
(*Eugenia
caryophyllus*)

Cloves are produced from a tree that is native to Indonesia. It is the dried flower bud of a tree that grows to about 40 feet in height. The trees come to bear at about 8 to 9 years and have a life span of about 60 years. The buds are picked by hand and dried in the sun for several days. It is mainly used as a spice for cakes, cookies, pies and pastry.

Variations

Add rind and juice of ½ lemon. Add more flour if necessary.

Substitute orange rind and juice for lemon.

Substitute ¼ cup concentrated sweetener for ¼ cup apple juice.

Add ½ teaspoon ginger to spices.

Add 1 teaspoon of mint (to taste) to spices.

RAISIN OATMEAL COOKIES

  1 cup raisins
    Juice or cider
  1 cup rolled oats
1½ cups sifted whole-wheat pastry flour
  1 teaspoon cinnamon
  2 teaspoons lemon rind
  ½ teaspoon salt
  ½ cup oil
  ¼ cup concentrated sweetener
  1 egg (optional)
  1 teaspoon lemon juice
  ½ cup chopped roasted pumpkin seeds

Soak raisins in juice to cover until soft. Drain (reserve liquid) and set aside for one hour.

Roast oats until very dark brown (almost burnt). Set aside to cool.

Combine flour, cinnamon, rind and salt, and set aside. Mix oil and sweetener together. Add well-beaten egg. Stir in raisins and lemon juice. Add dry mixture gradually, stirring until thoroughly mixed. Add oats and seeds. Mix well until stiff batter is formed (add more juice if necessary).

Preheat oven to 350°. Oil a cookie sheet. Drop from a tablespoon onto cookie sheet. Press down lightly with a fork. Bake 20 to 25 minutes. Place on rack to cool.

SPICE DROPS

  2 cups raisins
    Apple juice or cider
  3 cups whole-wheat pastry flour
  ½ teaspoon salt
  1 teaspoon ginger
  ½ teaspoon cloves
  1 teaspoon cinnamon
  1 cup chopped roasted walnuts or almonds
  ¼ cup oil
¼ to ½ cup concentrated sweetener to taste
  3 eggs

Soak raisins in liquid to cover until soft. Reserve liquid.

Sift flour, salt and spices together. Combine nuts, raisins and flour mixture. Mix well.

In a separate mixing bowl, combine oil, sweetener and eggs, beating in eggs one at a time. Stir in flour combination. Add reserved liquid, if necessary, to form a very thick batter.

Preheat oven to 350°. Oil cookie sheets. Drop batter from a teaspoon onto cookie sheet. Press down lightly with a fork. Bake 15 to 20 minutes, or until browned. Place on a rack to cool.

Molded Cookies

German and Danish cookies are so appealing because they are pressed with carved wooden molds or rollers into quaint designs and shapes. No matter what kind of technique you use for molding — pastry bags, cookie presses, wooden molds, carved rollers, or your hands — the more you make the better!

ALMOND
Rosaceae

Almonds are one of the fruits of the rose family. Originally, the almond is thought to have come from one of the Mediterranean countries, where it is still widely grown. Nearly all of the almonds grown in the United States are produced in California.

The tree is medium-size, related to the peach and grown chiefly for its nuts. The beautiful pinkish-white blossoms open in early spring before the long, pointed leaves appear. The edible seed or nut is enclosed within a small dry shell.

Almonds contain a large percentage of oil, and are also made into almond butter, used in baking as well as cooking. There are two kinds of almonds: sweet and bitter. Sweet almonds, a popular delicacy, are eaten roasted or salted, or are used in the cooking and baking of pastries.

The bitter almond is a variety of the common almond, but is usually not considered edible. Because of the large quantity of hydrocyanic acid it contains, the oil is most frequently used in medicines, or as a flavoring extract (almond extract) for baking, after the acid has been removed.

ALMOND COOKIES

2 to 3 tablespoons almond butter
  ¼ cup concentrated sweetener
  2 egg whites
  1 teaspoon vanilla
  1 cup sifted chestnut flour
  ¾ cup sifted whole-wheat pastry flour
  ¼ teaspoon salt
  ½ cup ground almonds
    Blanched almond halves (p. 46)

Preheat oven to 400°. Oil cookie sheet. Combine nut butter and sweetener. Mix until creamy. Separate eggs. Beat egg whites into nut butter combination until a smooth mixture is formed. Add vanilla. Sift flours and salt together and add to the mixture. Stir well until a thick moist dough is formed.

Use a pastry bag and a medium-size tube (p. 47). Fill the bag with cookie dough and press out into 2-inch kisses (see p. 134). Leave about 1 to 2 inches between cookies for expansion. Press almond halves into dough.

Bake 8 to 12 minutes, or until edges of cookie begin to brown. Remove from sheet, and place on rack to cool.

CHESTNUT BALLS

    1 cup sweet brown rice flour
    ½ cup chestnut flour
    4 tablespoons oil
    ¼ teaspoon salt
    1 teaspoon vanilla
    ¼ cup concentrated sweetener
1 to 2 tablespoons tahini
 ¼ to ½ cup liquid

Roast the flours separately in oil until they begin to smell sweet and are slightly brown.

Sift and combine flours and salt. Add vanilla and sweetener and rub in tahini with your hands. Add liquid until mixture begins to stick together.

Prepare steamer (p. 5). Shape mixture into little

balls before or immediately after steaming. Steam 10 to 12 minutes. Cool on a rack before serving.

Alternate Method

Pinch off walnut-size pieces of dough; roll into balls. Place on baking sheet. Flatten slightly. Stick a whole nut into the center of each cookie. Bake 12 to 15 minutes, or until firm.

Variations

Substitute 1 cup raisin purée for concentrated sweetener. Adjust flour content accordingly (see chart, p. 149).

Add 1 teaspoon cinnamon to mixture.

Add ¼ cup dried fruit. Soak fruit to cover until soft. Squeeze out excess liquid and dice. Add to dry ingredients.

Add ½ cup roasted sesame seeds to dry ingredients.

Add 1 teaspoon dried mint to dry ingredients.

Add 1 to 2 teaspoons orange rind or substitute for vanilla.

FINGERS

1 recipe for Rolled Cookies I or II
(p. 128)
Crushed nuts

Follow directions for Rolled Cookies. Shape dough into fingers, wrap individually in wax paper and chill overnight.

Preheat oven to 375°. Roll fingers in crushed nuts, and place on unoiled sheet. Bake 10 to 12 minutes, or until browned. Brush fingers with egg white if crushed nuts do not adhere to them.

Variation

Shape dough into long thin rolls, and twist these into a pretzel shape. Brush with egg yolk. Bake in a preheated 375° oven 15 to 20 minutes.

HEAVENLY RIBBONS

¼ cup oil
¼ cup concentrated sweetener
2 egg whites
1 teaspoon vanilla
1¼ cups sifted whole-wheat pastry flour
¼ teaspoon salt

Preheat oven to 400°. Oil cookie sheet.

Combine oil and sweetener, beating well. Separate eggs. Beat in egg whites slowly and continuously until foamy and well combined. Add vanilla. Sift flour and salt together, and fold into egg mixture. Stir until a very thick moist dough is formed.

Use a pastry bag and a medium-size tube (pp. 47–48). Fill the bag with cookie dough and press out thin strips of batter 2 to 3 inches long. Leave about 1 to 2 inches between cookies for expansion.

Bake 8 to 12 minutes, or until edges of cookies begin to brown. Remove from sheet and place on rack to cool.

Variations

Add 2 tablespoons grain coffee to oil-sweetener mixture, before folding in flour.

Add ½ tablespoon mint to oil-sweetener mixture before folding in flour.

Add 1 teaspoon cinnamon and ¼ teaspoon ginger to flour before sifting.

Shape into 2-inch rings, using a pastry bag (p. 47).

Add 2 tablespoons lemon rind and 1 tablespoon lemon juice before adding flour.

See Rolled Cookies for more variations (p. 128).

Suggested Dips for Serving with Cookies

Prepare squash-carrot filling (p. 65) or Chestnut Creame (p. 57) or consult Chapter 3 for more ideas for fillings.

Place filling in the center of a bowl, and trim with ribbons.

CHESTNUT SPIRALS

1 recipe for Heavenly Ribbons (p. 139)
  (substituting ½ cup chestnut or corn
  flour for ½ cup whole-wheat pastry
  flour)
2 tablespoons oil
1 teaspoon cinnamon

Roast chestnut or corn flour in oil, until it begins to smell sweet and turn light brown. Set aside to cool.

Follow directions for Heavenly Ribbons, adding cinnamon to flour before sifting. Fill pastry bag, and press out spirals (1 to 2 inches wide) on an oiled cookie sheet.

Bake in preheated 400° oven 10 to 12 minutes or until cookies are brown. Remove from pan immediately and place on a rack to cool.

Variations

Add 2 teaspoons orange rind and 1 tablespoon orange juice to batter before adding flour.

Add ½ cup ground pecans* to dry mixture after sifting but before combining it with egg mixture.

See variations for Heavenly Ribbons (p. 139) and Rolled Cookies (p. 128).

ICEBOX COOKIES

1 recipe for Rolled Cookies I or II (p. 128)

Follow recipe for Rolled Cookies. Prepare dough,

* Use only crushed or ground nuts or seeds when using a pastry bag; otherwise they may clog the hole of the bag, not allowing the batter to flow evenly.

shape into round or square log (see illustration). Wrap and chill at least 60 minutes. For Rolled Cookies II, chill overnight.

Preheat oven to 375°. Slice logs into ¼-inch thickness. Place on unoiled cookie sheet. Bake 10 to 12 minutes, or until lightly browned on bottom. (For a browner cookie, turn over after 8 minutes of baking.) Cool.

Variation

Molded Icebox Cookies

Prepare dough for Rolled Cookies I or II, shaping into a square or rectangle, and chill at least 60 minutes (for Rolled Cookies II, chill overnight).

Roll out to ¼-inch thickness, and a size slightly larger than your mold. Press the mold hard into the dough to get a good imprint. Separate the squares.

Bake in a preheated 375° oven 10 to 15 minutes, or until crisp.

MOLASSES COOKIES

4 tablespoons sorghum molasses
½ cup oil
1 egg
2 cups whole-wheat pastry flour
1½ cups corn flour
½ teaspoon salt
½ teaspoon cloves
1 teaspoon ginger
1 teaspoon cinnamon
  Juice to form dough
  Blanched almonds (p. 46)

Heat molasses until it becomes thin. Combine oil, egg and molasses in mixing bowl. Beat.

Sift flour, salt and spices together, and add to first mixture, stirring until dough is formed. Adjust liquid-flour content accordingly.

Preheat oven to 375°.

Roll dough into balls the size of a large cherry, and flatten slightly by pressing an almond in the center of each.

Place on unoiled sheet, and bake 15 to 20 minutes or until lightly browned.

Alternate Method

Steam 15 to 20 minutes (p. 5).

Variations

Substitute 1½ cups brown rice flour for corn flour.

Substitute 4 tablespoons any nut butter for oil.

Also see variations for Rolled Cookies (p. 128).

SESAME BUTTER FLAKES

4 tablespoons sesame butter
1 tablespoon concentrated sweetener
¼ cup oil
1 egg (optional)
1½ cups sifted whole-wheat pastry flour
Apple juice to form dough

Combine sesame butter, sweetener and oil. Add egg, if desired, and mix well. Add flour and roll into walnut-size balls. Add juice if necessary. Preheat oven to 375°. Place balls on unoiled sheet, and press with fork to flatten. Bake 10 to 15 minutes, or until browned.

Alternate Method

Heat oil (p. 6) and deep-fry.

Variations

Add one of the following suggestions to liquid mixture before combining with flour:

1 teaspoon vanilla
2 tablespoons orange juice and 2 teaspoons orange rind
1 grated apple
2 tablespoons grain coffee and 3 tablespoons orange juice

Substitute any nut butter for sesame butter. If using almond butter, add 2 teaspoons lemon rind and 1 teaspoon lemon juice to liquid mixture before combining with flour.

Cookie Bars

All children love finger things — any sweets they can pick up and eat. Cookie bars have the appeal of both cookies and cakes. They are quick to make, easy to handle and fun to eat.

Cookie bars should be baked in rectangular pans 1½ inches deep, or, for individual festive rounds, in muffin tins or cupcake forms. Any way you serve them, children and adults will keep coming back for more.

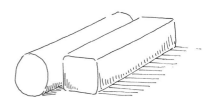

FILLED BARS

To make bars, use any rolled cookie (p. 128), and double the recipe.

Divide the dough into 2 uneven pieces (two-thirds and one-third). Roll out both pieces to the size of the pan. Line the bottom of an oiled baking pan with the thicker piece of dough.

Spread any filling over it (see Chapter 3, "Inside and Outside"), and cover with remaining dough. (Choose a filling that contains very little liquid.)

Bake in a preheated 350° oven 20 to 25 minutes.

LAYERED ALMOND BARS

3 cups whole-wheat pastry flour
1 teaspoon salt
½ cup oil
Apple juice, mint or mu tea to form dough

First Topping

2 eggs
2 tablespoons concentrated sweetener
½ teaspoon salt
1½ teaspoons vanilla
2 cups chopped almonds

Second Topping

4 tablespoons tahini

½ cup apple juice or 2 tablespoons concentrated sweetener plus 5 to 6 tablespoons apple juice

4 tablespoons grain coffee (p. 9)

Place flour and salt in a mixing bowl. Add oil, cutting it into the flour until it looks like fine bread crumbs.

Preheat oven to 375°. Oil an 11 x 16-inch rectangular pan or two 9-inch pans.

Add enough liquid to mixture to form a dough. Roll out dough (p. 71). Place in pan. Bake for 10 minutes.

First Topping

Beat eggs, sweetener, salt and vanilla. Add chopped nuts.

Remove crust from oven, spread egg mixture over it and bake 10 minutes longer or until lightly browned.

Second Topping

Blend tahini and juice. Cook over a medium flame, constantly stirring until boiling. Stir in grain coffee.

Spread on baked layer, and sprinkle with ground almonds. Cool. Cut into 1 x 3-inch bars or triangles.

Variations

Substitute Oat Creame for eggs (p. 55).

Substitute Chestnut Creame for second topping (p. 57).

Substitute any nut butter for tahini.

Substitute ½ to 1 cup fruit purée for first topping, or 2 tablespoons fruit purée for sweetener (p. 66).

Four-Layer Bar

Follow directions for Layered Almond Bars, using a smaller rectangular pan. After baking with first topping, divide pastry in half lengthwise. Place one layer on top of another and spread second topping over layers.

PEANUT
(*Arachis hypogaea*)

The peanut is an annual herb of the pea family, its fruit being a pod and not a nut. Peanuts are native to the South American Indians, who were growing peanuts there at least 1000 years ago. Today they are grown in semiarid regions as well as in other parts of the world and have the ability to endure long drought and grow when the rain comes.

The peanut contains pound for pound more protein than sirloin steak, more carbohydrates than potatoes and one-third as much fat as butter.

Peanut hulls have the food value of coarse hay, and the thin skin that covers the nut is sometimes used in place of wheat bran in cattle fodder. Also, the roots of the plant, if left in the soil, enrich it with valuable nitrogen products.

O'GEORGE BARS

While baking for stores and restaurants in New York, Sara and I baked these bars for our organic- and natural-food pushcart, which we wheeled around Central Park in the summertime.

4 cups sweet brown rice flour

1 cup rolled oats

1½ cups sesame seeds

2 teaspoons cinnamon

1 tablespoon orange rind

½ teaspoon salt

2 cups raisins

3 cups peanuts

½ cup peanut butter

½ cup apple juice or cider

1 teaspoon vanilla

¼ cup concentrated sweetener

Combine all dry ingredients. Blend peanut butter, ½ cup juice, vanilla and concentrated sweetener until smooth and creamy. Combine dry mixture with liquid mixture, adding more liquid if necessary to form a thick batter.

Preheat oven to 350°. Oil baking pan. Pour batter into pan.

Cover and bake 45 minutes (see "Moisture," p. 21). Remove cover and bake until firm. Remove from oven, cool. Cut into bars, squares or triangles, or whatever you wish.

Variations

Substitute almond butter for peanut butter and roasted almonds for peanuts.

Substitute sesame seeds for peanuts and sesame butter for peanut butter.

Substitute 1½ cups dried mixed fruit for raisins and peanuts, and tahini for peanut butter. Soak dried fruit in apple juice or cider to cover until soft. Dice and combine with dry ingredients.

Omit peanuts; substitute sesame or almond butter for peanut butter. Add 3 more tablespoons cinnamon and orange rind.

Boil ½ cup cider or juice. Add 4 to 6 tablespoons grain coffee to taste, and cook 2 minutes longer. Combine with peanut butter, vanilla and sweetener before blending.

Substitute 2 cups cooked couscous (p. 28) for 2 cups flour.

POPPY SEED BARS

1½ cups poppy seeds
    Apple juice
¼ cup concentrated sweetener
2 teaspoons cinnamon
2 teaspoons vanilla
2 cups raisins
½ teaspoon salt
½ cup oil
5 cups sweet brown rice flour

Soak poppy seeds with apple juice and sweetener to cover overnight.

Blend seeds, cinnamon, vanilla, raisins, salt and oil, until creamy and smooth (add more juice if too thick to blend). Add flour to blended mixture and enough juice or cider to form a thick pancakelike batter.

Preheat oven to 350°, and oil an 11 x 16-inch pan.

Pour batter into pan, and allow to sit 15 minutes.

Bake 45 to 50 minutes, covered (see "Moisture," p. 21); remove cover and bake 15 minutes longer, or until firm. Cool on rack. Cut into bars 1 x 4 inches before serving.

Variations

Substitute Lemon Poppy Seed Filling (p. 53) for poppy seeds.

Add grated rind and juice of 1 orange to flour mixture.

Substitute sesame or sunflower seeds for poppy seeds.

Substitute tahini, almond or sesame butter for oil.

PRUNE BARS

2 cups prunes
    Apple juice to cover prunes
2 cups sifted whole-wheat flour or whole-wheat pastry flour
2 cups sifted brown rice flour or sweet brown rice flour
1 teaspoon cinnamon
1 teaspoon ginger
½ teaspoon salt
1 cup oatmeal
    Juice and rind of 1 lemon or orange
¼ cup oil
½ cup chopped walnuts or almonds
¼ cup sweetener (optional)
    Sunflower seeds for topping

Soak prunes in juice to cover until soft; squeeze out excess liquid (reserve for batter), pit and dice. Toss prunes lightly with flour and place in mixing bowl. Sift dry ingredients. Combine with prunes. Add oatmeal, juice and rind of lemon or orange.

Mix in oil and nuts, and add apple juice or cider (and sweetener, if used) until a very thick batter is formed (adjust flour-liquid content accordingly).

Preheat oven to 350°. Oil a baking pan. Pour batter into pan, and top with unroasted sunflower seeds. Bake 20 minutes covered, remove cover and bake about 25 minutes longer or until firm (see "Moisture," p. 21). Cool and cut into bars 1 x 4 inches.

Variation

Substitute any dried fruit for prunes.

WALNUT
(*Juglans regia*)

The walnut tree is valuable not only for its fruit but also for its timber. Oil is extracted from the nuts, and is important for its edible qualities as well as being a preparation used in paints for artists. The walnut tree grows up to 100 feet high, with green fruit sometimes picked before it hardens and eaten pickled in vinegar. If allowed to harden, the fruit is then picked and used as nuts for dessert making and baking.

WALNUT BARS

½ cup oil
¼ cup concentrated sweetener
1 teaspoon orange rind
1 teaspoon lemon rind
1 teaspoon vanilla
2 eggs
2 cups roasted chopped walnuts
3 cups sifted whole-wheat pastry flour
1 teaspoon salt
1 teaspoon cinnamon

Preheat oven to 400° and oil a baking sheet or pan.

Combine oil, sweetener, rinds, vanilla and eggs. Mix well. Add nuts, flour, salt and cinnamon to egg mixture. Consistency should be that of a soft dough (adjust flour-liquid content accordingly). Cover and chill 15 minutes.

Divide dough into two pieces. Shape each piece into a log about 3 inches wide and 1 inch thick. Place on sheet and slit each log diagonally with a sharp knife or razor blade.

Bake about 20 to 25 minutes, or until logs are golden brown. Cool.

Alternate Method

After baking, remove from oven, cut diagonally into slices ½ inch thick. Place each piece on its side and reduce heat to 300°. Sprinkle on cinnamon and crushed nuts. Bake until lightly toasted and dry.

Variations

Substitute 1 cup roasted, sifted chestnut flour and ½ cup roasted, sifted whole-wheat flour for half of the flour.

Substitute 2 tablespoons almond butter for oil.

Substitute roasted chopped almonds for walnuts.

Add ½ teaspoon dry ginger and ¼ teaspoon cloves to flour before sifting.

Soak 2 cups raisins in liquid to cover until soft. Squeeze out excess liquid (reserve for dough). Add raisins to egg mixture before adding sifted flour. Adjust liquid content accordingly.

SUNSHINE BAR

3 cups roasted corn flour
½ cup oil
½ cup roasted whole-wheat pastry flour
½ teaspoon salt
Apple juice or cider
2 to 3 cups roasted, blended sunflower seeds
2 to 3 cups fruit purée

Roast corn flour in ¼ cup oil until lightly browned. Set aside to cool. Roast pastry flour in 1 tablespoon oil until lightly browned and set it aside to cool. When cool, combine the flours and add salt.

Begin to add the remaining oil, cutting it in until mixture resembles fine bread crumbs. Add just enough apple juice to moisten mixture.

Oil a cookie sheet and sprinkle mixture onto sheet. Press it into the bottom of the sheet.

Preheat oven to 350°. Prebake crust 5 minutes.

Roast and immediately blend sunflower seeds until they are almost at the nut-butter stage. Sprinkle a layer of seeds over the crust. Cover with a layer of fruit purée. Bake 10 to 15 minutes, or until fruit is dry. Cut into bars when cool, and serve as snacks.

Variations

Substitute sesame seeds for sunflower seeds. Add

1 teaspoon cinnamon or mint to flour mixture before cutting in oil.

Substitute any pressed pastry for crust.

Substitute any vegetable or fruit purée (see Chapter 3).

TRIPLE-LAYER BAR

2 recipes Pressed Pastry (p. 76)
Middle Layer
4 cups apricot purée (p. 66)
Topping
2 cups ground roasted sunflower or sesame seeds
1 cup roasted rolled oats
3 tablespoons roasted chestnut flour
2 tablespoons oil
¼ teaspoon salt
½ teaspoon vanilla
Apple juice or cider

Prepare crust. Preheat oven to 350° and oil a baking pan or cookie sheet. Press crust in pan or sheet and bake 10 minutes. Prepare apricot purée and spread over crust.

Topping

Combine all ingredients in a mixing bowl. Cut oil in thoroughly until mixture resembles tiny bread crumbs. Add a few drops of juice until slightly moist. Sprinkle topping on apricot purée. Bake 10 minutes longer or until slightly browned.

Variation

Substitute any fruit purée for apricot purée, and any pastry dough for pressed crust.

Appendix

Bibliography

Index

Appendix

Sweetness Equivalency Chart

Sometimes when preparing desserts, I like to vary the amount and kind of sweetener I use, in order to alter the taste, or the degree of sweetness. For very special occasions or guests, I often make cakes sweeter.

Here is a chart to help you substitute one natural sweetener for another. Remember always to increase or decrease the amount of liquid in the recipe according to the liquid content of the sweetener.

In all recipes, ¼ cup concentrated sweetener refers to ¼ cup maple syrup, or its equivalent according to the following chart.

¼ cup maple syrup = 2 tablespoons sorghum molasses
¼ cup apple concentrate
¼ cup honey
½ cup apple butter
½ cup raisin purée (p. 66)
¾ cup barley malt syrup
¾–1 cup amasake (p. 82)
¾ cup grain syrup (p. 52)
1 cup cider or apple juice

Ingredient Measurement Chart I

Almonds, whole, shelled	3 cups	= 1 pound	Pecans, shelled	3½ cups	1 pound
Almonds, ground	2¾ cups	1 pound	Raisins	3¼ cups	1 pound
Almonds, slivered	3 cups	1 pound	Rye flour	4 cups	1 pound
Almond butter	1¾ cups	1 pound	Salt (sea)	1 cup	12 ounces
Apples, cored and sliced	3–4 cups	1 pound	Sesame butter	2 cups	1 pound
Apricots, dried	3 cups	1 pound	Strawberries (fresh)	3 cups	1 pint
Arrowroot	3½ cups	1 pound	Sweet brown rice flour	3½ cups	1 pound
Brown rice flour	3½ cups	1 pound	Tahini	2 cups	1 pound
Chestnut flour	3 cups	1 pound	Walnuts, shelled, whole	4 cups	1 pound
Oats (rolled)	4 cups	1 pound	Water	2 cups	1 pound
Oil	2 cups	1 pound	Whole-wheat flour	3¾ cups	1 pound
Peanuts, shelled	2¼ cups	1 pound	Whole-wheat pastry flour	4 cups	1 pound
Peanut butter	1½ cups	1 pound			

Ingredient Measurement Chart II

Apples (raw)	3½–4 pounds	= 1 pound dried
Dried fruit	1 cup (dried)	2 cups (soaked)
Eggs (whole)	1 cup	5 eggs
Kanten (Agar Agar)	2 bars	1 tablespoon flakes
Lemon rind (dried)	½–1 tablespoon	1 medium lemon
Lemon rind (fresh)	1–2 tablespoons	1 medium lemon
Lemon juice	3–4 tablespoons	1 medium lemon
Mint tea	1 teaspoon	4–5 cups
Mu tea	1 package	8–10 cups
Orange rind (dried)	1–2 tablespoons	1 medium orange
Orange rind (fresh)	2–3 tablespoons	1 medium orange
Orange juice	6–8 tablespoons	1 medium orange
Vanilla (pure-liquid)	1 teaspoon	2½-inch bean
Whole-wheat pastry flour	1 cup unsifted	1⅓ cup sifted
Yeast	1 tablespoon dry yeast	⅔ ounce compressed cake yeast

Temperatures for Baking Pies

pie	min-utes	oven tem-perature (degrees)	pie	min-utes	oven tem-perature (degrees)
Unfilled pie shells	15–20	375–400	Filled one-crust fruit yeasted half-baked shell	10–15	375
Filled one-crust creame- or custard-type half-baked shell	25–30	350	Filled two-crust fruit unbaked shell	45–60	350–375
Filled one-crust creame- or custard-type yeasted half-baked shell	15–20	350	Filled two-crust fruit yeasted unbaked shell	20–30	350
Filled two-crust creame- or custard-type unbaked shell	40–45	350	Filled lattice-top unyeasted half-baked shell	30–40	350
Filled two-crust creame- or custard-type yeasted unbaked shell	25–30	350	Filled lattice-top yeasted half-baked shell	25–35	350
Filled one-crust fruit half-baked shell	25–30	375	Meringues	45	225
				25	325
				10–12	400

Baking time will vary according to the material of the baking pan. If using enamelware or glass, reduce the baking time indicated by one quarter; if using stoneware increase the baking time by one half.

Suppliers of Natural Foods

Northeast

Agress Nut & Seed Co.	3441 Kingsbridge Ave.	Bronx, NY 10463
Erewhon Trading Co.	33 Farnsworth St.	Boston, MA 02210
Good Nature Distributing Co.	Box 447	Export, PA 15632
Infinity Co.	173 Duane Ave.	New York, NY 10005
Like It Was	75 Hudson St.	New York, NY 10013
Miracle Exclusives, Inc.	16 W. 40th St.	New York, NY 10018
Mottel Health Foods	451 Washington St.	New York, NY 10013
Shadowfax	25 N. Depot St.	Binghamton, NY 13901
Sta-Well/All Diet	16 W. 40th St.	New York, NY 10018
Sundance Organic Food	R.D. #1, Box 146A	Coventry, CT 06238
T'ai Natural Food Flow	510–512 Hempstead St.	West Hempstead, NY 11552
Walnut Acres		Penns Creek, PA 17862
Weavers Natural Foods, Inc.	37 Market Square	Manheim, PA 17545

Southeast

Breads for Life	Box 663	Crossville, TN 38555
Cinagro Distributors	2239 Faulkner Rd., NE	Atlanta, GA 30324
Collegedale Distributors	Box 492	Collegedale, TN 37315
Laurelbrook Foods	Box 47	Bel Air, MD 21014
Sun Ray Products	169 NW 23rd St.	Miami, FL 33137
Tree of Life	Box 1391	St. Augustine, FL 32084
Whole Foods General Store	1404 17th Ave., Apt. 1, S.	Nashville, TN 37315

Midwest and Mountain States

Ceres, Inc.	2582 Durango Dr.	Colorado Springs, CO 80910
Cliffrose	129 Coffman St.	Longmont, CO 80501
Colorado Specialty Foods	4430 Glencoe St.	Denver, CO 80216
Eden Foods	Box 100	Ann Arbor, MI 48107
Food for Life	420 Wrightwood St.	Elmhurst, IL 60126
Great Plains Distributors	240 Oak St.	Kansas City, MS 64106
New World	347 Ludlow St.	Cincinnati, OH 45220
Northern Health Foods	Box 66–13 S. 4th St.	Moorhead, MN 56560

Southwest

Akin Distributors	Box 2747	Tulsa, OK 74101
Arrowhead Mills	Box 866	Hereford, TX 79045
Concord Distributors	Box 876	Snowflake, AZ 85937
New Century Foods	Box 45713	Dallas, TX 75235
Shiloh Farms	Box 97	Sulphur Springs, AZ 72768
Sunrise Distributors	Box 5216	Phoenix, AZ 83010

West Coast

Erewhon Trading Co.	8454 Steller Dr.	Culver City, CA 90230
Janus Natural Foods	1523 Airport Way, S.	Seattle, WA 98134
New Day Distributors	1242 S. Berendo St.	Los Angeles, CA 90006
Royal Garden Foods	118 105th St. NE	Bellevue, WA 98004
The Well/Pure & Simple	795 W. Hedding St.	San Jose, CA 95126

Outside of U.S.

Lifestream Natural Foods, Ltd.	724–26 W. 6th Ave.	Vancouver 9, B.C., Canada
Natural Foodstuffs	1 Main St., Box 27	Sutton, Quebec, Canada

Bibliography

Aihara, Herman. *Milk — a Myth of Civilization.* San Francisco: George Ohsawa Macrobiotic Foundation, 1971.

Aleco. *Simplified Cake Decorating.* August Thomson, 1929.

Bailey, Liberty Hugh. *The Standard Cyclopedia of Horticulture.* New York: Macmillan, 1917.

Beach, J. P. *You and Your Health.* Quoted in *Woodstock Aquarian.* Vol. 2, No. 1. Woodstock, N.Y.: Great Turtle Enterprises, 1971.

Beeton, Mrs. Isabella. *The Book of Household Management.* London: Jonathan Cape, 1861. New York: Farrar, Straus & Giroux, 1969.

Biale, J. N. "Fruit Ripening." *Scientific American,* May 1945.

Boston Traveller. Mary Jane's Book of Household Hints. Boston, 1915.

Bowman, Ann. *The Common Things of Everyday Life.* London, 1857.

Brown, Edward Espe. *The Tassajara Bread Book.* Berkeley: Shambala Publications, 1973.

Campbell, Helen. *Household Economics.* London: G. P. Putnam's Sons, 1897.

Carne, Charlotte. *Tea Time Tips.* Edinburgh: Ettrick Press, n.d.

Carque, Otto. *Vital Facts about Foods.* N.p. n.d.

Catanzaro, Angela. *The Home Book of Italian Delicacies.* New York: Collier Books, 1958.

Chase, A. W. *Dr. Chase's Recipes: or Information for Everybody.* Ann Arbor, 1863.

Clark, Linda. *Stay Younger Longer: How to Add Years of Enjoyment to Your Life.* New York: Devin-Adair, 1961.

Conn, H. W. *Bacteria, Yeasts and Molds in the Home.* Boston: Ginn & Company, 1903.

Encyclopedia Americana. International Edition. Vols. 12, 22, 23, 26. New York: Americana Corporation, 1971.

"Enquire Within," Editors. *The Family Save-All.* London: W. Kent and Company, Feb.–May, 1861.

Evans, Mary Elizabeth. *Mary Elizabeth's Wartime Recipes.* New York: Frederick A. Stokes, 1918.

Farmer, Fanny. *The All New Fanny Farmer Boston Cooking School Cookbook.* Revised by Wilma Lord Perkins. New York: Bantam Books, 1961.

Farmilant, Eunice F. *Macrobiotic Cooking.* New York: New American Library, 1972.

Ford Heritage Health Research. *Composition and Facts about Foods.* Mokelumne, Ca., 1971.

General Foods Cooking School of the Air. *The General Foods Cooking School of the Air Baking Book.* 1932.

Hale, Mrs. S. J. *The Good Housekeeper: or The Way to Live Well and Be Well While We Live.* Boston: Weeks-Jordan, 1839.

Harper's Household Handbook. New York: Harper & Brothers, 1913.

Harrison, S. G.; Masefield, G. B.; and Wallis, Michael. *The Oxford Book of Food Plants.* London: Oxford University Press, 1971.

Hart, Richard N. *Leavening Agents.* Easton, Pa.: Chemical Publishing Company, 1914.

Hawken, Paul. *The New Oil Story.* San Rafael, Calif.: Organic Merchants, 1970.

Hey, D. H. *Kingzett's Chemical Encyclopedia.* Balliere, Tindall & Cassell, 1966.

Hold, Emily. *The Complete Housekeeper.* New York: Doubleday, Page, 1917.

Holloway, Laura C. *The Hearthstone: or Life at Home, a Household Manual.* Philadelphia, 1840.

Hunt, William. *Good Bread and How to Make It Light Without Yeasts or Powders.* Boston, 1858.

Hunter, Beatrice Trum. *The Natural Foods Cookbook.* New York: Pyramid Books, 1967.

Jasny, Naum. *The Wheats of Classical Antiquity.* Johns Hopkins University Studies in Historical and Political Science, Vol. 62, No. 3, 1944.

Johnson, Arnold H. "Cracker Dough Fermentation." Ph.D. dissertation, University of Minnesota, 1924.

Leslie, Miss. *The Housebook, or a Manual of Domestic Economy for Town and Country.* Philadelphia, 1840.

Logan, Mrs. John A. *The Home Manual: Everybody's Guide in Social, Domestic and Business Life.* Boston: A. M. Thayer, 1889.

Macrobiotic, The, No. 83 (December 1972). San Francisco: George Ohsawa Macrobiotic Foundation.

Marl, Lee. *Crack and Crunch.* New York: Coward-McCann, 1945.

Morris, Josephine. *Household Science and Arts.* New York: American Book Company, 1912.

Parloa, Maria. *Miss Parloa's Kitchen Companion,* 12th ed. Boston: Estes & Lauriat, 1887.

———. *Miss Parloa's Young Housekeeper.* Boston: Estes & Lauriat, 1887.

Peck, Paula. *The Art of Fine Baking.* New York: Simon & Schuster, 1961.

Prevention Magazine. April 1971; March 1972; July 1972; Jan. 1973; June 1973. Emmaus, Pa.: Rodale Press.

Richards, Ellen H., and Elliott, Maria S. *The Chemistry of Cooking and Cleaning.* Boston: Home Science Publishing Co., 1897.

Richards, Paul. *Cakes for Bakers.* Chicago: Bakers Helper Company, 1926.

Rohe, Fred. *The Flour Story.* San Rafael, Calif.: Organic Merchants, 1970.

Rohe, Fred: *The Sugar Story.* San Rafael, Calif.: Merchants, 1970.

Rombauer, Irma S., and Rombauer, Marion. *The Joy of Cooking.* Indianapolis: Becker-Bobbs-Merrill, 1931.

Rose, Ian F. *Faith, Love and Seaweed.* New York: Award Books, 1969.

Skeats, A. C., ed. *Commercial Confectionary: A Practical Guide for Practical Men, by Many Expert Contributors.* London: Gresham Publishing Co., 1937.

Steffanson, Vilhjalmur. *Not by Bread Alone.* New York: Macmillan, 1946.

Sunset Cook Book of Breads, The. Menlo Park, Calif.: Lane Books, 1971.

Sunset Cook Book of Desserts, The. Menlo Park, Calif.: Lane Books, 1970.

Taussig, Charles William. *Some Notes on Sugar and Molasses.* New York, 1940.

Trager, James. *The Foodbook.* New York: Grossman Publishers, 1970.

U. S. Department of Agriculture, Agricultural Adjustment Administration. *Sugar Regulations, Series No. 1.* June 1934.

Van Nostrand's Scientific Encyclopedia. 4th ed. Princeton, N.J.: D. Van Nostrand & Co., 1938.

Wilcox, Estelle, in *The New Practical Housekeeping,* Subscription edition. Minneapolis: Home Publishing Company, 1970.

Wiles, Robert. *Cuban Cane Sugar.* Indianapolis: Bobbs-Merrill, 1916.

Williams, Henry T., and "Daisy Eyebright." *Household Hints and Recipes.* Boston: People's Publishing Company, 1884.

Wilton, McKinley, and Wilton, Norman. *The Homemaker's Pictorial Encyclopedia of Modern Cake Decorating.* Chicago: Wilton Enterprises, 1954.

Wright, Michael W., and Fred Rohe. *The New Age Old Fashioned Fertile Brown Egg Story.* San Rafael, Calif.: Organic Merchants, 1970.

Index